Reading Between the Lines

Decoding Handwriting

By Sheila Lowe

Note: This publication contains the opinions and ideas of its authors. It is intended to provide helpful and informative material on the subject matter covered. It is sold with the understanding that the authors are not engaged in rendering professional services in the book. If the reader requires personal assistance or advice, a competent professional should be consulted.

The authors specifically disclaim any responsibility for any liability, loss, or risk, personal or otherwise, which is incurred as a consequence, directly or indirectly, of the use and application of any of the contents of this book.

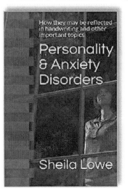

Introduction

Does something seem to be blocking you from getting where you want to be in life? Are you having trouble keeping a job? A relationship? Friends? We don't always know how to figure out the answers to these questions on our own, but the good news is, you're here, reading this book.

The proven fact is, your handwriting reflects your strengths and weaknesses, potentials and dreams, your fears and defenses; how you think, and your social persona. The way you arrange your writing on a page, the letter designs you choose to represent you, the rhythm, speed, pressure, and hundreds of other elements are a mirror image of who you are inside.

Maybe you've studied handwriting analysis before, but the method you learned didn't quite "click" with your thinking style; or maybe this is your very first exposure. Either way, you are about to gain an entirely new perspective on the marks you leave on paper.

Having studied handwriting and personality for more than 50 years, I have distilled the basics of what I've learned into these pages. The knowledge you gain from reading the material and putting it into practice will without doubt improve your self-knowledge and your relationships with yourself and others.

"But handwriting is going the way of the buggy whip," you might say. In 2009 when the Common Core Curriculum was introduced, it left out the requirement for public schools to teach handwriting. The American Handwriting Analysis Foundation has a detailed white paper available for a free download that details the research explaining why this was a very bad idea. But the good news is, since then, 18 states so far have seen the results and have returned handwriting training to the curriculum. For kids who still aren't learning in school an abundance of apps teach handwriting. So, it's not going anywhere soon. And as long as love letters and birthday cards exist, there will be handwriting to analyze.

Get ready to change the way you look at other people, yourself, and certainly, handwriting. I hope you enjoy learning to see behind the strokes and swirls into the depths of personality.

Happy analyzing!

Acknowledgements

My grateful thanks go to all whose handwritings have been included in this work, whether they knew they were contributing or not. I am especially thankful to the following friends for samples they provided: Roger Rubin, Linda Larson, Lena Rivkin, Edda Manley, Richard Kokochak, Steve Hodel, Hazel Dixon Cooper, Christopher Darden, Leslie Klinger, Sheldon Siegel, Raul Melendez, Louis M. Jason, Lionel Strutt, Lawrence Totaro. Apologies to anyone I have overlooked.

Some of the samples came from my book, *Handwriting of the Famous & Infamous* (Metro Books) and from my own collection.

When I took samples from Google Images, mindful of copyright, I used only small portions for the sake of education.

To the many thousands of people whose handwritings I have analyzed over since 1967, and pretty much anyone who ever picked up a pen and wrote, this book is inspired by you.

Sheila Lowe

Contents

Introduction 0

Acknowledgements 1

Handwriting as Body Language 2

What *is* Graphology, anyway? 3

Serious Fun 3

    In the Beginning: The Origins of Graphology 5

    Mais Oui! The French Approach 6

    The 7 main categories: 7

    Achtung! The German School 7

    Symbols Etched in Ink 8

    What Handwriting Can and Cannot Tell 13

The "Ideal" Sample 16

The Absolute Necessities: The least you need to know 17

The Tools of the Trade 17

    Books for the Budding Graphologist 19

School Copybooks 20

    A Room with a View? 24

    Eye Training: A how-to exercise 24

The "Ground" Work 26

    Figure-Ground 27

    A Fine Balance 28

What does a well-balanced page look like? 29

Pressed In 30

Spaced Out 30

    Taking up a collection 33

    Don't Stand So Close! Perspective 35

    Don't Fence Me In: Line Spacing 36

    Clear Line Spacing 37

    Narrow Line Spacing 37

    Crowded Line Spacing 38

    Tangled Lines 39

    Moderately Wide Line Spacing 40

    Extremely Wide Spacing 41

Irregular Line Spacing 42
Extremely Regular Line Spacing 43
Outer Space: Word Spacing 43
Balanced Word Spacing 44
Wide Word Spacing 44
Extremely Wide Word Spacing 45
Narrow Word Spacing 46
Extremely Narrow Word Spacing 47
Irregular Word Spacing 48
Inner Space: Letter Spacing 49
Wide Letter Spacing 49
Narrow Letter Spacing 50
Inconsistent Letter Spacing 50
Secondary Expansion 51
Somewhere in Time 52
Well-Balanced Margins 53
Extremely Wide Margins All Around the Page 54
Narrow or No Margins 55
Ghosts of Christmas Past: The Left Margin 57
Narrow Left Margin with Wide Right Margin 57
Wide Left Margin 57
Shrinking Left Margin 58
Growing Left Margin 59
Caving in or Bowing Out Left Margin 60
Rigid Left Margin 61
Irregular Left Margin 62
Future Perfect: Right Margin 62
Wide Right Margin 62
Narrow Right Margin 63
Expanding Right Margin 64
Shrinking Right Margin 64
Straight Right Margin 65
Extremely Irregular Right Margin 66
Your Majesty: Upper and Lower Margins 67
The Invisible Line 70
What's Your Angle? 70
Traveling The Underground 71
Following the Rules: the ruler writer 71
How About a Hug? 73
Pretending to Follow the Rules 74

Charting Your Goals 74
How to Measure a Baseline 76
Measuring Line Direction 76
Measuring Across the Baseline 76
Moderately Straight Baseline 77
Slightly Wavy Baseline 78
Extremely Wavy Baseline 79
Ready, Set, Goal! 80
Uphill Baseline 81
Downhill Baseline 82
Convex Baseline 83
Concave Baseline 83
Step-Up and Step-Down Baselines 84

Back to School with Freud 88
The Id Did It 89

Ergo, the Ego 91

Welcome to My World: The Middle Zone 92

Superego to the Rescue! 93

Soul Survivor: The Upper Zone 95

What Dreams May Come: The Lower Zone 96
Off the Beaten Path: unusual lower loops 98
Let's Blame Mom! 100

Leggo My Ego – back to the middle zone 103
Small, Medium, Large—As Opposed to What? 104

How About Those Loops? 106
Bigger Than Small, Smaller Than Big: medium 106

It's the Small Things That Count: small MZH 108
Small and Narrow 109
Very Small 110
Big Is Beautiful 110
Large but Narrow 111
Too Much of a Good Thing: extremely large MZH 112

Decisions, Decisions—variable MZH 113

Up, Up, and Away – the upper zone 113
Tall Upper Loops 114
Too Tall: extreme UZH 115
Narrow or Retraced Upper Loops 117
Tall and Wide 117

Look Ma, No Loops! 118

Down to earth: short UZH.. 119
Mix 'n match: variable upper loops..................................... 120
Down in the Boondocks – the lower zone 120
Short Lower Loops.. 121
Medium-long Lower Loops... 121
Long Lower Loops 122
Narrow Lower Loops 123
Moderately-Wide Lower Loops 123
Extremely Wide Lower Loops 124
Some Final Remarks About Zones................................... 125
Different Strokes for Different Folks: rhythm..................... 127

Energy Balancing: Contraction and Release 128

Willpower or Won't Power? 129

The Regularity Continuum...131
Irregularity Breeds Contempt... 133
Past, Present, or Future? Left and Right Trend.................. 133

Rhythm and Blues 135
Compensation 137

Do You Wanna Dance? 139
Extreme, Dude! 141

Ready for Action—Tensing and Flexing 145

External Influences..146

Internal Influences...147

A Gripping Tale: 3 types of pressure....................................148
Pussycat or Storm Trooper?.. 148

What Does It Weigh?..149

Breaking the Surface: Medium Pressure 150

Running on Empty: Light Pressure 150

Blowin' in the Wind: Extremely Light Pressure......................151
Pressure Fades Away 151

Slightly Heavy Pressure...152

Playing the Heavy: Extremely Heavy Pressure 152

Sudden Bursts of Pressure...153

Life's Hard Enough—Displaced Pressure..............................154
Pressure Displaced on the Horizontal.............................. 154
Pressure Displaced onto Upstrokes 155

Directional Pressure...157

In the Zone.. 158

Pastosity, No Marinara Sauce.. 158

Mud Wrestling... 159

Blocked Pressure 161

Shading and Sharpness 161

    The Age of Innocence...*163*

    Parlez-Vous Handwriting?...*165*

Speed Bumps... 165

Setting the Pace 167

Factors Affecting Tempo... 167

    Reading the Handwriting Speedometer...................................*169*

As Slow as Molasses.. 170

    Moderately Slow Writing *170*

The Tortoise: Very Slow Writing Speed 171

Steady as She Goes: Medium Writing Speed............................. 172

Moderately Fast Writing Speed.. 173

    Let's Play Jeopardy!..*173*

    Haste Makes Waste *174*

To Conform or Not to Conform, *That* is the Question!.............. 177

    Follower or Leader?..*177*

    Straying from the Straight and Narrow *178*

The Simplification-Elaboration Spectrum................................. 179

    Just the Facts, Ma'am: simplified handwriting......................*179*

    Ingenious Solutions *181*

Skeletons in the Closet: Neglect of Form................................... 182

Dressing Up Is Fun: Elaboration 183

    Artistic Additions...*185*

    Distinctive Details..*186*

    The Icing on the Cake..*187*

The Fab Four (Connective Forms)... 190

    Let's All Be Friends: Garlands...*191*

    Wilting Garlands *193*

    Fake It Til You Make It—Sham Garlands *194*

Cover Me, I'm Going In: Arcades.. 195

Fast Arcades 196

Slow Arcades... 198

No More Mr. Nice Guy: Angles.. 199

Your Guardian "Angle" Is Watching 200
Biting with the Shark's Tooth 201
Don't Pin Me Down: Thread 201
Primary Thread 202

Secondary Thread 203

The Double Bow 204
Combining Forms 204

Impulse Patterns 206

I Might Be Psychic: Airstrokes 207

Ties That Bind: Connectedness 210

Let's Stay in Touch: Connected Writing 211

Moderately Connected Writing 211
Highly Connected 212

Overconnected 212

I Need My Space: Moderately Disconnected Writing 213
Gimme A Break: Extreme Disconnectedness 215
I Want to Break It Off 216

Bring Me My Soldering Iron 217

Viva Variety! Printscript 218
The Fine Print: Printed Writing 218
I Don't Know How I Know It, but I Do: Intuition 221

Culturally Speaking 223

Gauging Slant 224
Feeling It in the Heart: The Right Slants 226
Moderate Right Slant 226
Strong-Extreme Right Slant 227

Upright, Uptight? 228

You'll Never Know How Much I Really Love You: The Left Slants 230
Moderate Left Slant 231
Extreme Left Slant 232

Every Which Way but Loops: Variable Slant 233
Lefties Are in Their Write Minds 234
Left Slant and the Sexes 235
Stuff About Slant That Doesn't Fit Anywhere Else 236
How Do I Look? 239
Changes in the signatures of world leaders. 240
Do You Read Me? 241
All in the Family 243

Signature Slant...*243*

All the Trimmings *244*

The Wrapping on the Package...*244*

Ups and Downs..*245*

Memories...*246*

The Man/Woman Behind the Curtain...*247*

Let's Get Personal: the PPI 248

Copybook PPI *249*

Common Types of PPI....*250*

In the Beginning: Initial Strokes.................................... 254

Can't Let Go *255*

Let's Get in Shape *255*

The End: Final Strokes... 257

I Love You, Period: Punctuation *261*

Yoo-Hoo! Here I Am! *263*

Don't Let Go! Hooks and Ties 263

Hooked on Handwriting: hooks and ties *264*

The Old School Tie: ties *265*

Making it in the Minors: trait strokes **267**

Don't t's Me: letter "t" 267

Stem Height..*268*

t-Bar Height...*268*

t-Bar Length *269*

t-Bar Pressure *270*

All sorts of t-Bars...*270*

"Different" forms of t-bars. *271*

Seeing i to i: lowercase "i" *273*

Let's Get Organized: lowercase "f"..*274*

The x-Files: lowercase "x" *275*

It's OK: lowercase "k"...*276*

Mmm Mmm Good: lowercase "m, n"...*277*

Mind Your p's and q's: lowercase "p"..*277*

r You Still with Me?: lowercase "r" *278*

Oh, My Dear! Signs of Culture 279

L. A. Confidential: The Communication Letters 280

Intrusions 281

Secrets and Lies: more "o's and a's"..*282*

e Is for Ear....*282*

I'll Believe Anything You Say....*282*

One True Thing: Honesty and Integrity 285
Read the Road Signs: clues to pathology 286
Felon's Claw or Cat's Paw 290
No Evil d Goes Unpunished: "maniac d" 291
Mack the Knife: "shark's tooth" 292
Unlovin' Spoonful: "spoon e" 292

The Awful Oval: "elliptical g" 293

Signs of Violence 294

Don't Drink and Write: Drugs and Alcohol 298
1. The First Impression 301
2. Finding the Guiding Image 302
3. Easy Handwriting Checklist 303
4. How Do You Do? Ask the Writing Questions 304
Other Kinds of Questions You Could Ask 307

Using the Gestalt Method to Analyze a Handwriting..............................307
The Synthesis 310
Typecasting: Using Typologies 311
Professional Is as Professional Does 312
Saying What You See—Writing the Report 313
1-2-3 314
Some Analysis Do's and Don'ts 315
The End of the Beginning 315

Glossary..317

Resources 321

Recommended Reading...322

About the Author 328

Chapter 1

Your Handwriting is You

Long before Sigmund Freud brought new meaning to the word "complex," people sought answers to the question of why we feel and act in the ways that we do. For many, the study of personality is as intriguing as a hall of mirrors. Just when you think you've got it figured out, another curve emerges to mystify and confound you. Fortunately, it isn't always necessary to spend years on the psychiatrist's couch or seated across from a therapist or even hours taking a battery of tests to find enlightenment.

If you've ever taken those tests, you know how intimidating they can be. There you are, sweating the 550 items on the widely used MMPI (Minnesota Multiphasic Personality Inventory), wondering whether you've given the right answers. Or you're trying to decide whether that ink blot is a sheep in wolf's clothing or merely a flower. Or you're madly making up stories that you hope will properly fit the TAT (Thematic Apperception Test), all the while wondering if the results will make you look like an ax murderer. And by the time you've finished, you're beginning to actually *feel* like an ax murderer.

There is an easier way to learn the truth about who someone really is, and that person doesn't have to answer even one test question. Since you are reading this book, it's fair to assume that you already have a pretty good idea that handwriting provides important clues.

As a projection of personality, handwriting is like a movie projected onto the silver screen. The trail of ink you leave behind on a sheet of paper vividly tells your story. From the moment of birth, your brain begins to record every experience, every sight, every sound. Millions of life events are stored in that miraculous computer in your head, waiting for just the right moment, the right stimulus, to recall them. No number of terabytes or RAM could match the memory functions of this computer as its highly complex system of programming keeps track of every single piece of information that comes your way.

Most experiences are not important enough to keep in the foreground of daily life, and some are just too embarrassing or too painful to *want* to remember. Recognizing that most memories are stored in the unconscious mind, Freud described the human psyche as being like an iceberg with most of its mass hidden below the surface. This is why, when a particular event, sight, scent, or sound jogs your memory, something that happened when you were, for example, 3 years old, pops right back into consciousness.

Tales from the Script...

Legend has it that when Gainsborough painted a portrait, he would place a letter written by his subject on his easel next to the painting. By studying her handwriting, it was as if he could glimpse the sitter's soul and "know" her at a depth not otherwise possible.

Handwriting as Body Language

Handwriting takes a "psychic photograph" of the hidden part of Freud's iceberg, a sort of EEG (brain wave recording) of personality. In fact, handwriting analysts believe that "brainwriting" is a more descriptive term than handwriting. Why is that?

When you pick up a pen and begin to write, the accumulation of all your life experiences travels from your brain, through the nerves in your arm, into your hand, and reflects how you have responded to those experiences on the paper in the trail of ink.

Body language, tone of voice, and facial expressions are also important projections of personality. But unlike those outward manifestations that can be changed to suit the occasion, handwriting always tells the truth, even when the writer is not aware of it.

Fine Points

The writing trail reveals a great deal about your past experiences and how you have integrated them into your life, but it cannot predict the future.

Imagine that...

In "The Picture of Dorian Gray," a 1945 movie, a man stays young and good-looking as he grows older, but a portrait of him changes to show his inner evil. Handwriting always tells the truth about the inner person.

What you say in an analysis can affect lives, so before we go further, please plant this idea firmly in mind: Regardless of whether a handwriting sample represents a sweet-natured, generous person, or an uptight, angry one, you must never forget that there is a human being behind *every* handwriting. When you look at a handwriting that makes you go "ugh!" remind yourself, the negative aspects are pain expressed on the page. So, always apply the age-old Golden Rule: treat others as you wish to be treated.

In fact, if you have not already done so, it would be to your benefit to start your study of graphology by having your own handwriting professionally analyzed. Giving a stranger the power to know so much about you is a humbling experience and may leave you feeling vulnerable. It's a feeling that I hope you will remember every time you pick up a new handwriting sample and begin an analysis, because it will remind you to treat the writer with kindness.

What *is* Graphology, anyway?

Graphology is the generic term for handwriting analysis. It derives from two Greek words that mean to learn about writing (if you're a Greek scholar, please don't write to me with the "real" definitions, I'm paraphrasing). Because the word "graphology" is sometimes confused by the uniformed with "astrology," in this book, we will refer to graphology as "handwriting analysis," whose meaning is quite clear.

Def·i·ni·tion

Graphology: The study of handwriting, and the inferring of character or aptitude from it [fr. Gk *graphein*, writing, + *logos*, discourse].

Serious Fun

It's fun to discover what your handwriting says about you and your friends, but it is also important to realize that handwriting analysis is serious business. One of the many applications is helping an individual gain greater self-awareness. The client already knows their personal faults and foibles, so it can be a pleasant surprise to learn from an objective third party about all the *good* qualities that they have taken for granted.

Compatibility is another application. An analysis of a couple in a relationship, or several people on a work team can teach them more about each other's needs and motivations. Educators can bring out better behavior in problem students. A vocational analysis might facilitate a career change to the client's dream job.

A "graphological autopsy" can help genealogists who want to understand ancestor they never knew, but whose letters and diaries they found in an old trunk in the attic. Therapists can track clients' progress in therapy; law enforcement agencies find handwriting analysis useful in determining dangerousness in certain suspects, as well as truthfulness of victim and witness statements.

> When you examine a handwriting sample, you hold the writer's psyche in your hands. Always wield this power delicately like a surgeon's scalpel, not carelessly, like a chainsaw. Remember, "With great power comes great responsibility."

One of the most popular uses of graphology is by employers. By having the handwritings of employees analyzed, they are able to build a more productive team whose members will work better together. New applicants are analyzed, too, to make sure they are a good fit for the team.

There is also a branch of graphology called "graphotherapy." Handwriting movement exercises are done to music to help facilitate changes in habits that the client has identified as problematic. Changes made to handwriting will result in changes to personality, so this process should be undertaken only after a thorough analysis of the handwriting and a discussion with the client about what *they* want to change.

The procedures of graphotherapy go beyond the scope of this book, but if you are interested in learning more about it or want to try it for yourself, you can find information about *Graphotherapy Manual*, which is a download available for sale at www.sheilalowe.com

In *United States v. Mara.* 410 U.S. 19, 41 LW 4185 (1973), the Supreme Court stated: "Handwriting, like speech, is repeatedly shown to the public and there is no more expectation of privacy in the physical characteristics of a person's script than there is in the tone of his voice." Although this case dealt with whether or not a person can be compelled to produce an example of their own handwriting for examination, it is important to graphology because it demonstrates that the courts consider handwriting to be an individual characteristic.

In the Beginning: The Origins of Graphology

Where did it all begin? The first recorded remarks about handwriting being related to personality are attributed to Aristotle in 330 B.C.E. What he wrote may be translated thus:

> Speech is the expression of ideas or thoughts or desires. *Handwriting is the visible form of speech.* Just as speech can have inflections of emotions, somewhere in handwriting is an expression of the emotions underlying the writer's thoughts, ideas, or desires.

Since Aristotle's time, graphology has had a long history of university research, beginning in France and branching out to other countries, continuing to the present. While it was generally accepted as a serious practice in Europe before WWII, Hitler outlawed handwriting analysis under the fortune-telling act. It went underground for many years, but today, graphology is back, full-force, all around the world.

Of all the important names in the history of graphology, foremost is abbé Jean Hippolyte Michon, considered the grandfather of modern graphology. Michon applied the classification system he had devised for studying botany to handwriting. It is known as "the study of fixed signs." All modern graphological thought has its foundations in his research. It was Michon who coined the French term *graphologie.*

Michon's student, Jules Crepieux-Jamin, recognized the need to view handwriting as a whole, rather than simply as a collection of fixed signs. Crepieux-Jamin taught that the "study of the school of fixed signs is to graphology as the study of alphabet is to reading prose."

Later, the German philosopher Ludwig Klages became a proponent of a more intuitive method of analysis, called the gestalt method, which is a forerunner of the method you will learn from this book.

Another name to remember is Dr. Max Pulver. A Swiss graphologist, Pulver applied the principles of Klages's system to the field of psychoanalysis and Jung's depth psychology. Perhaps Pulver's greatest contribution was his identification of three zones in handwriting, which parallels Freud's concept of personality structure: id, ego, and superego.

At the turn of the 20th century, handwriting analysis made its way to the United States through Louise Rice, an American newspaperwoman, who learned about it while on assignment in Europe. Her 1927 book, *Character Reading from Handwriting* (Newcastle Publishing Co., Inc., 1996), is available again after being out of print for many years.

There are many more greats to learn about, each of whom made his or her own valuable contributions to the scientific study of handwriting. From their research, the two major methods of analysis emerged that are in use today: the French and the German.

Mais Oui! The French Approach

Besides being a priest, Abbé Michon was a philosopher, botanist, geologist, archaeologist, architect, historian, and more. According to Edward B. O'Neill, translator of many French graphological works, Michon made some mistakes in his method, but "he gave us the very basis of the science and the art of graphology." O'Neill goes on to quote the eminent modern graphologist, Dr. Jean-Charles Gille Maisani:

"Michon believed in fixed signs but not in *isolated* signs, as one sometimes unjustly reproaches him for. Indeed, he mentions a "theory of the complex sign" and explicitly indicates that therein lies an immense field for investigation and the germ of future progress in graphological science."

Fine Points

The French method of graphology is atomistic (consisting of many separate, often disparate elements). Using Crepieux-Jamin's system of categories, the handwriting is broken into its various components and seen as if through a microscope.

Tales from the Script

Michon himself said this, which speaks volumes about the man and the way he viewed handwriting:

The slightest movement of the pen is a vibration of the soul in one direction or another. As soon as the graphic sign is known, it is, in application, a game of stating what the soul has produced, what it has felt, what it has wanted, etc.; more artfully still, what the nuance was in each manner of producing, feeling, wanting.

Although what follows is probably an oversimplification of the method, it will give you an idea of how French graphologists divide handwriting into several categories for analysis.

The 7 main categories:

1. *Layout:* how the writing is organized on the page
2. *Dimension:* how much space the writing takes up (size of letters)
3. *Pressure:* the depth component
4. *Form:* writing style
5. *Speed:* writing tempo
6. *Continuity:* types and degree of connections within and between letters
7. *Direction:* which way the writing is moving

Achtung! The German School

The German method, which came after the French school, is known as holistic or *gestalt* graphology, which means that the whole is greater than the sum of its parts. In other words, no single element of handwriting means anything outside the context of a given handwriting sample. In gestalt analysis, there is no "this means that" answer. Meanings can change and are dependent upon the context in which a particular feature appears.

Def·i·ni·tion
Gestalt: A pattern of unified elements that cannot be interpreted outside of the whole. The sum is greater than its parts.

In gestalt graphology, handwriting is composed of three big pictures, each of which relates to an aspect of behavior:

1. *The picture of space:* how the writer sees the world
2. *The picture of movement:* how the writer acts in the world
3. *The picture of form:* how the writer sees himself

The way these three pictures fit together forms the basis for understanding the core personality. Disturbances in one or more of the big pictures tell the graphologist where problems originate. This idea will begin to make more sense as we delve further into each of the three pictures.

Tales from the Script

In 1930s Chicago, Milton Bunker founded a school based on Abbé Michon's method (Michon was not credited) and coined the term "graphoanalysis." Only graduates of Bunker's school, the International Graphoanalysis Society (IGAS) can legally use the trademarked name. The IGAS system is known as the trait-stroke approach because it assigns a personality trait name to each writing stroke. IGAS students often quote the maxim, "A stroke is a stroke, wherever you find it."

Both atomistic and gestalt methods are used around the world, but the emphasis in this book will be on gestalt. Without a good grasp of the whole picture—*the gestalt*—all you have is a list of personality traits that need a context in which to place them.

Having said that, there is no "one and only way." Much depends on the thinking style of the user. A step-by-step left-brained thinker will be more comfortable with the atomistic trait-stroke method. On the other hand, a right-brained conceptual, "big picture" thinker will be more drawn to the gestalt approach. Bottom line, what's best is a good foundation in gestalt graphology, augmented by an understanding of atomistic graphology, for the most complete picture of personality.

Symbols Etched in Ink

If you are alive, you have needs. From the most basic biological, instinctual needs for food, safety, and reproduction, to the need for belonging and love, to the need to express one's creative urges, all humans share similar needs. We don't, however, express them in exactly the same way.

The most basic needs of life must be met before one is free to progress to the next level. A person who is literally starving is unlikely to think about going to a movie. When you are hungry, you think meeting that most basic need for food. Someone stuck at such a basic level cannot easily progress to the next stage of emotional growth.

Handwriting reveals the level of need at which the writer is operating. If, early in life, the writer's most basic needs for food, water, warmth, safety went unsatisfied, his handwriting will show it in a lack of development.

Fine Points

Psychiatrist Carl Jung said, *"A true symbol appears only when there is a need to express what thought cannot think or what is only divined or felt."*

The handwriting of one who has moved up the needs ladder but has not satisfied the need for love in positive ways will display the overly rounded forms of depending on others for emotional nurturing and love, never having learned self-love.

While the lower-level needs, the physiological ones, are innate and unconscious, other needs are conscious, such as the need for intellectual stimulation. Handwriting is a manifest symbol of whatever needs the writer feels compelled to express at the time he is writing.

Following is the handwriting of Christine Falling, a woman who, in her early 30s was convicted of murdering several children. Unattractive, abused as a child, after being hit in the head with a board by her young mother, she was mentally slow. Falling who was close to her cousin, became jealous when she had to share the cousin's attention with a new baby.

Left in the car with the infant for a few minutes, she accidentally smothered the crying baby. When the crime was successfully misread as crib death, Falling began to repeat the act again and again with people who employed her as a babysitter. Finally, someone began to connect the dots and she was arrested.

When interviewed in a 1999 CNN documentary film titled *Murder by Numbers,* Falling declared that if paroled, she would like to babysit again, saying, "I love kids to death." She was denied parole in 2007.

Through the pages of this book you will learn how handwriting like Christine Falling's reveal clear red flags for pathological behavior. You will come to understand that the writing, which uninformed people think pretty, is only part of the picture. Knowing how the "x-formations," twisted upper loops and other problems in the overly rounded forms and add up to danger.

Although no handwriting analyst could predict the terrible murders that Falling committed, if they had known what her handwriting revealed, the

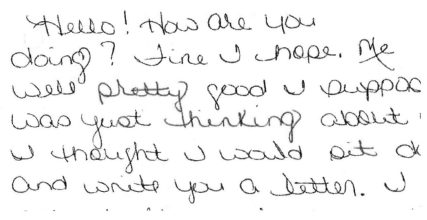

Christine Falling, serial killer

parents who hired her to care for their children might have been able to avoid the tragic losses that followed wherever she went.

Learning to measure and weigh the writing line in all its many expressions is an important key that unlocks the door to personality. The forms created in ink and the spaces around them reveal to the trained eye what motivates a particular type of behavior.

Last Words

Handwriting tells the truth about the writer. A body of research supports the validity and reliability of handwriting analysis. All methods begin with Abbé Michon's system, but do not end there. And remember: always be kind when analyzing someone's handwriting.

Chapter **2**

Getting Started: Your Handwriting Tells on You

The written forms created in ink and the spaces around them reveal to the trained eye what motivates a particular style of behavior. Similar to the way an artist uses line, color, and texture in his or her brush strokes, every movement of the pen uncovers something of the writer's temperament and style.

French impressionist Claude Monet daubed vivid colors on the canvas in thick, sensuous brush strokes. His slightly blurred style painting style reveals a love of natural beauty, color, and texture.

Claude Monet, artist

Contrast Monet's work with Dali's sharp edges, strong colors, and clearly defined objects often depict disturbing subject matter. The same is true of their handwriting as their art.

These artists and their works evoke distinctly different sensations because each creation was produced by a very different type of personality. Not surprisingly, the handwritings of artists—and musicians, too—are usually similar to the works they produce.

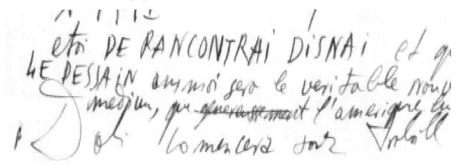

Salvador Dali, artist

Imagine that...

About 95 percent of people who learn about your graphology skills will offer one of four stock responses: 1) "I should let you see my handwriting!" 2) "You don't want to see my handwriting!" 3) "I wouldn't want to know what you would find out!" 4) "I have terrible handwriting."

As the writer guides the pen across the page, it is almost as if he is drawing a picture of what is happening inside him from moment to moment. By observing someone's facial expressions, body language, and tone of voice, you can probably figure out how he is feeling. An unhappy or depressed person's shoulders tend to droop, the spring goes out of his step, his eyes are lackluster. On the other hand, when things are going well and the same person is having a good day, she'll throw her shoulders back, put a smile on her face and a lilt in her voice.

Temporary changes in handwriting reflect changes in mood. Momentary excitement, anger, joy, or other strong emotions are reflected in the size of the writing, the direction in which it slants, and the baseline. However, like the basic personality, the fundamental character of the handwriting will remain the same.

Handwriting is as individual as a fingerprint. Regardless of the writer adds interesting symbols to their signature, there are many subtle ways in which

symbolic signatures of Joe Theisman & Greg Norman

the writing is unique. If that were not true, everyone would write exactly alike, the way they learned in school.

Imagine that...

Someone who identifies very strongly with their profession may create a symbol that represents what they do. Liberace drew a little piano in his signature; football hero Joe Theismann draws a football on a tee. Golfer Greg Norman, known as "the Great White Shark," draws a sharky-looking signature.

But personality *is* manifest in handwriting and we don't all write alike. When a letter arrives in the mail, the handwriting on the envelope can usually be readily identified as Cousin Ted, or Jenny's boyfriend Steve, or Grandma because the familiar script symbolizes the personality traits you associate with that writer.

Still, while handwriting does provide a great deal of important information about behavior, there are some things a graphologist cannot conclusively identify.

What Handwriting Can and Cannot Tell

Knowing what handwriting cannot reveal is just as important as knowing what it can. By recognizing your limitations as a graphologist, you can avoid creating unrealistic expectations in yourself and your clients.

You can't tell this from handwriting:

- *Gender:* If you assume that a pretty, rounded script was written by a woman, you may be surprised to discover that the author was a 45-year-old man. The reverse is also true. Rather than gender, we can only infer the degree of what is traditionally thought of as masculine/feminine in the script. Sexual preference cannot be determined, either. In modern times, a much wider gender spectrum, needs to be considered. Sticking to describing behavior in handwriting solves this problem. Regardless, gender cannot reliably be determined from handwriting.

- *Age*: Chronological age cannot be determined from handwriting, but emotional maturity can. That's why it best to get at least a ballpark idea of the writer's age before beginning the analysis.

- *Writing hand*: Non-graphologists believe it's possible to tell the writing hand by checking the slant. Contrary to popular belief, however, left-slanted writing is not preferred by left-handed people.

- *Race* or *religion:* not being able to make this determination makes it a nondiscriminatory personnel selection tool. Note, however, that sometimes there are features that point to country of origin.

- *The future:* Handwriting tells a lot about the past and the potential for certain behaviors, but it cannot tell the future.

But you can tell this:

- *Social style*: How the writer relates to other people. Is she friendly or reserved, sociable or antisocial, aggressive or submissive?

- *Thinking style*: Logical or intuitive? Does he create entirely new ideas or is he stuck in the mud of convention, afraid to move out and generate his own concepts?

- *Ego strength*: Is the ego strong and well-developed, or weak and battered?

- *Use of energy*: Does she carefully conserve energy or spread it around with wild abandon? Does she tire easily, with low vitality and stamina, or can she work all day and party all night without feeling the strain?

- *Fears and inhibitions*: How the writer employs what he has learned from past experiences?

- **Locus of control**: Does the writer's control come from conscious self-discipline, painful experiences, or from the old messages of childhood conditioning?

- **Potential**: Yes, but whether the writer will act on those potentials is a question the graphologist cannot answer. One would have to be omnipotent to do that—a responsibility most of us can do without.

> Someone who brags, "I can tell you everything about you from your handwriting," is either lying or psychic. People are far too complex for one tool—even handwriting analysis—to reveal 100 percent about them

It's never too soon to start collecting handwriting samples. And once you've got them, don't throw them away. You might want to study a particular characteristic at some later date. After more than 50 years of collecting, I estimate there are at least 15,000 samples in my personal collection and I continue to stumble across letter forms that I've never seen before. Nearly half of them are scanned into my computer.

Tales from the Script

I asked a client how she felt about her handwriting analysis report. She said, "It was great! It was really me!" Then she hesitated and added, "But it wasn't *all* of me." A humbling reminder of one's own limitations as an analyst: handwriting cannot reveal everything about the writer.

So, where do you get samples? Start with friends and relatives, your kids' teachers, your dry cleaner, the UPS guy who delivers the stuff you ordered from eBay. In other words, anyone who is willing to share their inner self with you. If you have difficulty coming up with enough good samples to practice on, Google Images has an unlimited supply. Just search on "handwriting" and whatever specific topic you want to study. For example, "handwriting, politicians." You'll come across some fascinating stories that way. Google is a rabbit hole. Once you start chasing down those stories, you're apt to get so involved that you'll forget why you were there.

The "Ideal" Sample

You always want to develop the most accurate report possible, which means you need a decent handwriting sample. You might not always get the *ideal* sample, but there are a few minimum requirements, especially if you are a beginner. After you have a few hundred analyses under your belt, you will be better equipped to work with less than the best.

- **Size:** a full page or more on unlined paper. Photocopies, faxes, or scans may distort some important aspects of handwriting, and a newbie could make some serious mistakes by working with less than an original. Printer paper is good.

- **Subject matter:** the writer's choice, but it should be free-flowing like a letter, not copied and not lyrics or poetry or a recipe.

- **Printing:** If the writer protests, "but I only print," let him print. Forcing someone to write in a way that is unnatural to them can skew the results.

- If **English** is a second language, a sample of writing in their original language would be helpful, as well as one in English.

- **Writing instrument**. Pen preference can tell a lot about the person, so let the client choose. However, only accept a sample in pencil if there is no other choice; some nuances may be lost.

- **Personal info:** approximate age, gender, and which is the writing hand. If possible, ask about medications or recreational drugs that might affect his handwriting. Recent physical or emotional trauma, too.

- **Writing surface:** a smooth surface, with the writer in a relaxed state. *However,* that relaxed state should not be due to alcohol consumption. Even one beer could affect the handwriting.

Def·i·ni·tion

- **Third-party analysis**: A request to analyze the handwriting of someone who has not first given permission is called 3rd party analysis.

Important note: Graphology is not a party trick or parlor game. Only someone with a genuine need to know should be privy to the information you uncover in a handwriting sample. If asked to do a third-party analysis, make sure that party has a good reason for requesting it.

Who, other than the writer himself, might have a need to know? Parents who suspect their teen might be in trouble with drugs; a spouse concerned about her mate's truthfulness; an employer investigating a sexual harassment matter, and so on. Such cases should be handled by an experienced graphologist.

The Absolute Necessities: The least you need to know

Handwriting analysis is about understanding and describing personality, so a basic knowledge of personality development is integral to being a good graphologist. Without it, you will not be sufficiently well-equipped to develop a meaningful report; it provides a context for the conclusions you reach from studying the various indicators and traits.

Besides understanding normal personality development, abnormal psychology is also a vital part of your education. You need to know what is "normal" and what is not so you can recognize pathology when you see it.

Get out your Psych 101 college textbook and brush up on the main schools of thought: psychoanalytic, Neo-Freudian, humanistic, behaviorism, and learning theories. If you did not attend college or take psychology courses, this would be a good time to make up for it.

If your schedule does not allow time to add external courses, some excellent ones are available online at no cost. Try Yale University's open courses: https://oyc.yale.edu/psychology. You won't get the diploma, but you will be getting the same information as if you had attended in person.

The Tools of the Trade

Fifty-some years ago, when I began reading books on graphology, I was confused by references to "long lower loops" or "tall upper loops," etc. *How am I supposed to know what's long or short or tall?* I wondered. It was not until ten long years later that I discovered Charlie Cole's Handwriting Analysis Workshop Unlimited (HAWU) course on the Roman-Staempfli

Psychogram chart and other instruments that had been invented to quantify handwriting.

I learned to plot the 40 handwriting factors on the circular Pyschogram, which led to a pictorial view of the personality that ended up looking like a Rorschach ink blot. The chart is comprised of eight syndromes that fall into four segments: left/right, up/down. On the left side are inhibiting traits, on the right side are social traits. The upper half has to do with the intellect, control, and ego aspects of personality, while the lower half deals with sex drive (euphemistically titled "Vitality"), repressions, and emotional release.

There are many things to recommend the Roman-Staempfli Psychogram, not the least of which is that the user is forced to carefully examine and measure the handwriting sample. That, of course, is more appealing to the left-brained step-by-step thinker, than the right-brained conceptual thinker.

Def·i·ni·tion

Psychogram: A scientifically based circular graph that was created in the 1930s by Klara Roman under the auspices of the Hungarian government.

Left-brain learners are the analysts who feel lost without a ruler and a protractor. Right-brainers, less enamored of numbers and measurements, prefer a conceptual approach. As a beginner learning how to measure certain aspects of handwriting is part of your education. But once your eyeball is trained, in most cases, absolute measurements are not necessary. Either way, when you know what the measurements mean and are able to recognize them in handwriting, you can experiment until you find the style of analysis that works best for you.

What tools of the trade?

- Ruler for measuring baselines and margins.
- Protractor to measure slant.
- Magnifying glass.

Why magnify handwriting? Because otherwise hidden features that could affect the analysis may be exposed under magnification. Little dots or "blebs" or miniscule breaks in the writing line, unseen by the naked eye, might point to a health problem.

As long as you can see through it clearly, it makes no difference whether the magnifying lens is round, square, or rectangular. The optimal degree of magnification is 2x-10x. You do not need to see the fibers of the paper, which is what you will get with a much stronger power.

Some magnifiers have a small inset with a higher magnification than the main part of the lens for getting up close and personal. Those with a long, flexible neck and attach to a desk or tabletop have a wider viewing area and a ring light. A photographer's loupe makes an excellent magnifier for the graphologist. eBay advertises them starting at under a buck.

Fine Points

Learning to measure provides a good frame of reference for beginners. Just don't to get so caught up in taking exact measurements that you forget to keep the whole picture in mind.

Do you need a microscope? Not unless you plan to branch out into the field of handwriting authentication, which is another story with an entirely different focus (pun intended). Also called document examination, handwriting authentication work requires additional specialized training and equipment. For recommended instructors see www.ahafhandwriting.org.

Books for the Budding Graphologist

Unlike the one you are reading, most graphology books on the market are trait-stroke oriented. They promise quick and easy shortcuts to learning your friends' and neighbors' secrets. Some even claim they will turn you into a graphologist in 10 minutes. If only it were that easy! Wouldn't it be great if you could just check off a list of traits and know that every time you saw a particular characteristic it always meant the same thing? Unfortunately, there are no shortcuts to becoming a competent analyst.

Appendix C lists some of the books I recommend. When graphologists retire or go to that great inkwell in the sky, their libraries often end up for sale at Mostly Books in Tucson, Arizona: www.mostlybooksazcom. They also sell monographs that may not be available anywhere else.

Another excellent resource is the American Handwriting Analysis Foundation, a nonprofit educational organization whose members have free access to a vast array of publications at no cost beyond the very reasonable dues: After being a member since 1977, I began serving as president in 2011. As of the writing of this manuscript, I still am. AHAF is probably the most progressive handwriting analysis organization in the world.

www.ahafhandwriting.org

School Copybooks

When you learn to measure handwriting, there is a basis for what is small-medium-large, long-short-wide-narrow, etc. Graphologists use the school copybook the writer learned as a standard. Most American baby boomers were taught to write with the Palmer or Zaner-Bloser methods. These were commonly in use prior to 1980. The more simplified D'Nealian method, which was released in the 70's has since become popular.

The client may write larger or smaller than copybook, more simplified or more complicated, or different in dozens of other ways. When you know the copybook he learned, you can use it as a frame of reference to determine how and how much he deviates from the norm. This gives you information about how original he is, or how much he needs to stick to standards.

Adults who stick to the school copybook they learned tend to work in administrative-type jobs where they must follow a specific structure—nurses, school teachers, secretaries, airline pilots, etc. Americans more than other nationalities do their own thing to suit their style. It is the alterations from copybook that clue us in on the writer's unique personality.

Those who have departed from the school model often say they feel bad that their handwriting is not as "beautiful" as it once was. The thing is, adhering to the way you were taught is not always a positive. While there is nothing wrong with doing so—we certainly need those pilots and nurses to operate within a narrow framework—there can be a downside.

Copybook writers as a group tend to be more conservative and conventional than groups who use a more simplified or a more elaborated form of writing. They may hesitate to step out of their mold and do something different, which can stunt their emotional growth. Luckily, there is room for all types in the world. To clarify, people of all types continue to use a school model writing. So, in this context, "conventional and conventional" means within the confines of that person's chosen social group, not necessarily the world at large.

Following are examples of the Palmer and D'Nealian copybooks, taught most commonly to those raised in the United States.

The Zaner-Bloser copybook is similar, but not shown here. Copybooks from Great Britain, France, and Germany are posted in the Resources tab on my website for free download: www.sheilalowe.com

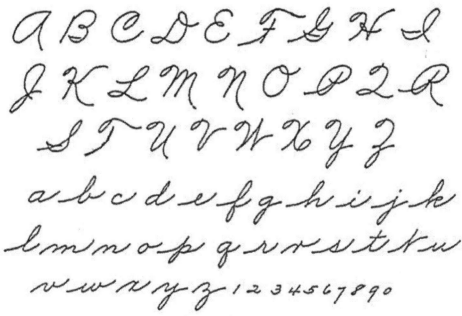

Palmer Copybook

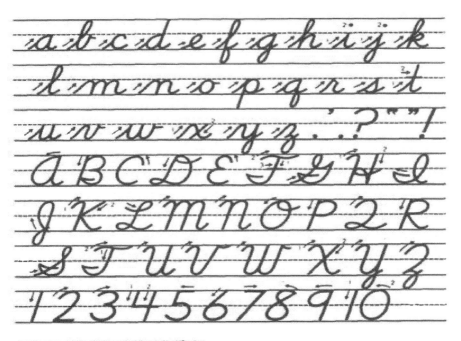

D'Nealian Copybook

Last Words

- Handwriting is symbolic of attitudes, gestures, and behaviors. You can learn a lot from handwriting, but it does not tell *everything* about a person. Handwriting cannot predict the future, but it does reveal a great deal about the past.

Chapter 3

The Preliminaries

Handwriting is rich with symbolism not readily apparent to the untrained eye. As part of learning to unravel its mysteries, you will discover what "environment" means in terms of the written word, and how to look for balance between the darkness of the ink and the lightness of the paper.

To the average person, "environment" might mean their living room, office, car. Essentially, your environment is wherever you are at the moment. To a handwriting analyst it means something different. From this point forward, get ready to start looking at a page of writing in a whole new way.

Def·i·ni·tion
Environment: The surroundings or conditions, influences, or forces, by which living forms are influenced and modified in their growth and development.

A blank sheet of paper takes on special significance as it waits to be filled with ink. The arrangement of writing on the page becomes a metaphor for how the writer organizes his daily affairs; his perspective on life, how he expresses his emotions, and much more.

A lion's natural environment is the jungle, where he can roam free. The zoo is an unnatural environment for a lion; yet, while he is probably not as happy in a zoo enclosure as he would be in the jungle, he can potentially live a long life there.

The same is true of humans, who also experience natural and unnatural environments. A person raised in an exurb inhabited mainly by well-off families would feel uncomfortable and out of his depth if suddenly transported to a federal prison. But, like the lion, humans can adapt and learn to live in a new environment when necessary.

What does this have to do with handwriting, you may ask? Everything. Your handwriting reflects how you behave within *your* environment, whether it is natural or unnatural to you. An analysis can help determine how well you have adapted to your environment, whatever it may be.

A Room with a View?

Visualize a piece of paper as a room waiting to be filled with the furnishings you choose. Until you begin laying ink on the paper, the room is empty. Mentally plan the decor of your imaginary room. Pick out the color and style carpeting and paint or wallpaper that appeals to you, the type of furniture you prefer; consider where you might hang the artwork, the personal knickknacks and ornaments that make it uniquely yours. You can have anything you want here. It's just a mental exercise, so live a little! Be as extravagant as you like.

Just as your personal style and taste determine the design and final look of a literal room, so the way you have integrated your past experiences and relationships into your life will influence how your handwriting appears in your symbolic room.

It doesn't matter whether you use a sheet of lowly notebook paper or expensive watermarked vellum. You can turn that environment into a jungle, a desert, a cozy den, or a sophisticated drawing room. It's entirely up to you.

Analyzing handwriting is a way of exploring the writer's reality. Doing it accurately requires learning looking at handwriting in an entirely new way. And that requires a change in your frame of reference through "eye training."

Eye Training: A how-to exercise

When it comes to your environment, changing your frame of reference can be as easy as turning off a light. The same objects you saw with the lights on are still there, but things look very different in the dark.

Or you could look at an object from a different perspective. As a kid you may have lain on your back and hung your head off the end of your bed to

find that the floor and ceiling look completely different from that angle. In the
context of handwriting, to change your
frame of reference means scrapping
what you think and looking from a different point of view—at handwriting as
a whole picture, rather than a collection
of individual words or strokes.

Fine Points

Exercises in Betty Ed-
wards's book, *Drawing
on the Artist Within* (J.P.
Tarcher, Inc., 1979), can
help you get in touch
with your creative side
and change your frame
of reference.

Before we begin, we want to activate the
right side of the brain. In an earlier chapter you read that graphotherapy
exercises can make changes in the brain using simple form drawings like
the propeller exercise found here.

Take a sheet of lined paper or graph paper and make several rows of infinity
symbols turned on their sides like the ones above. Try to make them a little
more even than I did, focusing on the movement until you feel the percep-
tual shift. You'll know it when you feel a little dreamy. Your conceptual
self—the right brain—has taken over. You can even use your nondominant
writing hand if you like. Adding baroque music such as Pachelbel's Canon
in the background is even better.

Right-brain exercise

After achieving the shift, your eye training begins. You will need a full-size
sheet of paper covered with writing, your own or someone else's; any old
page of writing will do.

Take a good look. What do you see? At this point it's just a collection of
words, so we need to change your perspective. For this exercise it would be
okay to scan the page and look at it on the monitor. Or, prop the paper up
on a stand or tape it to the wall. Move far enough away that you cannot
read the content. Stare at it for a while. Try to see the page as if it were a
painting, your own personal Picasso or Rembrandt.

Force yourself to look past what you think you know about handwriting.
Like an artist, see the shapes, the colors produced by the flow of ink, the

textures, the area between the shapes, the white space that creates a border around the image. Let your eyes relax and become unfocussed until there is an "Aha!" moment where the marks on the paper seem to shift and change. Now you aren't seeing words, but a whole picture, which may be somewhat different from your original impression.

Next, turn the page of writing upside down and once again step away. What happened? You lost your original frame of reference and were forced to see the writing as a whole object instead of as single words, letters, and parts. Even if you wanted to, you could not identify individual elements of the writing. And that is our goal—to force you to look at the whole object rather than words on a page.

 Tool Tip

If you studied the trait-stroke method of handwriting analysis and consequently find it difficult not picking out individual strokes and traits, turn the writing upside down. This tricks your brain into seeing the whole picture.

> When analyzing someone else's handwriting, you can actually experience the emotions that the writer experienced while drawing the trail of ink across the page.

When you are able to see the writing as a whole, you will get an instinctive feeling about it that has nothing to do with logic. It takes practice, but if you allow your intuitive sense to take over, you will learn to perceive the *patterns* of the writing, the *rhythms*, the symbols that appear—slashing knives, hearts, whirling tornadoes, and so on.

The "Ground" Work

We are about to put our toes into a concept that may at first seem strange—gestalt psychology. But by the end of this chapter, hopefully, you will understand why the gestalt terms "figure" and "ground" explain the basic principles of gestalt graphology.

Gestalt psychology is a school of thought with roots in 1930s Germany, and grew popular in the United States around World War II. Its originators were Kurt Koffka, Max Wertheimer, Wolfgang Kohler, and Fritz Perls, researchers who based their theories on the concept that nothing exists in a vacuum. In other words, when something affects one part of an organism, it affects all of the other parts in some way, too. Think of the last time you stubbed your toe. It wasn't just your toe that hurt, was it? The pain shot through your entire being and made itself felt from head to foot.

> In gestalt psychology there is no meaning without a context in which to put all the elements.

If you were to place some handwriting under the lens of a microscope, your field of vision would be limited to a few words or letters. How that tiny bit fits into the whole, which is vital to an accurate understanding of personality, would be beyond your ability to see. Thus, picking out a single letter or stroke, or analyzing just a scrap of writing and trying to reach a conclusion about the whole person, makes little sense. We need the page to provide a context for the writing.

Figure-Ground

According to gestalt psychology, we see things as solid objects—a *figure* against a background—the *ground*. For example, you see your friend Linda as a whole person against the background of her house; she is not simply an inventory of body parts. Likewise, a computer is made up of CPU, cables, monitor, keyboard, mouse, and many other peripherals, but unless you are a computer geek, you are likely to view all those parts simply as "the computer." Likewise, handwriting is made up of many different parts: strokes, letters, words, sentences, and paragraphs, but we want to see it as a whole object—handwriting.

In handwriting analysis, the ground is the paper and the ink is the figure. Thus, in a sense, we see the finished trail of ink as an object against the background of the paper. While, pulling out individual letters or strokes contributes some superficial information about the writer, *the sum is always greater than its parts*. Outside the context of the whole writing, individual bits and pieces of writing reveal little of the whole person.

Take the letter t. You might examine a handwriting where the t's are crossed very high on the stem. In the trait-stroke handwriting analysis system, the small letter t relates to one's work and goals. The height at which the t is crossed tells how high the writer sets his goals.

Theoretically, if the t is crossed high on the stem, the writer sets his goals at high levels. A well-trained stroke handwriting analyst will add and weigh many other factors against the t-crossing in order to reach a conclusion, but beginners often base their judgment on individual strokes alone. And, unfortunately, in my own experience, many students who take the "8 Basic" beginner course never progress beyond it.

With this approach, important information is omitted. We don't know what types of goals he might have, or how firmly he is committed to them. We don't know whether the writer has the energy to follow through on his goals and see them to completion. But viewing the handwriting as a whole, the answers to those questions are apparent.

> Handwriting is like a microcosm of the human body:

In order for a human to live and breathe, he needs a circulatory system, nervous system, respiratory system, skeletal system, and all the other systems working together as a whole entity. If a few parts of a system are missing or not working properly, it affects the way all the other parts work.

At what point can we say we have a person? When the heart is pumping blood? When the lungs are sucking in air? When synapses are sparking in the brain? There is no such point. None of the individual organs or other parts by themselves, or even one or two together, are representative of the whole, living human being. Not until all the pieces are working together can we say, "It's a person." Of course, it's true that sometimes some of those systems break down and other systems (or outside systems) must compensate.

The strokes that make up the letters, the letters that make up the words, and the words that make up the paragraphs are analogous to the various organs and systems that make the body work. Just as the organs must all function together within the framework of the body, all parts of handwriting must be seen as working together as a whole within the context of the piece of paper they are written on.

A Fine Balance

"You never get a second chance to make a good first impression." When looking at a handwriting sample, you are meeting the writer for the first time. That first impression is a very important one. Handwriting is as individual as those who write. The first glance at a sample speaks volumes to the well-trained handwriting analyst, even before starting the analysis.

Pay attention to your gut reaction. Ask yourself, how well balanced is this page? Is the figure/ground relationship (the amount of writing compared to the white space on the paper) at least moderately even, or does one overpower the other so much so that viewing it is disturbing?

What does a well-balanced page look like?

Exaggerations of any kind disturb the whole picture. Your eye should not be drawn to any one particular element on the page.

There are some ways to quantify balance, such as measuring the margins, the space between words and lines (which we will cover later), but mainly, it "just feels" balanced. Nothing jumps out at you. The writing is framed by even, balanced margins on all sides; the lines are clearly spaced, no loops hanging down from the line above to interfering with the writing on the next line. There is a pleasant harmony between the writing and the paper on which it is written.

On the other hand, if you look at a writing and your first response is "Eww!" it's your first clue balance is lacking somewhere. A lack of balance makes you feel uncomfortable, as if you need to fill in the blank spaces with something, or erase some parts because there is too much writing and too little white space.

The "Eww" factor might not sound like a very scientific approach, but handwriting analysis, while using the scientific method, is also partly an art that requires eye training and intuition. The intuitive part will be more difficult for left-brain thinkers who prefer to follow rules. But even the intuitive analyst must learn to be objective when it comes to interpreting what he sees, not allowing personal biases to affect the outcome.

Looking for balance involves seeing not only the handwriting itself, but also the negative space. Yes, the blank spaces in and around the writing can be just as significant as the writing itself.

Pressed In

When the page is unbalanced because of a problem with the writing, you will know it because very little of the paper is visible. Words and lines are pressed in, compacted, crowded together, leaving little breathing space. The writing overtakes the entire page.

What type of person uses up all the space on the paper? Someone who feels the need to dominate and control the environment. His living area may be just as cluttered with furniture and other objects as the written page he produced. The writer may be a collector of fine art or a greedy hoarder. Other aspects of the writing that we will cover later will reveal which is more likely to be the case.

Spaced Out

If lack of balance is caused by too much white space, the paper has over-whelmed the writing. Rather than too much, there is too little writing, with lakes of space between words that draw the eye. In some samples, a pattern of wide spaces moves down the page, creating a river of space, line by line.

There are various ways the picture of space can cause imbalance. Maybe one of the margins is extremely wide and the other extremely narrow, re-sulting in the page looking lopsided. Or, the margins all around may be too wide, so the writing looks like a sad little island in a sea of space. Any of these problems create a lack of balance in the spatial arrangement.

Def·i·ni·tion

Negative space: The space *around* the words that helps define the figure/ground relationship.

What kind of writer leaves big holes in their writing? In some circumstances this phenomenon may be the result of vision problems, so it would be wise to check with the client.

If vision is not the cause, the writer probably needs an abundance of space in her day-to-day life. This person does not appreciate being micro-man-aged or having someone hanging over her shoulder while she works. She does her best work when left alone

She tends to arrange her personal space with an aesthetic eye. Her house may be sparsely furnished, or he may isolate himself and avoid contact with other people. Interestingly, while it is her choice to separate herself, she feels lonely and alone.

You probably already know much more about handwriting than you think you do. Test yourself with the following three handwriting samples.

Which writing is balanced? Which is too spaced out? Which is too compressed? Check the amount of white space on the paper against the dark area of the writing to see if there is good figure/ground balance.

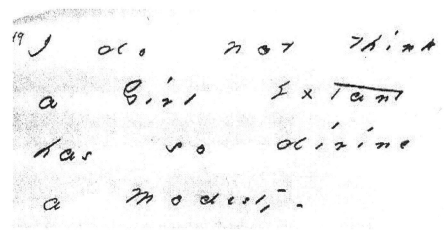

Sample A: Emily Dickinson, poet

Sample B: Dame Maggie Smith, actress

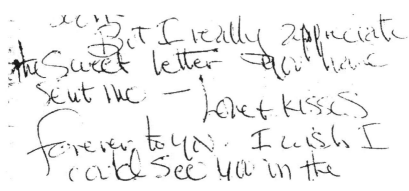

Sample C: Jimi Hendrix, musician

It's probably not too difficult to recognize which samples lack balance in the black/white space, is it?

If you picked A, those enormous spaces Emily Dickinson left between the words probably distracted you. But if you chose C, you need some more eye training. Jim Hendrix's script is as wild as the (dis)harmonies he was so good at creating. If Sample B, Maggie Smith, was your choice for the balanced one, well done! You were correct.

This table provides some pairs of opposites that will you can use to describe the writing space you are analyzing.

Harmonious	Inharmonious
Orderly	Disorderly
Clear	Confused
Light	Heavy
Lively	Sluggish
Elegant	Crude
Simplified	Complicated
Regular	Irregular
Original	Commonplace

Taking up a collection

To begin the process of analysis, you will need to collect as many hand-writing samples as you can for practice. Use the guidelines in Chapter 2. With each sample, do the exercise described earlier in this chapter, where you looked at your own handwriting from a distance. The better you train yourself to look at the writing as a picture, the easier it will be to determine whether the picture is balanced or not. For one thing, the answer will tell how well the writer organizes his life.

Fine Points

View the handwriting as if it were a painting. Don't try to analyze it yet. Analysis takes eye training, and that means observing many handwriting samples before you can expect to "get it."

Without exercise, muscles get weak and atrophy. Strengthen your graphology muscles by continually looking for ways to exercise your perception and eye training. Ask everyone you know to get their friends and acquaintances to volunteer handwriting samples for you to use for practice. Collect samples of as many different writing styles as you can.

Always remember, we take on the awe-inspiring task of putting ourselves into someone else's reality. *It is vital to remain objective and neutral.*

Let's say you are going to analyze my handwriting. We just met for the first time and I remind you of someone you don't like. If you project what you feel about that *other* person onto me without letting me show you by my actions who *I* am, you may well form a wrong impression of the real me.

> We must "become" the writer, become one with his handwriting, and *listen to the story that it wants to impart.* The analyst who imposes on the handwriting sample what he wants to hear is likely to get the wrong message.

The good analyst is required to put his 'self' aside and ask the writing questions, then be ready to receive the right answers. Letting the writing speak to you helps you to connect naturally with the personality behind it.

Returning to the opening concept of this chapter, look at your handwriting and ask yourself, "How do I behave within my environment?" Picture yourself in a crowded room at a party where you don't know anyone. The guests seem to be having a good time, eating hors d'oeuvres and dancing, enjoying their conversations. Do you make a grand entrance, jump right in, and introduce yourself? Or do you feel awkward and sit shyly in a corner on your own, waiting for others to introduce themselves? How about when you are alone? How do you use your environment then? Or at work, at school, on the road in your car, or in the supermarket?

Tales from the Script

Graphologist Tam Deachman and his companion went to a small bistro. The daily specials, handwritten on a chalkboard in a flamboyant script, had an obvious flourish and many embellishments and ornamentations. His companion issued a challenge: "Who wrote it?" Tam glanced around the restaurant at the various employees. Just then, the kitchen door was flung open and into the dining room stepped a man dressed like a French chef, complete with floppy toque and curled moustache. "There's your writer!" Tam declared. He was right!

Handwriting is the body language of the mind. It reflects in a very real way how people act behave their environment. The way Italian film star Roberto Benigni clambered over the seats, nearly trampling Steven Spielberg on his way to accept his 1999 Oscar for *Life is Beautiful,* suggests the exuberance of a large, right-slanted writing with loose rhythm. A timid, retiring person, is likely to have small writing, crammed up against the left side of the page.

People come in all shapes, sizes, and types, and their handwriting shows it. The one-dimensional person who understands only those who are just like him makes for a bad handwriting analyst. The greater the variety of personalities you can find to study, the faster you will grow into a competent analyst. You can have fun along the way, too. You'll be helping people, and they will think you're terrific for doing it. And they'll be right!

Last Words

Handwriting symbolizes how you behave in your environment. Seeing handwriting as a whole is more important than identifying individual strokes. Balance (or not) between writing and paper is the first thing to check. To begin your journey to being a good graphologist, collect as many different types of samples as you can find.

Chapter 4

A Space Odyssey

Interpreting the meaning of the empty spaces on the page is just as important as an understanding of the writing movement. In this chapter we will address the following aspects of space:

> ➤ Relationship to the environment
>
> ➤ Relationship with self
>
> ➤ Relationship with others

As we learned in Chapter 3, space in handwriting is the empty area *around* the writing on the page (the margins), and the areas *between* words and between lines. Space reveals much about our perspective on life, the invisible boundaries we set between ourselves and others, and how well we respect those boundaries. It has to do with how we arrange our environment and how we see the relationship between ourselves and others.

Don't Stand So Close! Perspective

Imagine being 2 feet away from the Sears Tower and looking up. Would you be able to tell how tall the building was? Of course not; standing too close to an object makes it impossible to get a correct perspective of its size. You need to stand back, but not too far back. If you drove 50 miles away and tried to gauge the height you would not be any more accurate than standing too close. Either way, your perspective would be skewed.

When we write, we don't take the time to stop and measure the distance between each letter, word, and line—to do so would make communication impossible. The brain takes over our use of space. The most unconscious element of handwriting, the picture of space evolves over time without our being aware of it.

Def·i·ni·tion
> **Perspective:** The ability to judge relationships between ideas or dis-
> tances.

Handwriting is limited by two physical factors: the available space bounded by the edges of the paper, and the energy invested when writing on the paper. A small sheet of paper creates artificial boundaries that are tighter than those of a larger sheet, forcing the writer to limit himself.

The writer's actions within the boundaries of paper size provide clues about how she views time, space, and money. Is he generous or stingy? Is she a profligate time waster, or one who jealously guards every minute of the day, the way Scrooge hoarded pennies?

A small amount of writing space constricts the writing movement. That's why we prefer the writer to use an ample sheet of paper the sample. One who crams a few words into the top left-hand corner of an 8 ½ x 11-inch page has a quite different personality from someone else who takes up every bit of white space on the paper.

Don't Fence Me In: Line Spacing

At the end of each line of writing, you must decide where you will place your pen to begin the next line. If you are relaxed and have plenty of time, you may feel free to use up more space. The writer who feels pressed for time is more likely to start writing the new line closer to the previous one.

Believe it or not, there are no rules about how much space should be left between each line of writing. Not even a school model provides guidelines on that issue. So, the choice of line spacing is a very personal one that provides the graphologist with several pieces of information about the writer:

- ✓ How she uses time
- ✓ How she uses her material resources
- ✓ How well-ordered are her thinking processes

Writing is a form of communication, so clarity should be a high priority. One who communicates clearly wants to make sure he is properly understood by leaving a reasonable distance between the lines of writing. No lower loops should hang down and interfere with the next line.

> When the lines are jammed too close together, it's like being in a crowd with someone whispering in your ear.

Line spacing is one of the indicators for self-control. The amount of space left between the lines establishes how well the writer recognizes the need for order and how well he organizes his life.

Clear Line Spacing

Clear line spacing indicates mental clarity and a sense of order. The person who leaves moderate distances between the lines is able to plan ahead and organize her life and time effectively. He knows the importance of contingency planning—that is, leaving enough time and space in which to handle the various emergencies of daily life without leaving herself in a pinch.

Fine Points

Balance is always the key. The interpretation changes when the line spacing becomes too wide or too narrow.

When someone feels free to leave ample white space between the lines, it shows that he's not afraid to use his environment to his advantage and implies self-assurance.

Clear line spacing demonstrates an ability to assimilate the impressions and experiences one accumulates from day to day and to express them appropriately. The writer is objective when dealing with a situation or problem, and considers a variety of potential responses and how they might affect the outcome. She reasons well and uses good old-fashioned horse sense to help her make decisions.

Narrow Line Spacing

When the spacing between the lines of writing is narrow, the writer's perspective becomes impaired. If other aspects of the writing support it (such as close word spacing, which we'll get to later) he may be an impulsive person who goes with his gut reactions, rushing ahead too quickly without taking time to reason things out. A subjective viewpoint allows this person to see things only in terms of how he feels about them and how they affect her, rather than keeping the bigger picture in mind.

Narrow line spacing also reveals something about the writer's spending habits. Jammed-together writing suggests compulsive caution in spending (that's a nice way of saying "cheap"). Just how careful he is with his resources depends on how closely the writing is packed. When there is little or no white space to be seen, one of several options will be true:

> ➤ The writer has a "poverty consciousness," which means he expects to be poor, therefore, fears spending.

> ➤ The writer is a stingy cheapskate.

> ➤ The writer is genuinely conscious of the need to be very careful in the use of resources.

The writing below is Herb Brenk, who was paroled in 2009, 16 years after admitting to killing and dismembering his wife. There are many problems with this handwriting, but here, illustrates narrow line spacing, which interferes with an ability to keep a clear perspective.

Narrow line spacing
Herb Brenk, convicted of killing his wife and sawing her body in half

Crowded Line Spacing

The writer whose spatial arrangement is impacted by extremely narrow, crowded lines is driven by impulse and lack of ability for abstract thinking and objectivity. In some cases, he may be more imaginative than someone who chooses wider line spacing. He is certainly less interested in taking time to reason things out than going by his gut instincts. He tends to live in the moment. Even in speech, his words are more impulsive and less discreet, and he has plenty to say! The trouble is, instead of thinking far enough ahead to measure his words, he gets so caught up in his ideas that when the words come tumbling out, he isn't always clear, so the meaning is obscured. Many good ideas can be lost this way.

Imagine that...

Please note: In this instance I've used the handwriting of a killer to illustrate narrow line spacing, do not interpret this as meaning that narrow line spacing by itself is a sign of psychopathology. Remember, no single element means anything outside the context of that particular handwriting. Herb Brenk's handwriting is filled with many danger signs.

Tangled Lines

When lines are written so close together that loops and/or parts of letters hang down and collide with writing on the next line (or several lines) we call it "tangling." The writer is suffering from a loss of perspective because he is too busy acting on his instincts and emotions to take the time to keep things in their proper place. Thoughts, ideas, feelings, actions are all jumbled together. There is always so much to do and he fails to plan ahead. The trait-stroke school calls it "confusion of interests."

The tangled writer's many activities spill over into each other. He's at the barber when he should be at a meeting, or he's off playing golf when he was supposed to have lunch with mother. Without a strict schedule (which he hates), he does what feels good at the moment. The vital but mundane routines that keep life running smoothly—like paying bills or doing laundry—are delayed, or in some cases ignored entirely.

Life with this type of person can get pretty chaotic and almost impossible for a partner who needs a steady routine. The tangled writer continually involves himself in situations that have nothing to do with him, not always using the best judgment. His prejudices may cause him to overrule his common sense, even when he means well. You simply cannot count on him to be where he said he would be, when he was supposed to be there. He's rushing around somewhere else, trying to cram more activities into his day than humanly possible.

The tangled writer's motto might be, "You only go around once." Don't expect him to listen if you try to offer constructive advice on how to better organize his life. He simply doesn't hear you. Oh, he may nod and say, "M'hm," but his eyes will either glaze over or be bouncing around the room instead of on you.

As always, the whole picture will help you decide whether to interpret this characteristic positively or negatively.

While author Nora Roberts has some tangling, the overall gestalt of her writing says this is simply a very busy person who needs a good organizer to keep her schedule on the straight and narrow.

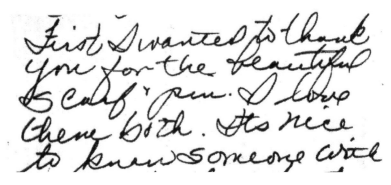

Slightly tangled lines: Nora Roberts, mystery and romance author

Moderately Wide Line Spacing

The writer who leaves moderately wide spaces between the lines of writing has a logical, orderly mind and a preference for keeping things clear. She is good at analyzing situations and concepts, and always plans ahead.

Her thinking is measured and orderly and she considers the consequences before acting. She is unlikely to act spontaneously or on impulse. Her tastes tend to be elegant and refined, with a strong sense of aesthetics, a love of beauty. She might be more at home at the Met than the local wrestling arena.

Whether or not they actually have money, there is a tendency of some people who leave wide spaces between their lines to be extravagant. They may feel less constrained to hold on to their resources, so they spend more freely.

The key to a positive interpretation for wide line spacing is that it should not be *excessively* wide. When spaces between the lines becomes so wide that you notice the white spaces between the lines more than the writing, we interpret it differently.

Below, you will find some handwriting whose wide line spacing plus linear letter designs and simplification (to be discussed later) reflects good taste, but the extreme word spacing suggests a sense of isolation.

tennis   as   a   career   goal

years   of   school   I   we

circuit   and   injured   m

then   finished   school,   ta

Moderately wide line spacing (and very wide word spacing)

Extremely Wide Spacing

Line spacing that is far too wide is a sign of one who has lost the capacity to act spontaneously. This is not an active joiner, but one who stands back and observes rather than participates. Permanently anxious, he feels isolated, separate from his fellow human beings and the world at large.

Do not expect this writer to do anything on the spur of the moment. He quickly puts the kibosh on any possibility of a rash act, needing time to consider how a future action might affect his comfort before making a move.

Fine Points

One who leaves excessively large spaces between the lines may be trying to bring order to an inner world that feels as if it is falling apart. The wide spaces are an attempt to create some kind of structure and order.

This might be the absent-minded professor who goes around with his head in the clouds, forgetting to take a lunch break because he is too busy working out a formula in his head.

He tends to see things more in discrete pieces than as whole concepts. Or, to put it another way, he sees the individual trees more than the whole forest. Being more concerned with maintaining his own space, he is not especially considerate of other people. With supporting evidence, he would rather do his own thing by himself than include more than one or two others, if that.

The handwriting of actor Jeremy Irons embodies the need for plenty of elbow room in his extreme word and line spacing.

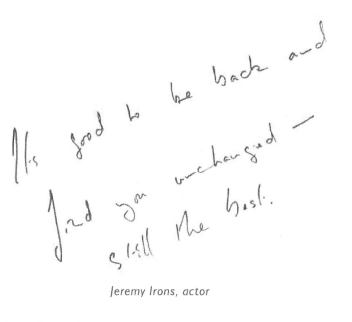

Jeremy Irons, actor

Irregular Line Spacing

The writer who sometimes uses wide line spacing and sometimes narrow, who sometimes lets his loops get tangled and at others keeps them separate, is inconsistent in his use of time, money, or other resources. His reactions depend on the circumstances and how he feels at the moment.

This writer may start out with the best of intentions (clear line spacing), but soon gets carried away with what she's talking about or the project she's involved in (the writing gets more crowded). If the line spacing is wider at the top of the page and narrow at the bottom, the more she gets swept up in her daily activities, the more difficult it is for her to maintain a clear perspective. She wavers between organized, abstract thinking and the need to go with her gut.

She wants to be generous, but that conflicts with a resolve to be conservative and thrifty, so it depends on the moment. In any case, the writer lacks good self-discipline and is unsure of herself, engaging in a continuing struggle between the limitations of time and resources and what she would like to accomplish.

Extremely Regular Line Spacing

Extremely regular line spacing is made by the inflexible, obsessive person who feels compelled to follow a strict routine. He finds it impossible to vary from the daily rituals he has established to help him get through life. If you come across someone who writes this way, refer him to a counseling professional. You'll know this type of writing by its machinelike look. Yes, the following sample is a font, but it illustrates the point.

I have left the instruction manual for the washer/dryer but it is not plumbed in as it was originally just for display. You may have to get a plumber for this. The clothes line is in the shed and fits into the pole (which also fits an umbrella).

Tales from the Script

The handwriting of one America's best-loved poets, Emily Dickinson (seen in Chapter 2), is an excellent example of extremes in spatial arrangement. She isolated herself, and during her 30s saw few people besides her family. Even those closest to her sometimes had to communicate with her through a closed door for long periods of time. The excessively wide spaces between letters, words, and lines reflect her isolation.

Outer Space: Word Spacing

Inhale. Exhale. Inhale. Exhale. We speak and we pause to breathe at the end of a thought. Some people speak quickly with less breathing space between their words than others do. Some speak so fast that their words run into one another. The spaces between words have been compared to taking a breath in speech and reveal one's need for social distance. How much space do *you* need in order to feel comfortable around other people?

The amount of space a writer leaves between words is a pretty good indication of how much personal space she demands from others and the degree of self-restraint she uses in social situations.

What is a "normal" amount of space between words? A good rule of thumb is to use the width of a letter m in the writing you are analyzing.

Fine Points

Measuring word space by using the width of the letter m is not an absolute measure, but is proportional depending upon the sample. A large handwriting will have a larger m, but proportionally, the space between words where the m fits may be the same as a small writing.

Balanced Word Spacing

The writer whose word spacing is well balanced is fairly comfortable asserting his need for space. He expects other people to respect his privacy and is willing to give them the space they deserve. Comfortable around other people, he is fine spending time alone, too. More or less conventional when it comes to social interaction, he likes to feel that his behavior conforms to the norms of his social group, whether that group is a book club or a motorcycle club.

Balanced word spacing: Bill Gates, Microsoft magnate

This small sample of Bill Gates' writing shows balanced word space.

Wide Word Spacing

Moderately wide spaces between words (wider than the letter m in the particular writing sample you are analyzing) tell us that the writer is a clear thinker who likes to step back and pause for reflection. That willingness to pause for a breath shows also that he is considerate of others, because he takes the time to see if his listener understands where he is going in the conversation.

As in wide line spacing, wide spaces between words have an effect on the writer's ability to act spontaneously. He may be charming and sophisticated, but he is also socially reserved and literally keeps his distance. Don't run up to this person and give him a big sloppy kiss in public.

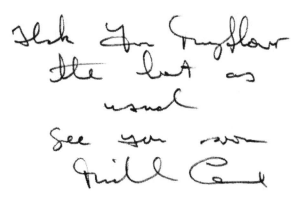

Sir Michael Caine. actor

This writer is not easy to get to know. His standoffishness keeps him from becoming too involved on an intimate level. Relationships are viewed more in the abstract than the personal, and you can expect her social circle to consist of a carefully chosen few. Jackie Onassis, who we viewed above, would fall into this category, as does Sir Michael Caine.

Extremely Wide Word Spacing

Extremely large spaces between words disrupt the flow of communication and indicates problems in the writer's ability to string ideas together in a logical progression. Socially isolated, he has difficulty expressing his thoughts clearly. He probably has some wonderful concepts

Fine Points

 Teenagers with a wide spatial arrangement in suffer from feelings of loneliness and isolation, which they try to cover with indifference.

in his head, but they may not make it out of his mouth, because he gets lost in the unimportant details.

When words become islands in oceans of space (remember Emily Dickinson's handwriting), it implies a profound inability to connect with other people on their level. This is not a voluntary condition. The writer may have a deep desire to make contact but the fear of intimacy is stronger. Long pauses between words, rather than taken as a moment to reflect, become a social crevasse. Awkward and insecure around people, he is uncomfortable in crowds, and withdraws into a shell of shyness.

In extreme cases, mental illness may come into play. The writer may not even be aware of what is appropriate in social relationships. All he knows is the need to protect and defend his ego, which means shunning physical and social contact.

Extra-large word spaces are sometimes found in the handwritings of developmentally delayed people who feel isolated and cut off from the rest of the world. Unable to communicate what they want to say, they are helpless to express their inner needs.

Princess Grace Kelly of Monaco adopts extremely wide word spacing, but of course, this feature needs to be interpreted within the whole picture.

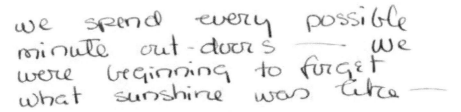

Extremely wide word spacing: Princess Grace Kelly, actress

Narrow Word Spacing

As in narrow line spacing, narrow spaces between words signify an impulsive, spontaneous person who doesn't take the time to reason things out. He acts and reacts as the mood takes him. So many impressions bombard him all the time that it is hard for him to sort them out. Step back and take an objective look before deciding? I don't think so! The word "rational" isn't part of this writer's vocabulary.

He is driven by a strong need for involvement and socializing, so don't expect him to keep his distance. This is an in-your-face, touchy-feely person who expresses himself through physical contact. He may pat you on the shoulder, hug you, or thrust his face close to yours when speaking. His conversation is stream of consciousness—whatever pops into his head one minute comes out of her mouth the next.

The narrow word spacing of Colonel Sanders of KFC fame reveals his desire for close social contact and difficulty with proper boundaries.

It may not look like it on the outside, but the person who writes with narrow word spacing is insecure, looking outside himself to get his needs met. He cannot stand to be alone for very long and will soon be looking for ways to connect with someone, anyone. Unfortunately, he is not always sufficiently choosy about whom he calls friends.

Colonel Harland Sanders - founder of KFC

Extremely Narrow Word Spacing

The purpose of spaces between words is to create boundaries. The letters form groups that are framed by the spaces between them. When someone disregards appropriate boundaries, he is behaving like the character on the subway who stands so close that you can hear him breathing in your ear, even though the train isn't all that crowded. You want to elbow him out of your way.

Words so close together that they almost (or do) touch suggest the writer with an extreme need to surround himself with other people. He leaves no space for self-exploration and, since he requires no space for herself, also has no regard for the space of others. His social boundaries—his sense of what is appropriate—are blurred.

Fine Points

Extremely narrow word spacing, especially when combined with narrow letters, can be one sign of obsessive thinking. Stalkers may adopt this type of spacing (not everyone with extremely narrow word spacing is a stalker!).

Like a puppy always on the heels of whoever walks into the room, he needs constant attention and approval to feel good about himself. He acts purely on instinct.

Without continual reassurance from others he gets anxious. The moment he is not getting attention, his self-esteem plunges. The problem is, when it comes to the need for approval, the writer of very close word spacing is a bottomless pit. Too much will never be enough.

Murderer of three little boys, Westley Allan Dodd, whose handwriting appears below, had such a need to talk to the media (and anyone else who would listen) about his crimes that during his trial, the judge took away his telephone and mail privileges. Dodd requested to be executed because he believed that if he was released, he would continue to hunt children.

As for being receptive to new ideas, and giving the benefit of the doubt to someone who may be able to help, I don't think you had to really analyze the writing itself to know that. The fact that I responded at all, and what the words actually said should prove that point.

Extremely narrow word spacing: Westley Dodd, killer

Irregular Word Spacing

Irregular spaces between words suggests behavior that changes unpredictably from moment to moment. You cannot count on this writer to act consistently. Filled with inner conflicts, he is unsure of how to behave, either in the company of others or when he is alone.

He's always on the move, can't sit still for long (especially when irregular word spacing is combined with extremely long lower loops). His movements, though, may not have any particular purpose. When the letters spill over their proper boundaries he doesn't mean to be impulsive, but the confusion that drives him is more compelling than the ability to control himself.

Inner Space: Letter Spacing

Spaces between the letters provide clues about the degree of freedom the writer allows himself internally and his receptiveness to others. They show the writer's gut reactions to emotional situations and his ability to act on them appropriately.

Def·i·ni·tion
> **Intraletter spacing:** The amount of space between the letters.

The ideal amount of space between the letters should be about the width of the letter n. In "ideal" writing, this amount of space would indicate adaptability, a capacity for give-and-take relationships. The writer is spontaneous and friendly, with the appropriate amount of warmth in relationships. She has the capacity to learn new ideas and is open to changing her mind when she finds a better way of doing things.

Wide Letter Spacing

If the letters themselves are also wide, you can be sure the writer is talkative, spontaneous, and outgoing, open to everything. He does whatever comes naturally without a lot of restraint. This is not someone who takes the time to analyze a situation using logic, but prefers to "let it all hang out," responding according to what's happening from moment to moment. Newsman Sam Donaldson's handwriting exhibits wide letter spacing and is otherwise wide open to the moment, ready to receive and act on whatever comes next.

Wide letter spacing: Sam Donaldson,
ABC News correspondent

Narrow Letter Spacing

Letters crammed too close together reveal an impetuous person who rushes to judgment and overreacts. Impulsive and often confused about what she feels and what others feel, her need to fit in with a social group can push her to behaving inappropriately. She desperately wants acceptance, so she'll do anything she thinks will help her fit in. This is the type of person who will give in to either internal emotional pressures or external peer pressure.

The handwriting of Susan Smith appears below.

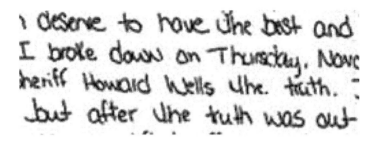

Narrow letter spacing: Susan Smith, killer mom

In 1995, Smith drove her two young sons into a lake, allowing them to drown because the man she was seeing did not want children (he was unaware, as was her husband, of her plan). She claimed to authorities that a black man had attacked her, but later confessed to her incomprehensible crime. She is still serving out her sentence.

Notice that Smith's letters are so close together that they actually bump up against each other, a big red flag for de-

Fine Points

When letters bump up against each other, the writer may be stingy with affections and emotions, especially when the letters themselves are narrow.

pression and possibly suicidal thinking. Several other signs must also be present before reaching such an extreme conclusion, and in her case, they are. Certainly, this feature always suggests a lack of good boundaries.

Inconsistent Letter Spacing

Inconsistency in any area of writing symbolizes ambivalence. In letter spacing, the ambivalence is about whether the writer should move forward or stay back in the shadows. He is uncertain and worried about what to do. An internal tug of war keeps him unsettled most of the time.

Secondary Expansion

A special situation is secondary expansion, where the letters themselves are narrow but the spaces in between them are wide. We interpret this feature as the writer having learned to appear to be outgoing, but privately shrinking from social contact.

> **Def·i·ni·tion**
> **Secondary expansion**: Narrow letters with wide spaces between them.

So, despite insecurity and shyness, the writer of secondary expansion pushes himself to interact, at least in groups where he knows people. We call this type of person a "converted introvert" because while it isn't natural to her, she's learned how to behave as an extrovert in social situations.

Britain's Prince Charles's handwriting is a good example of secondary expansion.

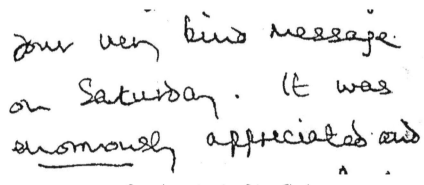

Secondary expansion: Prince Charles

Last Words

Spatial arrangement is the most unconscious aspects of handwriting. Clear line spacing suggests clear thinking. Word spacing shows your need for closeness. Letter spacing shows how much space you give yourself. A person who does not have a good self-image, yet writes with a clear spatial arrangement can usually get along in the world.

Chapter **5**

Back to the Future: Margins

Are you punishing yourself for the past? Raring to race into the future? Ambivalent about what lies ahead? The margins that frame the handwriting sample are about time—past, present and future. They reveal whether you have left the past behind, how you approach the future, and how you view authority, among other things.

When you look back over your childhood, are the memories mostly happy, with just a few experiences you might rather forget? Or do you recall what should have been a carefree time with regret that it was filled with sadness and pain? The margins on the page reveal the degree to which you have moved on from the past or it holds you back from emotional growth.

Def·i·ni·tion
Margin: The perimeter area that borders a page of handwriting.

Somewhere in Time

Handwriting in English and other Western languages begins on the left side of the page and progresses to the right side. A margin is created when the writer makes a conscious decision about where to place the pen. As he moves toward the right side of the page, two new decisions are called for—where to end that line and where to start the next. The result of these decisions is the creation of a pattern of blank space—the margins—that forms as the writing moves down the page from top to bottom.

An average margin leaves 1 inch of blank space on all sides of the writing. As a handwriting analyst, you will be confronted by samples that have virtually or literally no margins at all, and others with margins so wide that they form an ocean of space around a relatively small amount of handwriting.

The left side of the paper, where the writing effort begins, is symbolic of the writer's past. Moving across the page toward a goal, the writer reaches the right side of the page (however far he decides to go), which represents the future. What happens with the line of ink along the way, therefore, represents the present.

Fine Points

Margins are the blank spaces *around* the handwriting. This is a reminder that blank spaces on a page can be just as revealing as the writing that rests between them.

The left margin also represents the self ("me"); the right margin, other people ("you"). As the writer moves from "me" to "you" we can see whether he faces the future and other people with hopeful optimism, or fear and trepidation.

The space we leave on the right side of the page shows how we view the future. Do you look forward to the future with a hopeful, optimistic outlook or as something to delay facing as long as possible?

The paper can also be divided into three sections. The top third symbolizes the past, the middle third the present, and the bottom third the future. You will be able to see where in a project or a relationship—beginning, middle, or later—the writer begins to lose or gain confidence. Just look for the point where the writing either pulls away from or toward the margins.

Well-Balanced Margins

A handwriting that is well framed by nicely balanced—not perfect— margins on all sides looks like a picture in a frame. Balanced margins reveal a careful planner with a good sense of timing. Such a writer creates structure and order in his environment and doesn't appreciate it when disruptions threaten to mess things up. He prefers to carry out his activities according to a plan. He is neither stingy nor likely to spend lavishly. Using common sense, he budgets his resources (time, energy, and money).

The illustrations that follow are vastly reduced in size to train your eye to look *around* the writing and see the white space.

Novelist Dean Koontz sets his writing within margins that are not perfect (that's good; we don't like "perfect."), but are nicely laid out. The writing looks as though it is framed.

Balanced margins:
Dean Koontz, author

Reserved, with slightly formal manners, this type of writer is polite and courteous, but because he feels most comfortable within familiar limits, probably will not go too far beyond the boundaries of what he knows.

When the margins are too exact, too careful, we can infer that appearances mean more to the writer than substance. His home is likely to be just as orderly as his handwriting. This is the kind of person whose motto might be, "A place for everything and everything in its place." When things get out of place or unexpected events happen, his anxiety skyrockets. He is a bit of a perfectionist who cannot stand for anyone to see him at less than his absolute best.

Extremely Wide Margins All Around the Page

The person who places a relatively small amount of handwriting in the middle of a vast desert of space fears getting involved with life. Feeling inadequate, he keeps himself apart from others in an effort to hide what he believes are his deficiencies. While his limits are self-imposed, that does not make it any easier for him to reach out and make connections with others.

Extremely wide margins in an undeveloped or immature script may simply be a writer who is showing off and attempting to pass himself off as sophisticated and cultured when in reality he is not at all.

Keeping in mind that we must always look at the whole writing before reaching a conclusion about the writer, we need to look at whether the writing is otherwise well developed or not.

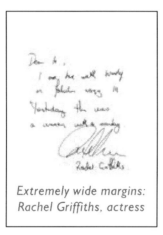

Extremely wide margins:
Rachel Griffiths, actress

For the writer of extremely wide margins, physical contact is especially difficult. The only way he is likely to allow physical touching is when he initiates it. If you reach out for a hug or to pat him on the back, he'll shrink away from your touch, possibly without realizing it. He might even take a step backward to put more distance between himself and the other person—a greater margin of distance, that is.

Narrow or No Margins

Looking for someone to take on that tedious project? Ask the person with no margins. Running a few bucks short for the rent? No problem, ask the guy with no margins (unless his letters are narrow, then he's stingy). He may not have the time or money, but he gets involved in anything and everything, whether he can afford to or not.

He doesn't know when to say no, which means he's often overextended. This habit can become problematic when his time and energy is wasted on trivia that doesn't get him anywhere. Not only does he waste his own time,

he'll make demands on yours, as well. This person is the juggler of innu-
merable activities and tries to keep so many balls in the air at the same
time that it would be a miracle if he could complete half of what he takes
on.

The writer with no margins usually crowds other parts of writing, too, such
as lines and words. If that is the case, he feels compelled to control "all
space," which includes other people's space, too. He gets involved in others'
lives to the point of intrusiveness.

If handwriting without margins is also large in its overall size, money probably burns a hole in the writer's pocket. No matter what resources he has
at his disposal, he feels obliged to use them up.

Next is another mother who wanted to rid herself of her children for the
sake of a lover. Diane Downs, a postal worker, was convicted of the 1983
attempt to kill her three children. She *still* claims a bushy-haired stranger
shot the family and attempted to carjack them. With one daughter shot
dead and the other two injured, she shot herself in the forearm and drove
to a local hospital. Her son was paralyzed from the waist down, her other
daughter disabled. In 2010 she was turned down for parole and cannot
apply again until 2020.The story was made into a book by Ann Rule and
1989 movie titled *Small Sacrifices,* starring Farrah Fawcett.

Extremely narrow margins:
Diane Downs, killer mom

Downs's sample lacks any margins on any side. Writing from edge to edge,
she leaves zero space. This type of writer sucks all the air out of the room.

Ghosts of Christmas Past: The Left Margin

Life experiences begin at birth, and the initial placement of the pen symbolizes that magic moment. The left margin represents how the writer feels about the past.

Narrow Left Margin with Wide Right Margin

A narrow left margin combined with a wide right one suggests that the writer finds the past a more comfortable place than the present or the future. Safety and security are very important to him, and he is afraid to spend his resources. The need to economize nags at the back of his mind.

Going into unfamiliar places and situations or trying new things is stressful, so in order to keep the stress at bay he limits himself to whom and what he already knows. Old friends and family are where he goes when he needs support. The downside is, he may miss out on opportunities for growth when they threaten to take him out of his depth.

Narrow left margin with wide right

> The writer of small or narrow writing with no margins hoards everything. This is the person about whom it can be said, "He still has the first nickel he ever made."

Wide Left Margin

A wide left margin shows a strong desire to move forward and leave the past behind. Willing to get involved with life, the writer welcomes opportunities to meet new people. He takes hold of new ideas and projects without hesitation. That he does not use all the space he reasonably could indicates some degree of extravagance. That is, he will spend the time and money it takes to get where he wants to go, but he is not overly concerned about utilizing all of his resources.

Especially when the *right* margin is narrow, the writer courageously forges ahead into new territory and charts new goals. Rather than being overly concerned about conforming to convention or doing things the way they were always done before, he is more interested in what is coming up in the future than worrying about the past.

Extremely wide left margin, wide right margins

An extremely wide left margin suggests that the writer may be running away from something in the past—something so upsetting that he cannot bear to think about it. The painful event could be in the distant past or it might be something that happened recently. It would be necessary to examine a series of samples written over a period of time to determine whether this was a habit or related to a specific situation.

Shrinking Left Margin

When the left margin starts out wide but shrinks back toward the left edge of the paper as it progresses down the page, the writer shows plenty of enthusiasm at the beginning of a project or relationship, but doubts soon begin to creep in. He starts to back off, second-guessing himself, wondering whether he is doing the right thing, or maybe that new project was not such a good idea, after all.

Shrinking left margin

He looks for ways to return to the safety of the past, which could mean going home, maybe calling old buddies, or following some ritual that makes him feel secure. His misgivings will have to be put to rest before he will return to his original plans.

Growing Left Margin

As you might guess, a left margin that gets wider as it moves down the page has an interpretation that is the opposite of the shrinking left margin. The writer is a slow starter but his enthusiasm grows by leaps and bounds the more he gets involved with a new situation or project.

President Richard Nixon's Growing left margin

If the handwriting with a growing left margin is also large, there is a tendency toward extravagance. The writer may not show the appropriate restraint when it comes to spending his time, energy, and money.

In the case of the next sample, written by Richard Nixon, the left margin starts out wide and only grows wider, while the right margin weaves back and forth. Along with other aspects of the writing that you will learn about later, the margins reflect his paranoia regarding his perceived enemies.

The left margin gets wider, while the right margin gets narrower, giving the writing as a whole the look of a tornado, swirling around and around. This a reflection of the way his thoughts must have been spinning at the time of writing this letter to newsman Ted Koppel.

Caving in or Bowing Out Left Margin

Imagine you are in a department store with your girlfriend, and she's about to splurge on a $75 black lace teddy but changes her mind at the last minute because it's just too extravagant. Check her left margin for the concave pattern.

Def·i·ni·tion

Concave: Concave dips inward toward the middle or "caves in."

Convex: Convex bulges outward and away from the middle.

A **Concave** margin starts at one point, pulls in for a few, or many lines, making it wider. Then, somewhere down the page it begins to pull back again. We find this phenomenon in the basically thrifty person who battles a desire for extravagance and pulls himself back before getting carried away.

Concave left margin   Concave right margin

Convex is the opposite of concave. Something convex bows outward, like a lens. Thus, the left margin starts at one point, moves further to the left for a while, making the margin narrower, then moved toward the right again, making the margin wider.

You have probably already figured out that the writer continually puts the brakes on his behavior, which tends to be a bit more openhanded than he can afford. He recognizes his tendency to be extravagant and tries to control it. Yet, because the end result is movement toward the right, we know that he can't always resist the temptation for a more freewheeling lifestyle.

Rigid Left Margin

There is less control over the right margin—we're not always certain of how much space will be left as we move across the page—but the left margin is always consciously chosen.

The left margin represents the ideal self—who the writer would really like to be. Just as significantly, the right margin is more symbolic of his real self—who he actually is.

Fine Points

A rigid left margin is less significant than a rigid right one, which has a greater degree of choice. A rigid margin is interpreted the same as any element of writing that is rigid: fear and inflexibility.

Strong self-discipline and willpower are needed to begin every new line in exactly the same place under the previous one. It also takes longer to maintain a strict left margin, suggesting someone who does not decide anything without first taking his time to consider all of the potential outcomes.

Rigid left margin

Convex left margin

Convex right margin

A rigidly straight left margin is made by a writer who is highly conscious of appearances and who doesn't allow himself or others any slack. Just as his margin is inflexible and premeditated, so are his attitudes and behaviors.

Someone this rigid is not easy to live or work with. He insists on following the rules (his rules), and that can sometimes refer to adhering closely to a literal lined rule when writing on notebook paper. Chances are, there will also be signs of fear and/or perfectionism.

Irregular Left Margin

A left margin that has a different starting point with practically each new line signifies either conflict about what to do next or that the writer cares little about society's convention and standards. He would rather improvise as he goes along. Likely a poor manager of his resources, it would be no surprise for him to run out of money long before payday.

Writing done to the left of a ruled line suggests one who literally makes up his own rules. Among the writers who ignore the left margin are juvenile offenders who refuse to follow the standards and rules of polite society. Yet, they may be easily influenced by their peers.

Writing that pushes beyond the left margin's printed line is a fairly uncommon phenomenon and is mostly seen in those who push the boundaries.

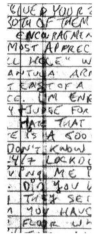

The illustration on this page is from a sample of music producer Phil Spector, convicted in 2009 of killing a woman visiting his home. He is currently serving a 19-year sentence. An HBO movie starring Al Pacino, who played Spector, aired in 2013. Notice how he writes far to the left of the ruled line, but there are far many more red flags in this handwriting than just its left margin.

Phil Spector, producer

Future Perfect: Right Margin

Courtesy of the left margin, our virtual time machine has taken us on a voyage through the past. Now we are about to move forward in time and explore the writer's attitudes about the future. The right margin reveals how ready he is to face what is ahead, as well as more about how he handles his time, energy, and money, and how he feels about social contacts.

Wide Right Margin

Leaving an extra-wide right margin is like stopping your car about 15 feet behind the stop sign; it's just a little too soon. The person who stops so far back is letting us know he is being cautious—*very* cautious. He wants time to see what's coming before figuring out how best to proceed.

Wide right margin

Past experience has taught this writer to view the future as an unfriendly place where he can get hurt if he's not careful. He feels overwhelmed by life and fears he won't be able to cope with any additional stress.

Steering clear of the right margin allows the writer to avoid reality for a while. By creating a safe framework for himself, he is able to stay inside those self-imposed limits, rarely extending his reach beyond them.

> A wide right margin may be temporary, related to a particular situation, such as job loss. An out-of-work single parent, worried about how she's going to feed her kids, may pull back from the right margin (the future). With a regular paycheck again, the right margin will return to a more norm al width.

Narrow Right Margin

The spontaneous, action-oriented person leaves a narrow right margin. Eager to set new goals and work on them, he cares about progress and is constantly looking ahead to see what he should do next. Outgoing and at ease meeting new people, he wants to try out new things.

If a wide *left* margin is balanced with a moderately narrow right margin, we can assume that the writer is poised, ready to jump at the chance to move forward on his goals.

When the right margin is overly narrow, almost to the edge of the page, it can be a sign of an eager beaver who lacks self-discipline. His impulses take over and he fails to consider the consequences before acting.

Extremely narrow right margin

Imagine that...

When the words actually careen off the edge of the paper, the writer is rushing headlong into the future. At the extreme end of the future is death. The writer whose words fall downward and crash right into the edge may be having thoughts of suicide. Or, he may just be suffering from temporary financial embarrassment because he has spent beyond his means. Take care how you interpret this characteristic and as always, look at the whole picture.

Expanding Right Margin

What if, as the writing proceeds down the page, the right margin begins to pull back (like Nixon's), so it is wider at the end of the writing than at the beginning? Although he may jump in with enthusiasm, the writer needs encouragement to keep on going.

Expanding right

He reverts to behavior that has proved safe and effective in the past rather than travel into uncharted waters. Completing new projects on his own may be a bigger challenge than he can comfortably handle. With other positive aspects in the writing, it may be that encouragement from his support system—the people he loves or respects—will help him complete what he started.

Shrinking Right Margin

When the right margin moves ever-closer to the edge of the paper, the writer welcomes new challenges. The more he gets swept up in his interests, the more his excitement grows.

Progressive and goal-directed, he is willing to involve himself in things he's never done before without a second thought. He may be shy on a first introduction, but his reticence soon disappears. In a group he watches everyone until he understands the power structure, then he'll put in his two cents.

Fine Points

A long, horizontal end stroke that fill in the ends of lines and touch the right edge of the paper is like carrying out a superstitious habit for protection, like "touching wood."

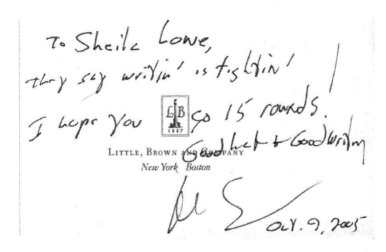

To Sheila Lowe,
they say writin' is fightin'!
I hope you [L|B] go 15 rounds.
LITTLE, BROWN AND COMPANY
New York Boston
Good luck & Good writing
MC
Oct. 9, 2005

Shrinking right margin: Michael Connelly, author, producer

Straight Right Margin

Making a straight right margin is much harder than making a straight left margin. The writer has to hyphenate words and take great care to line up last words of lines. Someone who goes to this much trouble has plenty of self-control. He also needs a tremendous amount of structure to function comfortably.

Whatever this person does, it's going to be something he's done before and will be done strictly by the book. Don't expect him to act independently or quickly. He's self-protective and has trouble adapting, so he needs time to adjust to new situations and people. He can't trust others because he doesn't trust himself. In an effort to safeguard his ego he creates the most predictable environment possible.

The next sample, written by the famed psychiatrist Sigmund Freud, is filled with contradictions. There is a tremendous amount of energy in the writing, which indicates a strongly emotional person. At the same time, the overall narrowness pulls him back from easily expressing his deepest emotions. One thing is certain, he was as complicated an individual as any of the patients he analyzed.

Straight right margin: Sigmund Freud

Extremely Irregular Right Margin

Some variability is expected on the right margin because it's not always possible to predict how the line will end. However, when the irregularity is extreme, the writer is guaranteed to be emotionally unreliable.

A poor planner, he's unsure of how he feels about other people or the future. An adventurer who is content with the turbulent life he creates, he'll take whatever comes next, and the more exciting the better. Pressured by a strong need for variety (especially when combined with very long lower loops), he vacillates from one position to another, unable to stick with a steady point of view about anything or anyone.

Extremely irregular right margin: Jon Benet Ramsey ransom note

In the late 1990s, six-year-old child beauty queen, Jon Benet Ramsey, was found murdered in her home, a 3-page ransom note discovered.

Jon Benet's parents, John and Patsy Ramsey came under microscopic scrutiny, as did their son, who was only 9 at the time. The police also came under intense fire for the way the crime scene was handled. For one thing, they allowed the parents to see the ransom note in preparing their hand-writing for comparison purposes. This is the opposite to what a document examiner should do.

Patsy Ramsey later died of breast cancer. After more than 20 years of con-troversy, her killer has never been brought to justice. Note the irregular left and right margins of the ransom note.

Your Majesty: Upper and Lower Margins

In bygone days it was customary to leave a very wide upper margin when addressing a letter to an important personage, such as royalty. It was as if the writer were putting a respectful distance between himself and the re-cipient of the message. Although that rule does not seem to apply in the twenty-first century, it is still appropriate to leave a respectful margin at the top of the page.

As a gauge of personal space, a narrow upper margin is like starting the conversation in the middle—the writer cares little whether or not you un-derstand the context. This inconsiderate kind of behavior may show a lack of discretion and appropriateness, especially with other supporting factors, such as narrow word and line spacing.

Because there is no set standard for the lower margin it is viewed as less significant. A narrow margin at the bottom of the page indicates enthusi-asm and spontaneity. The writer is so wrapped up in the message that he doesn't want to take the time to stop and turn over the paper or start a new sheet. Or maybe he's just impatient.

A lower margin that is too wide for the message, on the other hand, may indicate that the writer is more concerned about appearances than what he has to say. He reveals little about himself, and may not be telling the whole story.

Last Words

Margins reveal where you are in time and space. To learn how the writer feels about the past, check the left margin, while the right margin shows how eager you are to meet the future. Upper margins indicate your respect for the reader. Lower margins reveal enthusiasm about getting ahead.

Chapter 6

Stand Your Ground:
The Baseline

The baseline, whether printed or imaginary, may seem insignificant, but the fact is, it gives the graphologist several things to consider. We look at how well the writer adheres to the writing line; whether it goes up, down, or straight across, and what it has to do with reaching one's goals. In addition to all that, there are aspects of physical health that are reflected in the baseline.

The graphologist examines the baseline of writing to determine how much it fluctuates. In this chapter, among other things we'll cover how to measure the baseline and what baseline direction really means.

First, the baseline represents the very ground on which you stand. The question is, how steady is your ground as you move from one place to another? Are you walking on solid concrete, loamy soil, asphalt, quicksand?

Solid ground, not trembling and shaking ground, offers a measure of security. If you've ever been caught in an earthquake or hurricane, when terra is not so firma you feel insecure and anxious. All you can think of is keeping your balance, finding something substantial to hold on to or hide under for protection. When the earth stops moving, you breathe a sigh of relief.

Def·i·ni·tion

Baseline: The invisible or printed line on which handwriting rests and is created by the bottoms of the individual letters and their connections.

The Invisible Line

Thanks to the Common Core Curriculum, which was adopted in 2009 by 48 states, little attention has been paid to teaching children to write, with many states dropping the requirement altogether. Happily, since then, many states (mostly Southern ones) have returned the requirement for children to learn how to write to the curriculum. We hope that eventually all of them will. But I digress...

The person who used to be called the penmanship teacher supplies paper with printed with ruled lines, which provides a road map of where the child needs to go and how to get there. Without that printed line, and left to their own devices, there's no telling where those little writers would travel. The empty page offers an unlimited playground where anything goes.

Later on, once the child understands the rules (literally and figuratively), he begins to form a mental picture of the baseline he needs to follow and becomes less dependent on the ruled line.

What's Your Angle?

The baseline of writing may be an actual ruled line on the paper or it may be invisible. The bottoms of letters and the ligatures that connect them form an imaginary line that moves across the page.

Def·i·ni·tion

Ligature: Something that binds The strokes that tie one letter to another..

The position of the paper on the writing surface (desk, table, or other) directly affects the direction and shape of the baseline, as does the position of the writer's body.

Some people turn the paper at an angle to the writing surface, which tends to push the writing uphill and produces a rightward slant. It may also force the body to turn to the left, which affects the tension/release pattern (we'll discuss that in a later chapter). This position allows the right-hander more freedom of motion, which in turn means a greater release of tension. The same is true of the left-hander, but from the opposite direction.

The person who places the paper square to the edge of the desk and sits very straight generally produces writing that is upright or left-slanted.

Try this experiment:

Sit straight, facing the table or desk on which you are preparing to write. Put both feet flat on the floor and the writing paper square in front of you. If you're right-handed, you'll find that your writing arm is pulled leftward, while your hand is slightly torqued to the right, producing tension in the writing movement.

Traveling The Underground

Whether invisible or ruled, the baseline separates the handwriting into two areas: above the baseline and below the baseline. Since the baseline is symbolic of the ground, it follows that the area below the baseline represents "under the ground."

Plants that feed and nourish the body grow under the ground, an area we normally don't see. Remember, we're talking in symbols. In handwriting, the area below the baseline corresponds to the subconscious, where unseen forces motivate behavior and either stimulate personality growth or stunt it.

Fine Points

The baseline is the dividing line between reality (the conscious) and fantasy (the unconscious), the dividing line between the present and the past.

Logically then, it follows that the area above the baseline represents above the ground, where the fruits of the underground growth are visible. In terms of the writer's personality, this area represents the conscious aspects or expressed behavior.

Following the Rules: the ruler writer

The response to a request for a handwriting sample on unlined paper is often met with unmitigated horror: *"You want me to do what?"* The person who insists on having a ruled line on which to write has a strong need for direction, for specific rules, structure, and a pattern to follow.

More compulsive still, though uncommon, is the person who chooses to write on ruled paper, placing a ruler on the ruled line to boot!

The "ruler writer" is an example of extreme insecurity. Imagine how it feels to enter an unfamiliar room in the dark. You cautiously feel your way around the perimeter, afraid to step out into what might be empty space or a space filled with unfamiliar objects that might trip you. That is how the ruler writer experiences life. She doesn't know what might be waiting for her in that empty room, and that is intolerable. Thus, she sticks like glue to what is familiar—the baseline.

The ruler writer may have unresolved difficult sexual issues and uses the ruler to separate the middle and lower zone (the lower zone is the area of sexuality). In some cases, she pushes entire lower zone letters up into the middle zone. In other cases, the writer will cut lower zone letters (usually the letter g) into two segments.

Jittery and high-strung, the ruler writer lives with the continual threat that her internal chaos will overwhelm her. She fears that if she lets go for an instant, her life will spin out of control. Returning to the baseline—something familiar and safe—is like a ritual that gives her a point of reference she can count on (like the person in chapter 5 whose margins are extremely straight). Knowing what to expect allays her anxiety to some degree.

"Ruler writers" in essence cut off the lower loops, both literally and figuratively. Anything represented by those loops (we will cover that area of writing later) is consciously eliminated from the script and from one's own life. This is frequently found in those who are repressed, rigid, and overcontrolled. They avoid spontaneous emotional response and may use chemical substances to help loosen their controls.

Cutting off the area below the baseline also cuts off one's past and memories. That type of control means that the script is usually slow, and almost drawn rather than written. Some who write with this degree of rigidity are adults who were abused as children, emotionally, physically and sexually.

In this example, a man in his early thirties cuts off the area below the baseline, which is symbolic of his actual attempt to cut off his penis. The root cause of this extreme behavior is unknown.

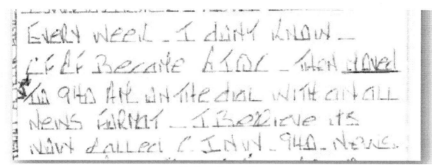

Male ruler writer

Female ruler writer

The writing above is a female in her 30's. It may be the extremely difficult domestic situation she was in that caused her strong need to cling to the baseline. Notice that what should have been lower loops appear above the baseline and look like hearts.

How About a Hug?

Among other things, the baseline tells the graphologist how much stability and security the writer needs. The degree to which the letters cling to the baseline indicates how firmly he needs to keep his feet planted on the ground.

Motivated by a strong need for security, the writer who hugs the baseline is pragmatic and believes only what she sees. Not particularly imaginative, she takes things so literally that she misses the irony in subtle humor.

The baseline hugger makes sure she handles the basic essentials—making sure there is plenty of food in the fridge, getting insurance coverage, and building up a bank account—before attending to anything else. Yet, no matter how much she stockpiles those material goods and money, it never seems to be quite enough to make her feel really secure.

Fine Points

Bottoms of letters that look very even and always return to the baseline are said to hug the baseline. This type of writing usually shows strong regularity and low variation.

Pretending to Follow the Rules

Then there are those who choose to write on ruled paper, then fail to follow the ruled lines. They write above or below the line. This writer wants us to believe he is going to follow the rules, but in reality, prefers to be independent.

Writing that hovers *above* the ruled line suggests mental interests, enthusiasm, and a spirit of adventure. The writer is particularly intrigued by what the future might hold. She focuses more on the possibilities and what might be, rather than what actually exists. She is not someone who needs to see something to believe in it.

The person whose writing falls *below* the ruled line focuses almost entirely on the tangible, material realities of life. There is little or no interest or energy left for spiritual matters, as he exhausts himself in pursuing her most basic needs. Depression or illness may be a factor in this case, as psychic heaviness drags him down.

Charting Your Goals

As we saw in the chapter on margins, the beginning of a writing line symbolizes the beginning of an effort, starting out toward a goal. The end of the line stands for the end of the effort, or completion of the goal. So, we might say that the baseline, which is created by the writing crossing the page toward the goal, is a major indicator of how goal-oriented the writer is. The *way* the writing progresses across the page reveals how the writer sets about attaining her objectives.

The steadier the baseline, the more focused the writer is on achieving her goal. Let's say you decide to take a road trip. How much preplanning do you do? Are you the type who decides on a destination, then download a map, check weather.com to make sure you have the appropriate dress, pack a cooler with snacks and drinks, fill up the car with gas, plan each stop carefully to make sure you have the proper amount of fuel, and let those who are expecting you know exactly what time you'll arrive?

Fine Points

 A rigidly straight baseline is an extreme, which is always interpreted negatively. A rigid baseline is made by a writer who feels anxious and insecure.

If this describes you, you are highly goal-oriented. You focus on what you want, making certain that you won't run out of resources before reaching your goal. At the same time, unplanned events are difficult for you to deal with. If you run into a roadblock and have to make a detour, or traffic is unexpectedly heavy and delays your arrival time, you may overreact with anger and frustration. Your baseline is probably quite straight.

> Balance means steady, not rigid. A rigidly straight baseline is an extreme, and extremes are always interpreted negatively.

Tales from the Script

Sally, who uses lined paper but writes well above the line, seems like a pretty conventional lady. She dresses conservatively, holds a respectable job as an executive assistant. Her manner is quiet and reserved. In her "other life" her individuality bloomed. Sally's night job is acting! On stage, she is flamboyant, ebullient, and totally outrageous. Like her handwriting, outwardly, she follows the rules, but only to a point.

Maybe you are the type who suddenly decides you want to go somewhere, though you're not sure where. You grab a jacket, jump in the car, and head out on the road, not bothering to check the gas gauge. You just might end up sleeping in the car because you run out of gas and have no hotel reservation.

When you arrive at your unknown destination, it might be somewhere exciting and wonderful. Or, you might discover the less attractive side of society in a yucky part of town. But to you, it doesn't matter because the freedom to act is more important than the goal. Your baseline probably wavers quite a bit.

How to Measure a Baseline

There are two ways to measure baselines. Each provides a different type of information. The first is to determine in what direction the line is going (rising, falling, straight across). The second is how well the writer adheres to the baseline. (See the following illustrations.)

Fine Points

Never mark up the original. Make a copy and drawn your line on that.

Measuring Line Direction

Place a ruler or any straightedge on a page of writing. Slide the ruler until its left edge rests on the bottom of the first letter on the line.

Measure across to the last letter on the line and draw a line between the two points. This technique tells you the direction of the baseline, whether it is straight across, rising, or falling.

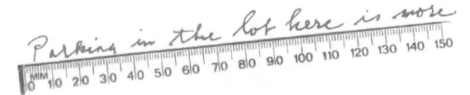

Measuring line direction using the rising handwriting of comedian Shelly Berman.

Measuring Across the Baseline

Now place the ruler on the page of writing so that the end of the ruler touches both the left and right edges of the paper. Place the ruler at the bottom of the first letter of a line and then lay it straight across the page. Draw a line to see if the words stay on the baseline, rise above it, or fall below it.

As you can see in the illustration below, the writing is quite regular.

Measuring across the baseline.

Imagine that...

Researchers have found that blood-sugar levels can have an effect on the baseline. When blood sugar is low, as in hypoglycemia, the person's mood plunges and the baseline may be erratic until the blood sugar increases. Blood pressure and muscle tension likewise affect the straightness of the line.

Moderately Straight Baseline

A moderately straight baseline varies to some degree. Overall, though, it proceeds directly from one side of the page to the other. It goes where it is supposed to go (from left to right in English; from right to left in Hebrew or Arabic), but is reasonably flexible about how it gets there.

The writer has good willpower and can be relied upon to pursue her goals persistently, using common sense. She handles unexpected events without getting too distracted, finds a way around obstacles, and quickly gets back on track.

The generally straight baseline (though it does tend downward towards the ends of lines) of former First Lady Eleanor Roosevelt illustration someone who knows how to set and meet goals. The downward trend can be a sign of fatigue or discouragement. Here is where the analyst needs to follow up and see if additional samples over time can be obtained. This will let you know whether the writer is just tired or has a pessimistic outlook on life.

Mrs. Roosevelt had a lot to contend with, so either could be true. But considering the dynamic movement in the handwriting, fatigue seems the most likely explanation.

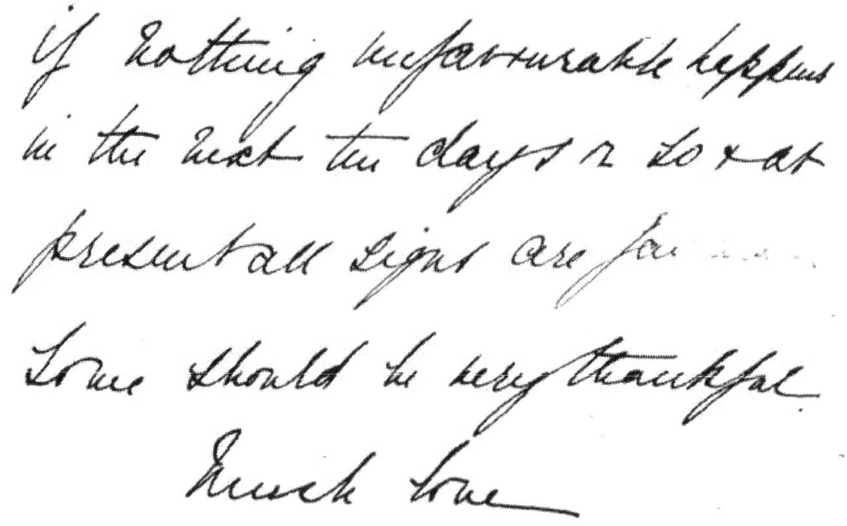

Fairly straight baseline: FIrst Lady Eleanor Rosevelt

Slightly Wavy Baseline

The writer whose baseline meanders casually across the page is easily distracted. He doesn't have a problem stopping what he's doing to handle something else. We call that multi-tasking. This writer probably welcomes interruptions. But will he return to finish the original project? Maybe. Maybe not.

Sensitive to what is going on around him, the wavy baseline writer easily adapts to people and circumstances. He is emotionally responsive with suddenly aroused emotions that are quickly expressed. Because he experiences more emotional ups and downs than the writer of a straighter line, you can expect him to laugh and cry easily.

We see this type of personality in the wavy baseline of former British Prime Minister Tony Blair. The gestalt—the big picture shows him to be clever and intellectually extremely bright. We don't know when this sample was written, so circumstances might have made the baseline wavier than usual.

> *political power throughout the U.K.*
> *and put the [?] of political part*
> *in a proper and accountable basis.*
> *). We will give Britain the leadership i*
> *Europe which Britain and Europe nee*

Slightly wavy baseline: British Prime Minister Tony Blair

Extremely Wavy Baseline

A snakelike baseline is formed by one who cannot make up her mind on even the smallest detail. She can't decide whether to go east or west; to the movies or play video games; wear green or pink, cotton undies or silk. It doesn't matter what she chooses anyway because the moment after she decides, she'll change her mind. Her fear is that as soon as she makes a choice something better might come along; then, oh dear, what would she do?!

Fine Points ————

The excessively wavy baseline is sometimes seen in the writings of criminals, but you must never judge criminal behavior or *any other type* of person based on only one sign!

As one who avoids conflict at all cost, don't expect this writer to take a firm stand on anything, even when her point of view is challenged. As aimless as a little boat adrift on stormy seas, tossed here and there by the waves of emotion that threaten to capsize her.

The writer of an extremely wavy baseline is something of an opportunist, always willing to quit what she's doing if something else looks like it might be more fun or more profitable. It doesn't matter who was counting on her to meet the original goal. You have to wonder about her ability to plan coherently, not to mention her sincerity.

You cannot apply the negative values to the teen whose baseline is extremely wavy. We expect teens to have loads of conflicting feelings and find it hard to stick to a course of action. Hopefully, the kid will grow out of it and their baseline will straighten out. One thing is for sure—the adult writer of an excessively wavy baseline is probably unreliable and not to be trusted with important decisions.

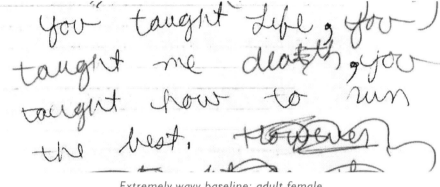

Extremely wavy baseline: adult female

Extremely wavy baseline of a teenage girl.

Ready, Set, Goal!

The direction of the baseline is strongly affected by mood or emotional state. A sudden welling up of emotion may cause a change. We look at whether the baseline as a whole moves up, down, or stays even across the page. Enthusiasm and optimism are factors, but other influences will also affect it.

As always: if you see something unusual in the direction of a baseline, ask for other samples of writing done over a period of time. This will allow you to better determine whether the baseline direction is related to a specific issue or it is the writer's habitual state of mind.

Uphill Baseline

Most graphology books claim that an uphill baseline means the writer is optimistic. This is not necessarily true. Much depends on the degree of the uphill slope. A slight uphill slant reflects spontaneity, optimism and enthusiasm, someone excited about the future. On the other hand, an extremely slanted baseline, if supported by other factors, suggests that the writer may be fighting depression.

We saw the handwriting of novelist Dean Koontz in an earlier chapter. Here it is again, this time demonstrating the uphill baseline of enthusiasm. Why is this not a sign of fighting depression, as some uphill baselines are? Because the rest of the writing has strength and dynamic energy.

Uphill baseline: Novelist Dean Koontz

When the uphill slope is moderate, we interpret it as eagerness, ambition, and hopefulness. To interpret optimism there must also be self-confidence and self-assurance. The writer is not unduly influenced by his emotional state.

An extreme uphill baseline rises about 45 degrees from the edge of the paper, which suggests impulsiveness. The writer is excitable and driven by her urges and emotions. It takes a certain amount of forcefulness and aggressiveness to produce this type of baseline, so it's a good guess that he pushes to get his way.

Imagine that

Remember Sisyphus of Greek myth? As a punishment for offending the gods, he was doomed to push a massive boulder uphill. Once he reached the top of the hill, the boulder would roll back down to the bottom and he had to begin all over again, forever. That's how the person who creates an exaggeratedly uphill slope feels: as if life was an unending uphill battle. His attitude is "If I just keep on pushing, things are bound to get better tomorrow."

Downhill Baseline

In general, a baseline that points or falls downward is a sign of fatigue or illness, or it could indicate a generally pessimistic outlook on life. Again, only by examining a series of handwriting samples done over a period of time will you know which is true.

Fine Points

When a word falls below the baseline or jumps up above it, the word may have a strong emotional association for the writer and provide an important clue.

The bottom line, however, is that the writer is suffering from weakness for some reason, and lacks the energy and enthusiasm needed to effectively pursue the goals he has set. If the writer is in reasonably good health, you can infer that he is probably feeling discouraged and worn down by external events. The falling baseline of Hitler on the next page reveals his depression and well-deserved feeling of defeat.

Falling baseline: Adolph Hitler

Convex Baseline

Earlier, we discussed convex margins, which bow outward. There are also convex baselines. This baseline rises in the middle like a hill, then falls back down by the end. It signals someone who starts out with passion about a new thing, but her interest and enthusiasm quickly die out. In other words, she's a better starter than a finisher.

Actress Miranda Richardson has a sort-of convex baseline in this small sample. It goes up, then goes back down. Her enthusiasm ebbs and flows. She may have been tired or feeling down at the time of writing.

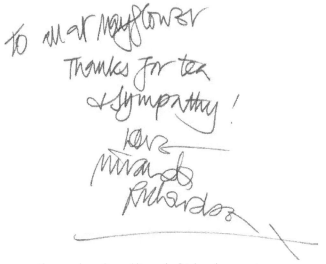

Convex baseline: Miranda Richardson, actress

Concave Baseline

We have also discussed concave margins—the kind that actually cave in and form a valley. The concave baseline writer is a slow starter who belly-aches about how much he has to do, and how put-upon he is, but who nevertheless finishes what he starts. Bit by bit, as his enthusiasm and confidence grow, he pulls himself up out of his negative attitude and does everything he can to meet his goal on time.

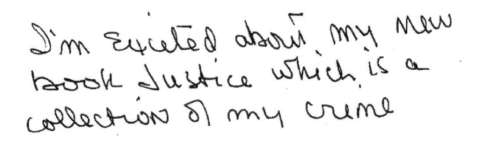

Concave baseline: Dominick Dunne, TV personality and author

Step-Up and Step-Down Baselines

It is unlikely that the step-up or step-down baselines will appear over an entire page of writing. They show up more or less sporadically, so we think of them as the baseline of individual words.

The *step-up* baseline is created when the baseline of each word rises, producing a tiled effect. In this case, the writer struggles to keep strong emotions and enthusiasm under control.

Fine Points

Words that step up or down may be emotionally charged and can help you understand the writer's emotional state at the time of writing.

The *step-down* baseline is made by one who experiences life as a constant struggle. He expects things to go badly and must pull himself out of depression on a daily basis. No matter how much he fights the tendency towards discouragement, and no matter how many times he picks himself up, he just seems to fall back down into a dark pit of despair.

Step-up (above) and step-down (below) baselines: Convicted killer Herb Brenk, whose handwriting we saw earlier, creates a new baseline for almost every word.

Herb Brenk - step-down baselines

Sometimes a baseline will be reasonably straight, but suddenly turn downwards right at the end of the line. This can indicate a lack of planning on the writer's part—he didn't see the end of the page coming.

Fine Points

Before deciding that the falling baseline writer is a pessimist with a negative outlook, ask if he has been ill recently, or experienced a major life event, such as becoming unemployed, which might have a temporary effect on the baseline.

This writer is often unrealistic and extravagant, getting into financial hot water by spending beyond his limits and having to pinch pennies to make ends meet. By using up most of his resources at the beginning of a project, he soon exceeds his budget and is forced to skimp later.

Last Words

The baseline of writing is the invisible line that you write on. Slight variations in the baseline mean flexibility. A super-straight baseline isn't a good thing, but neither is a super-wavy one. An uphill baseline doesn't necessarily mean an optimistic outlook. As always, balance is the key.

Chapter 7

In the Zone

Handwriting is divided into three zones that mirror various parts of personality. Each serves its own function, but none acts independently of the others. When one or two zones is either overdeveloped or underdeveloped at the expense of the others, the effects span the entire handwriting and thus, affects the entire personality. In this chapter we explore the zones and learn how they interact with each other.

You have learned that the baseline is the dividing line between conscious reality (the present) and the unconscious (the past). The middle zone sits on this dividing line.

Def·i·ni·tion

Reality: the state of things as they actually exist, rather than an idealistic idea of what might be.

Middle zone

- The self
- Day-to-day life
- Interactions with other people
- Communication
- Expression or control of emotions
- Acting out moral principles
- Ego needs and ability to satisfy them
- Ability to adapt

Middle-zone letters include the vowels a, e, i, o, u, and other small letters that have no upper or lower extensions. These are c, m, n, r, s, v, w, and x. Some letters have upper and lower extensions, but parts of the letters fall into the middle zone. They are the circle parts of b, d, and g, and the hump on h and y. Any stroke passing through the middle zone counts.

> Handwriting has three zones, which represent different areas of personality, but there is always an overlap. What affects one zone will have a corresponding effect in the other zones. Letters or parts of letters from other zones that wander into the upper zone where they don't belong are given special attention.

Like the middle zone, the upper zone is part of the conscious area of personality. Upper-zone letters have extensions that rise out of the middle zone: b, d, f, h, k, l, and t.

The movement the hand makes going into the upper zone is up and away from the middle zone, away from the body, then back down to the baseline. When we move into the upper zone, the upward movement of the pen symbolizes reaching up into the mental sphere, where the mind is free to wander, unfettered by the material world.

Fine Points

In a mature personality, the energy is distributed throughout the writing, producing symmetry and balance.

Upper zone

- Mental processes
- Spirituality
- Standards, principles, conscience
- Abstract reasoning
- Ambition
- Intellectual pursuits
- Imagination
- View of authority figures, such as one's father, boss, or God

The unconscious, hidden, instinctual aspects of personality, as well as our attitudes toward work and productivity, are stored in the lower zone. We are taught to write lower-zone letters by making a downstroke from the baseline into the lower zone, then a smooth turn to the left that forms a loop, then an upstroke that ends to the right for a return to the line of reality (the baseline).

Lower zone

- Biological imperatives: food, sex, money, physical activity
- The past, including experiences and memories that influence our behavior in the present
- View of mother or other close female, and nurturing
- Dreams and fantasy
- Release or repression of anger
- Susceptibility to stimulation
- The energy of the personality
- Productivity

Lower-zone letters have extensions that reach down under the baseline: f, g, j, p, q, y, and z.

Back to School with Freud

Handwriting analysis requires an understanding of personality. Without at least a basic foundation in developmental and abnormal psychology, the best you can expect is to identify a few traits, which is not helpful to your client. To develop a meaningful, helpful analysis, you must not only identify traits, but also recognize how they work together as a dynamic system.

Fine Points

 Letters or parts of letters that don't normally belong in the lower zone but appear there are a sign of unresolved pain and frustration.

Def·i·ni·tion

Psychoanalytic Model: Freud's personality development theories about the id, ego, and superego.

Freud's ideas have been hotly contested over the years, but it is generally accepted that most systems of personality development have their roots, at least partially, in his time-tested concepts of id, ego, and superego. Because his psychoanalytic model of personality fits so nicely with the concept of handwriting zones, we go there next.

> **Note:** while useful for our purposes, please understand that what follows is an oversimplification of psychoanalytic theories.

The Id Did It

Every living organism uses psychic energy (basic life force) to meet its needs in the physical, emotional, and spiritual areas of life. Energy cannot be destroyed, but it can be transformed for different uses and redistributed as needed.

Picture a lake that has been dammed. Some of the water is redirected into another area. The same amount of water still exists but is not all available at the same time for the same purpose. The same is true of the human organism. We expend some mental energy at work, then go to the gym and use some for physical exertion, and an entirely different kind in socializing when we go out for dinner with friends.

> Energy is transformed for use in different parts of the personality at different times.

Freud called the energy available to the human system the *id*, and identified it as the earliest part of personality to appear after birth. The id serves one purpose: to reduce tension and produce pleasure. It does not think or reason, it simply seeks ways to provide relief from discomfort and it doesn't matter what form the relief takes. If the source of discomfort is hunger, cold, sadness, or sexual tension, it makes no difference. The id's sole function is to make you feel good.

Def·i·ni·tion

Id: The pleasure principle.

The id knows only that it wants what it wants, and it wants it now! "Wait" is not a word the id understands. Like an infant who is not interested in putting off the urge to eat, the need to have its diaper changed, or the desire to be cuddled, the id demands instant gratification. Hungry, wet, or scared, a baby will scream to get relief, and that's appropriate for a baby. The same type of behavior in an adult draws stares of disgust.

We have all seen adults who, when they don't get their own way, have a tantrum. They yell and pound the desk and jump up and down, making unreasonable demands. We say to ourselves, "What a baby!" Such people act like babies because their emotional development never progressed past the infantile stage. Their id impulses drive them, rather than the mature adult quality of self-control.

Tool Tip

Hooks, knots, twists, and angles in the lower zone, indicate an unhappy id. The writer's basic urges are not satisfied in the usual, standard ways.

Although the distribution of id energy in the personality is seen throughout the zones of handwriting, we start with the lower zone, where it is stored.

The handwriting of one who remains at the id stage of emotional development runs wild. Unevenness and variability appear in every area: size, style, baseline, slant. Loops may balloon as the energy bursts into places where it doesn't belong. Life is all about doing what comes naturally without restraint. Id writing explodes into impulsive action.

Id handwriting: Marianne Faithful

For the id energy to be used effectively, it must be properly channeled. And that is the job of the ego, the next area of personality to develop.

The "id writing" of singer Marianne Faithful on the next page is all over the place. It goes where it wants and refuses to be restrained. True, there is tremendous creativity in the unique letter designs, but there are few, if any, controls. Everything in her world is *Big! Exciting! New!*

Ergo, the Ego

The ego is the "traffic cop" of the personality. It directs the energy where needed and as long as there are no other elements interfering, will help the individual make appropriate choices based on common sense and reasoning.

Def·i·ni·tion
Ego: The reality principle. The executive part of personality.

A healthy ego uses self-discipline and self-control to ensure that the appropriate amount of energy is available as and channeled where needed.

San Francisco attorney Sheldon Siegel is the author of five critically-acclaimed best-sellers: Special Circumstances, Incriminating Evidence, Criminal Intent, Final Verdict and The Confession. Mr. Siegel's novels feature criminal defense attorney

Healthy ego writing: Sheldon Siegel,
author of the Mike Daley & Rosie Fernandez mystery series.

If you are playing racquetball, you need more energy for the physical than for the intellectual area. In handwriting analysis class, you need more intellectual than emotional energy. But when you and a couple of your classmates decide go out for a latté together after class, the ego channels the energy into the social area.

Imagine that...

A large middle zone does not signify a strong ego, but a weak one. Overemphasis in the middle zone of an adult handwriting, especially with a high degree of roundedness, is a sign of immaturity. As you might expect, many teenagers write only in the middle zone. Short upper and lower extensions are made by those who live in the moment and have less interest in the past or the future.

So. The ego. You're walking by a bakery early in the morning. The aroma of warm, fresh bread curls into your nostrils. Your stomach grumbles longingly and your conscious mind starts a debate with your biological urge to eat something delicious: "You're on a diet and need to cut down on carbs," the mind says. "But it smells wonderful," argues the id. What to do?

A well-developed ego gains the upper hand and says, "Not now. You need to wait until you've lost 5 more pounds. Eat salad instead."

A handwriting with good overall balance suggests common sense and self-discipline, a strong ego. The writer is generally even-tempered and has learned to delay gratification until the appropriate time.

Fine Points

Middle-zone letters that suddenly flare up over other letters paint a picture of sudden outbursts. This phenomenon is known as jump-up or pop-up letters. The writer may normally be mild-mannered and low-key, but without warning, comes on strong.

Although its effects are imprinted on the entire handwriting, we look for the ego in the middle zone, where day-to-day routines and social interactions take place. That is where the traffic cop directs the energy where it needs to go.

> Everything passes through the middle zone. The middle zone is also where letters connect.

If a handwriting sample seems fairly neat and organized; nothing pops out to hit you in the eye, chances are the writer has a healthy ego and the ability to get his needs met in socially acceptable ways.

Welcome to My World: The Middle Zone

The middle zone, where the ego resides, reveals how the writer acts around other people, how well adjusted he is, and whether all the parts of his personality are working together harmoniously.

In the middle zone we act on the goals that were conceived in the lower zone (unconscious) and planned out in the upper zone (conscious). When one zone is much larger or smaller than the others—for example, a tiny middle zone with an extremely tall upper zone, or a large middle zone and stunted lower zone—the writer's goals conflict with his ability to meet them.

$$\mathscr{aeioucmnrsvwx}$$

Middle zone letters

How consistent the size of middle-zone letters tells something about the writer's sensitivity to the needs of others. The middle zone represents how we interact socially, so some variability in size shows ability to deal with various types of people. Some fluctuation is normal and expected, but when letter size (height and/or width) varies too much, the writer's ego is in a constant state of flux.

How much variation is too much? When the middle zone looks very uneven, with letters randomly jumping up and squishing down, it's too much. Are the words "look for balance" becoming your mantra yet?

Middle-zone letters of more or less the same height indicate a degree of self-confidence and ego strength. But too much regularity is no better than too much variation. The rigidly consistent middle zone writer is so fixed on his own protecting his ego that he cannot understand or is not able to concern himself with what others need.

Superego to the Rescue!

As the superego evolves through childhood, the child learns to live by the rules of society, he (hopefully) begins to develop a conscience. Its only function is to reward and to punish. The superego acts like the parent who peers over your shoulder when you want to do something and says, "Don't do that!" A little reminder goes a long way. If you constantly hear a little voice in your head whispering "you should" or "you shouldn't," it's a sign of an overly strong superego.

A super-strong superego is like a strict dean of discipline and Santa Claus rolled into one. It punishes you with guilt feelings when you fail to do what you were supposed to. For example, you give in to the id's temptations and overspend your credit limit. If, on the other hand, you fend off the naughty urge, the superego might reward you with the glow of pride and self-satisfaction that you controlled yourself.

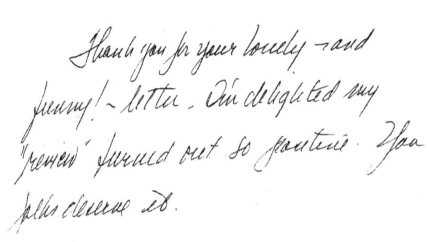

Superego writing: Radio personality Dr. Laura Schlessinger

Def·i·ni·tion
Superego: The Morality Principle. Conscience.

The handwriting of the person with a too strict superego looks rigid and overcontrolled. It is brittle and stiff, with tall upper loops and many angles. The writer's internal parent is a stern taskmaster that never relaxes. It rarely allows the writer to experience anything that might be pleasurable.

> Unlike a "strong ego," a "strong" superego is not desirable.

Machinelike rigidity

The superego writer is serious and has a hard time allowing himself to have fun, unlike the id writer, who wants *only* to have fun.

Soul Survivor: The Upper Zone

The upper zone is where the writer can expand his knowledge, let his imagination run wild, explore various philosophies and satisfy his intellectual curiosity. To effectively use the ideas of the upper zone, the writer must bring them back into the middle zone. Otherwise, he is simply building castles in the air.

Upper zone letters

When too much emphasis is placed on the upper zone, either by making the loops disproportionally tall or wide, it is often a sign that the writer has difficulty functioning in the real world (the middle zone), and compensates for his problems in the realm of the ego. It may be because he feels socially inferior that he escapes into the upper-zone world of the intellect where he can create his own reality. It feels safer.

As we look at some of the possibilities in different types of upper zones, always keep in mind that no single element of handwriting means anything outside the context of the writing you are examining. As with every other aspect of writing, you must confirm the interpretation of the upper zone with the rest of the sample.

Fine Points

A UZH that is too tall in proportion to the other zones, may reveal an intellectual dilettante who lacks the ability to manifest his ideas in middle-zone reality.

An **extra-tall** upper zone is like someone standing as proud as if he just won an Olympic gold medal. Whether or not the pride is deserved and based in reality depends on how well-developed the other zones are.

❖ A **very narrow** upper zone allows little room for the writer to expand his ideas. In a very real sense, he is narrow-minded and may be afraid to explore philosophies that threaten to draw him outside the realm of his own experience.

❖ A **tall and narrow** upper zone is often adopted by the writer who was raised in a strict or authoritarian household. and the writer of tall, narrow loops views authority figures as extremely powerful, towering over him. Feeling inferior to those in authority, he compensates by dominating others over whom he feels superior.

Tool Tip

A well-formed middle and lower zone are needed for balance. An overemphasized upper zone means the writer is unable to properly meet the demands of everyday life. Everything is filtered through the intellect, so reality testing is poor.

❖ **Overly wide** upper loops are often made by those who expend too much time and energy thinking about things rather than doing them often make. The imagination is given free rein. The writer is also hypersensitive and imagines others are talking about him in a critical way. The wider the loops, the more unrealistic he is.

❖ A **short** upper zone indicates a writer who generally doesn't have strong religious or spiritual beliefs, and who isn't interested in questioning his values. More materialistic than intellectual, he is interested in people and things that he can see and touch, not what he views as "airy-fairy" abstract ideas and philosophies.

> One's attitude toward authority figures (father, boss, minister, superior officer, etc.) is found in the upper zone,

What Dreams May Come: The Lower Zone

Keeper of secrets, gateway to the unconscious, the lower zone holds the mysteries of the psyche. The lower zone begins at the baseline and descends into the darkness of the past. This is where expression of sexual and material desires is found. Whether the writer is inhibited, moderate, or freewheeling, whether he feels inferior or powerful when it comes to sex, the lower zone tells an important part of the story.

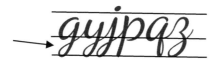

Lower zone letters

It reveals whether he is more likely a sensitive, considerate lover, or one who prefers to use brute force to subdue a partner. Sex is more than just a physical expression, so other aspects of sexuality will be seen throughout the handwriting, not just in the lower zone.

Note whether the loop is weakly falling into the lower zone or the downstroke has a strong, purposeful thrust. Is the writer easily led, or does he do the leading?

The downstroke that moves decisively from the baseline into the lower zone symbolizes going down into the basement of the unconscious. This is where we explore all the old junk that is kept there, as well as some bona fide treasures. We choose the lessons we have learned and bring "back upstairs" in the upstroke, to use in the reality of daily life.

But what if your basement is a dank and scary dungeon where there's nothing you want to use? What if, in fact, you have a strong aversion to going there at all? You might get to the door and decide to rush back upstairs as fast as you can, pretending you never visited. That is what the writer does who, mid-word, makes a straight downstroke into the lower zone with **no return loop.**

Fine Points

A straight downstroke with no loop only at the ends of words is a form of simplifying and does not have the same meaning as when it appears consistently mid-word.

As we consider various types of lower zone formations, always be mindful of the context in which they appear.

❖ **Moderately full** lower loops, when balanced with the other zones, indicate a capacity to satisfy sexual and other biological urges. There is the ability to plan ahead (upper zone), call on past experience and draw on the necessary energy (lower zone), and effectively act on his plans (middle zone).

❖ The writer of **extremely long** lower loops has dug his basement deep under the ground. He likes to delve into the past and is very interested in learning about his heritage, his roots, and if the loops are at least medium width, even the skeletons in his closet.

❖ **Very short** loops are found in one who may be uncomfortable in the contents of his basement or, simply not interested in exploring the past. He quickly returns to the middle zone. Such a person has difficulty learning from past mistakes. All that counts is the present. He would rather think about what he's going to have for dinner, or whether he has email. Last year, last month, or even yesterday is all in the past. What might or might not happen tomorrow is just a bother.

Tales from the Script

The late graphology great Felix Klein noted that sometimes a tick in the lower zone of a male writer indicates impotence. That would cause irritability, for sure!

Off the Beaten Path: unusual lower loops

The copybook lower loop that you learned in school goes below the baseline, makes a left turn and returns directly to the baseline.

Commonly, however, loops veer off in a different direction. When the lower loops have unusual twists or ties or other shapes, chances are, the writer suffered sexual abuse, probably (though not always) in childhood. As a result, the emotions attached to sex are not always expressed in the usual, standard ways. What should have been a natural expression of the basic urges turns into something self-conscious, shameful, and humiliating.

There exists a great **variety** of lower-loop formations that represent unconscious needs. Suffice it to say, any twists or unusual forms suggest that the writer has been unable to resolve the past painful events, whatever the cause. (This topic is addressed in greater depth in *Advanced Studies in Handwriting Psychology*).

❖ **Extremely wide** lower loops that look like an inflated balloon are made by writers with an overblown fantasy life. They'll talk ad nauseum about their sexual prowess, but when it comes down to it, they're usually full of hot air. The writer feels sexually inadequate, and the extra wide loops help him put up a big bluff.

❖ Lower loops ending in a **short, sharp hook** suggest a cranky, short-tempered nitpicker. When found in combination with other negative signs, such as very heavy pressure, he may also be a bully.

❖ A lower zone pulling **strongly to the left** (more often seen in men's writing) signifies a strong attachment to mother or a need for mothering that was not satisfied in childhood.

❖ Lower loops that **pull to the right** (more often seen in women's writing) are usually made by those who rebel against male authority.

Examples of non-standard lower zones

Claw-shaped lower-zone forms symbolize unconscious feelings of guilt that the writer has been unable to release. She unconsciously sets herself up for punishment because deep down, she believes she deserves it. One such writer had a habit of gossiping about a particular friend to others in a way that the talk would inevitably get back to the friend, which would lead to an angry confrontation that made her feel guilty.

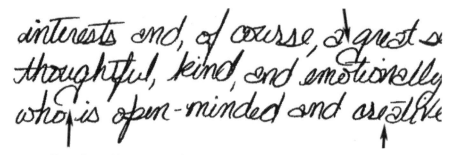

Claw-shaped lower zone (sometimes misnamed "the felon's claw")

Let's Blame Mom!

Because the lower zone represents the past and birth and mother are at the very beginning, lower zone formations can represent the writer's feeling about the mothering and nurturing they did or did not receive. When the latter is true, it may show up in left-pulling or cradle-like forms.

❖ A **triangular-shaped** lower zone with sharp corners pointing to the left (past) indicates unresolved issues—possibly with mother—that can affect relationships with other women in the writer's life. This form has hidden aggression or hostility because it is below the baseline (the line of reality), in the unconscious. The aggression may take the form of nagging and constant criticism. When the angles have soft edges, it mitigates the implication somewhat.

> When the upstroke crosses the downstroke too soon (before the baseline) it may indicate a lack of the proper emotional release in sex, resulting in frustration.

President Bill Clinton's two terms in office were marred by accusations of sexual misconduct. What does his handwriting reveal? A combination of hard and soft triangles in the lower zone. The triangles represent hostile feelings towards women of which he is probably unaware. The rounded forms in the middle zone blend with angles, which soften the aggression.

President Bill Clinton

❖ Large, rounded lower extensions that look like **cradles**. Instead of returning to the baseline, the downstroke stays in
the lower zone. It ends in a leftward movement towards the
past and mother. The writer
missed the nurturing, loving
care she would like to have had.

Fine Points

A well-developed lower
zone, balanced with the
other zones, shows
good coordination, self-
confidence, and an abil-
ity to relate effectively
with other people.

Growing up and as an adult, she seeks it in relationships with men (mostly women adopt this form, but not always). She might be quite competent in her career world, but in emotional matters is as vulnerable as a kitten.

Cradle form lower zone

❖ Loops that **curl inward** like a snail's shell show strong self-involve-ment. Everything comes back to the self. This is literally an example of being self-ish. These forms, assuming there are supporting signs, are generally made by the egocentric, insincere person who cannot be trusted to tell the truth. The snail's shell keeps things hidden and locked up. In relationships, this writer only has room for himself.

Lower zone snail shell forms

Last Words

Handwriting is divided into three zones—upper, middle, and lower—which correspond to areas of personality. The middle zone is considered the most important because all parts of handwriting pass through it. The upper zone represents conscious thought (how you think). The middle zone represents where you live (how you feel). The lower zone represents the unconscious (how you act). Although each zone has its own significance, all work together and affect each other. *As in every aspect of handwriting, no zone should be interpreted separately from the others.*

Chapter 8

Size does matter:
Writing Size

Now that we know the general areas symbolized by each zone, it's time to learn how writing *size* affects the writer's activities. First, though, let's define what "size" means.

Def·i·ni·tion
> **Size:** A thing's overall dimensions or magnitude; how big something is.

Absolute size encompasses the entire scope of writing, from the tops of the upper loops to the bottoms of the lower loops. What's more important, though, is *relative* size, which refers to the ratio of the height of middle-zone letters to the height of upper-zone and length of lower-zone letters.

The most important measurement is middle-zone height because several other measurements are based on it. If you are no mathematician you are in good company, but no need to worry. Exact measurements are not needed; ballpark is good enough.

Leggo My Ego – back to the middle zone

The middle zone, the zone of the ego, answers the question, "How tall does the writer feel?" One who is not very tall in a literal sense but has a healthy ego can seem like a giant. Robert Reich served in the administrations of Gerald Ford, Jimmy Carter, and Bill Clinton. His 4'11" height did not stop him from serving as Secretary of Labor or being a professor, author, or political commentator. Clearly, he did not feel small.

Def·i·ni·tion

Ego needs: Degree of self-esteem.

Ego strength: Ability to deal with stress and maintain emotional equilibrium; to get one's ego needs satisfied.

On the other hand, you might be as tall as Kobe Bryant, but feel like a little person. What counts is how tall you feel inside. The middle-zone height (MZH) is an indicator for how tall the writer *feels* and how much recognition he needs.

> MZH measures *ego needs.*

Positive ego needs reflect a sense of autonomy, personal worth, and the self-respect that comes through the respect of others.

Middle-zone width (MZW) is the movement from left to right (from me to you). It indicates whether the writer feels free to move out into the world and satisfy his ego needs without undue stress or upset. One who is not afraid to ask for what he needs has a somewhat fuller middle zone than the one who is shy and shrinks back.

> MZW measures *ego strength.*

Small, Medium, Large—As Opposed to What?

Since everyone has their own idea of what small/medium/large looks like, we need an objective measure. In this case, the American Palmer school copybook (CB) has been the standard measure of what is small-medium-large for at least fifty years. Other copybooks, such as the Zaner-Bloser and D'Nealian copybooks have similar proportions. The key word is "proportion," not so much the absolute measurement. What you want to know is how the upper zone and the lower zone relate to the middle zone.

MZH (middle zone height)

For the MZH, the letters o, a, and e are the easiest to measure. Select several from various areas of the handwriting sample and measure them with a metric rule from top to bottom as in the illustration.

Measuring middle-zone height.

If most of the middle-zone letters measure 3 millimeters, as the copybook requires, the middle-zone height is *medium*. Middle zone letters taller than 3 millimeters high are *tall*. Shorter than 3 millimeters is *small*. A wide variation in measurements means that the MZH is *variable*.

MZW (middle zone width)

Next, again using the letters o and a, measure MZW. Copybook dictates that MZW should be about the same as MZH or slightly less, a ratio of 1:1. A fairly close (doesn't have to be absolute) MZH/MZW is *medium*. Letters that measure less than 3mm wide are *narrow*. If the measurement is greater than 3mm, the middle zone is *wide*. A wide variation in measurements means the MZW is *variable*.

The following is a summary of the abbreviations we use in handwriting measurements. That way, you don't always have to write out the whole long term.

Abbreviation	Handwriting Factor
CB	Copybook
LZ	Lower zone
LZL	Lower-zone elaboration
LZW	Lower-zone width
MZ	Middle zone
MZH	Middle-zone height
MZW	Middle-zone width
UZ	Upper zone
UZH	Upper-zone height
UZE	Upper-zone elaboration
UZW	Upper-zone width

How About Those Loops?

The CB upper-zone height (UZH) is one-and-one-half times as tall as the MZH, That means the upper loops would measure 4 ½ mm from the baseline to the top of the loops. Using the letters l, b, or h, measure several of the tallest ones. To be considered medium, the width of the upper loops (UZW) should be only about one-half as wide as the middle zone height.

Now, let's turn to the lower zone. Measure the longest loops on g or y from the baseline to the bottom of the lower-zone loops (LZL). The LZL should be twice as long as the middle zone is high, and the

Fine Points

Someone who wants to appear taller puts on high-heeled shoes or poufs up her hair. In handwriting, she writes a tall middle zone. But without self-confidence, the middle zone width will be narrow.

lower-zone width (LZW) should be half as wide as the middle zone height. That means loops measuring 6 millimeters long and 1½ millimeters wide are medium. Measure lower loops at their widest point.

In the illustration below, which is the *Dancing Script* font, the proportions are incorrect, but at least you will see where to measure.

Measuring upper and lower loops

Bigger Than Small, Smaller Than Big: medium

A middle zone that is medium in height and width suggests a writer who is generally well adjusted, realistic, and conventional. She is able to focus on what she wants to do and gets it done with adequate self-confidence. Socially, she knows her place in the world and does what is expected within her chosen social group. Your social group might consist of workmates or classmates, friends, book club, gang, etc.

As one who follows instructions well, it drives her crazy her when others break the rules or step too far out of line.

A more or less uniform middle zone height and width implies a degree of inner security. Most of the time, the writer doesn't seem to be affected by the external environment. Her relationships with others are based on give-and-take; she feels pretty comfortable in her own skin.

Fine Points

With moderate fluctuation in the middle zone, the writer is responsive and reacts to emotional events. With little or no fluctuation, check for a pulse!

> A middle zone much wider than it is tall is made by someone who tends to be indiscriminate in relationships and spending (time and money). Quantity becomes more important than quality. The wider the middle zone, the more important it is to the writer to be accepted by others.

and trial pieces in Vanity Fair. They tell me I get too personally involved in my stories. So what I say. Dominick Dunne

Slightly larger than medium middle zone:
author and television personality Dominick Dunne

When the MZW is much wider than it is tall, the writer may have a habit of oversharing, telling anyone who will listen about everything she wants to do, where she wants to go, who she wants to become. Her unfortunate fear of not being liked or accepted sets her up for disappointment due to a desperate need to fit in and be approved by those she views as superior. She can be too pushy, intruding where she is not welcome.

> Describing the middle-of-the road, average writer is one of the biggest challenges for the graphologist. It's like giving a description of a man in his mid-20s, with a medium build, brown hair, and brown eyes. There are too few distinguishing characteristics.

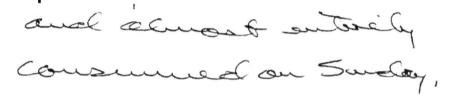

Wide middle zone: Supreme Court Justice Sandra Day O'Connor

It's the Small Things That Count: small MZH

The writer of a small MZH with medium width cares little what others think. Her manner is restrained around other people, and when it comes to social situations she recognizes her limitations. More intellectual than social, she is content to spend long periods of time on her own, concentrating on things that interest her. In her view, there's nothing wrong with being an introvert, so don't try to talk her into being more sociable. She won't appreciate it.

Fine Points

With wide spaces between the letters, the interpretation of very wide MZW is mitigated.

Assuming supporting elements in the writing, he prepares ahead for a project, making to-do lists and checking of the items as they are completed. You can expect him to show up on time and work well under pressure, especially when small details are an important component of the work. Because his satisfaction comes from successfully completing an assignment, accolades are less rewarding to her than a job well done.

Small and Narrow

The narrower the MZ letters are, the greater the insecurity. When the writer pulls back from moving toward the right, the letters become ovals instead of circles and "from me to you" becomes "from me to me."

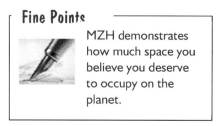

Fine Points

MZH demonstrates how much space you believe you deserve to occupy on the planet.

A lack of confidence restricts the writer, causing him to feel tense and apprehensive in an unfamiliar environment.

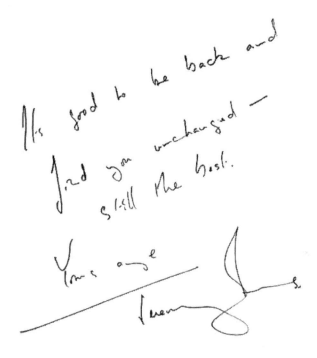

Small middle zone: actor Jeremy Irons

Despite what he might display to the outside world, the short MZH says his self-concept may not be so hot. He feels he doesn't deserve to command very much space. Add to that narrowness in the middle zone and his emotional world becomes limited to what and who he knows. He may outwardly display few great passions or strong emotions. In fact, others may see him as impassive or apathetic. An actor, such as Jeremy Irons in the above sample, may be able to express his deep emotions through acting roles.

Very Small

A middle zone that is less than 1mm high sometimes signals mental or emotional problems, so be sure to get additional information before attempting an analysis.

In an otherwise positive handwriting, it is a sign of the shrinking violet who rarely ventures out of his own space. She prefers her own company to that of others, perhaps because her great fear is that others will see her for what she believes she is—nothing.

When forced into the company of others, expect him to pick nits and generally be petty. We could call this the porcupine defense—I'll attack you before you get a chance to attack me. As soon as he can, he will retreat to the security of his safe little shell.

Miniscule middle zone: author William Faulkner

In some cases, this is a temporary sign caused by profound depression. The writing reflects the wish to disappear.

Big Is Beautiful

The large-middle-zone writer is less of a realist than the smaller writer. The tallness of her strokes takes her away from the baseline (the line of reality) so she sees things less pragmatically. She thinks big, and, because she believes she can't fail, gladly takes on assignments that others might feel are beyond their capability.

If there is also adequate width (approximate 1:1 proportion), she will have the confidence to carry out her plans. This is the extrovert who wants to act upon the world, rather than have the world act upon her. Determined to stand out in a crowd, she behaves in ways that will put her at center stage with the spotlight pointed directly on her. Her large ego, as reflected in her large MZH, reveals a need for approval and admiration.

Large but Narrow

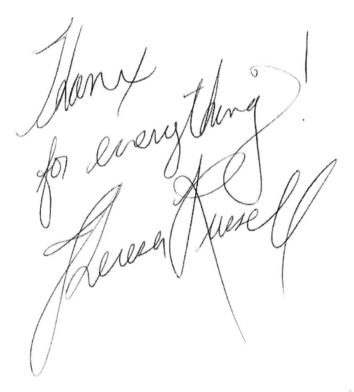

Large (variable width) middle zone: actress Theresa Russell

This ebullient personality can sometimes be more show than go. The tallness in the middle zone compensates for the feelings of anxiety demonstrated by the narrowness. He need reassurance of his worth, so remember to give him genuine compliments from time to time.

The large/narrow writer may talk grandly about things he wants to accomplish, but when it comes to performing, is afraid to try unless he knows with certainty that he will succeed. With a habit of looking at the big picture and ignoring the small, but important details, he may start better than he finishes. But of course, there may be redeeming factors, as in the sample below.

Robbie Coltrane, who plays Harry Potter's friend Hagrid the giant, has more than just a tall, narrow middle zone. Yes, it is all over the place, but energy (though it fluctuates) and enthusiasm push him forward.

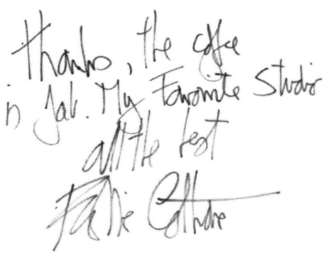

Large, narrow middle zone: actor Robbie Coltrane.

> As always: *consider the whole handwriting.* There is no "this means that." All features of a writing are modified by other fea-tures.

Too Much of a Good Thing: extremely large MZH

It may seem counter-intuitive, but an extremely large middle zone (larger than 5 millimeters high) does not represent an extremely healthy ego. Quite the opposite. The writer believes the world revolves around her and that she is better than others, she has a right to anything she wants. If called upon to do a job that she believes is beneath her, and she can find someone else to do it, it won't get done.

This know-it-all behaves as if whatever or whoever fails to serve her ego simply does not exist. Refusing to listen to anyone who might know better, she is right about everything (despite the nagging little voice reminding her that her bragging isn't based on truth). When she fails, and she is likely to fail often and spectacularly, it's always someone else's fault (especially with a crowded spatial arrangement). She makes mountains out of molehills—nothing is too small for her to turn it into a major issue.

Decisions, Decisions—variable MZH

Variable middle-zone height is an indicator for a wide range of emotions on a continuum from sensitivity or touchiness. Whether the writer is emotionally lively or simply unstable depends upon the degree of variability. A moderate amount is normal and indicates the ability to adapt to the needs of the moment. When variability becomes extreme, the writer is a victim of his own moods.

Typically, a variable middle-zone height range is from 2 to 4 ½ millimeters. When the MZH fluctuates too much, it infers a changeable level of self-confidence. He feels sure of himself now, but in 5 minutes will be chiding himself for his inadequacy.

If he's feeling good, he might get involved in a project, then suddenly fear he won't be able to handle it and want to back out. Life is never dull around this type because you never know what to expect.

The writer of changeable MZW is likewise unpredictable. You never know what he's going to do next and neither does he. He might seem friendly and welcoming one moment, then withdrawn and aloof the next.

Variable middle zone: Ludwig Von Beethoven

Up, Up, and Away – the upper zone

If you want to know about someone's values and principles, check the state of their upper zone (UZ). The upper loops show the degree of interest the writer has in ideas, philosophy, and spirituality.

One would think that the higher the loops reach, the more the writer seeks

Fine Points

For mental activity to be productive, the UZH must be balanced with the LZL and the MZH.

to reach into the theoretical domain. However, the writer of extremely tall UZH tends to be more interested in theory than the practical application of a field of study. Other factors need to be considered, such as loop width, etc.

The upstroke moves away from self and out toward other people before returning to the baseline, bringing back what it has learned. If the writer is successful in incorporating the new information into her life, she will make a strong downstroke. A weak downstroke shows avoidance of reality and the writer has trouble integrating what is real (MZ) with what is theoretical (UZ).

Imagine that...

Pilots often have upper zones that reach up toward the sky. Charles Lindbergh's handwriting, which appears in this chapter, is a good illustration. You won't be surprised that to be of practical value, the lower zone length needs to be in balance with the upper zone height.

Tall Upper Loops

A moderately tall upper zone height (UZH) suggests that the writer is searching for greatness—literally reaching for the stars. Whether he is likely to achieve that goal depends on several other factors. The height simply shows the leaning toward the mental or academic aspects of life.

If the UZH is twice as tall as the MZH, the writer is more concerned with the theoretical than the practical. He's a glutton for information who is driven to understand the universe. If he thinks (the keyword is: "think") there's more to know about a subject he finds interesting, he will be driven to ferret out every atom of information available. This writer wants to continually add to his mental database, which, depending on other factors in the handwriting, can negatively impact his social life. As he lives mainly in his head, he often forgets appointments, birthdays, or other important "people events."

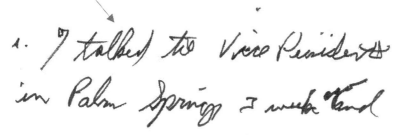

Medium UZH: Hazel Dixon Cooper, Cosmo's Bedside Astrologer

Too Tall: extreme UZH

Loops that reach too far into the upper zone tell us that the writer is dissatisfied with who he is. The movement is strongly away from the self, towards something else, something "out there." He is looking outside himself

Too tall upper zone: Elvis Presley

to get his needs met, rather than seeking self-satisfaction. Interestingly, while the writer of too-tall upper loops has a self-image that could use some help, he has an exaggerated sense of his own importance and abilities.

The loops seem to be reaching up as if aspiring to please an authority figure, either the writer's father or a father figure, whether he is aware of it or not.

An extra-tall and narrow upper zone is very often found in someone who had an ultra-strict religious

Fine Points

It takes longer to make extra tall loops. The writer wastes time expounding on theories that have little basis in reality. The more he thinks, the less time there is to act.

upbringing with an overabundance of rules and regulations to follow. An authoritarian personality is likely the result.

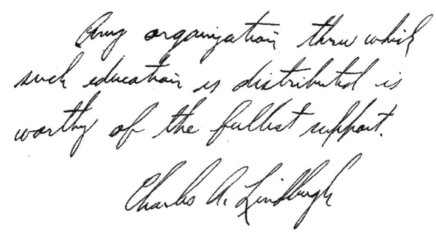

Too-tall, narrow upper zone: aviator Charles Lindbergh

Many pilots have a disproportionately tall upper zone, which may reflect their desire to fly up-up-and-away.

Another famous person with disproportionately tall upper loops is King of Pop, Michael Jackson, whose father was known to be extremely strict and demanding.

Too-tall upper zone, singer Michael Jackson

Def·i·ni·tion

> **Authoritarian personality:** One who insists upon blind obedience
> to authority (father, government, paramilitary organizations, etc.).

The authoritarian personality type has a disproportionately tall, narrow upper zone height. Personality characteristics of this type include rigid loyalty to certain values (ones the authoritarian person sets). The rigidity extends further as fear is used as a ruling force.

This personality type possesses a degree of narcissism, in that they promote success only in themselves. They are aggressive, lack empathy or interest in the needs of others. Viewing the world in terms of black/white, their outlook is rather simplistic, leaving no room for another viewpoint. They are often attracted to law enforcement, the military, or paramilitary types of organizations where there are strict rules to follow or they can be in charge and set the rules.

Narrow or Retraced Upper Loops

Retraced loops, where the downstroke covers the upstroke, leave no room for intellectual growth. The writer is as narrow-minded as his loops, and closed to new ideas. Opportunities to broaden his horizons or come up with something innovative and revolutionary leave him cold. Instead, he continually recycles ideas and concepts he learned while growing up.

Def·i·ni·tion

> **Retracing:** the downstroke is laid on top of (retracing) the upstroke
> stroke, or vice-versa, and may be found in any zone.

Tall and Wide

Tall, *moderately* wide loops are a sign of imagination. The writer leaves room to create new thoughts and listen to someone else's ideas. She is able to learn from experience and keep a reasonable perspective on what others have to say. Unafraid of someone else's opinion, even if it runs counter to hers, she finds it easy to visualize unfamiliar concepts.

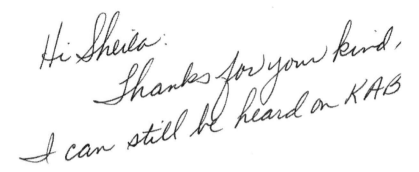

Tall, moderate upper zone: astrologer Lee Holloway

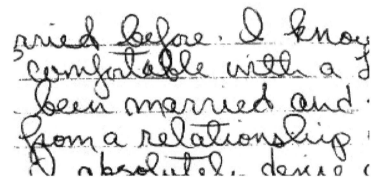

Extremely wide upper loops

When the loops grow to more than twice the MZH, the writer lacks discrimination in what she takes into her mind. An overdeveloped upper zone is a way of compensating for dissatisfaction in one or both of the other zones. It takes extra time to make a very wide loop, and the writer prefers to escape into daydreams or intellectual woolgathering, rather than return to the reality of the middle zone. Her ideas are many, but tend to be impractical and unrealistic. It's doubtful they ever get off the drawing board and into reality.

Look Ma, No Loops!

Some writers simplify by making straight downstrokes without loops. They think in a direct manner, no frills, preferring to cut to the chase rather than spending time in the imagination. This is not to say they are lacking imagination; they just have a more straightforward thinking style

The unlooped downstroke cuts off emotions, too. The straight-stroke writer is uncomfortable with big, emotional scenes. Certainly, they have feelings, and don't necessarily repress them; they just don't want to look at them. It's a case of, "Okay, that happened, now let's get on with it."

I understand that you have volunteered for my campaign. I am grateful to have you on my team.

Unlooped upper zone: President George W. Bush

Down to earth: short UZH

The person who doesn't rise above the middle zone is rooted in the real world. She finds the intellectual discussions of the upper zone boring and will quickly seek an excuse to leave when the conversation turns to abstract ideas. People and things are far more interesting topics for this writer, who concentrates on her day-to-day activities. Don't bother giving her a book for her birthday, as it will never be opened (unless it's a picture book, of course).

Fine Points

If the middle zone is much larger than the upper and lower zone, the writer is avoiding the intellectual and material areas of life in favor of social relationships and emotional concerns.

The short upper zone writer cares that things happen, not *why* they happen. Rather than spending a lot of time planning the next activity, she would rather "just do it." Nonetheless, she finds it frustrating when pushed to do *new* things without time for advance preparation. At her best with uncomplicated, straightforward projects, she uses what she already knows and stays within a familiar framework.

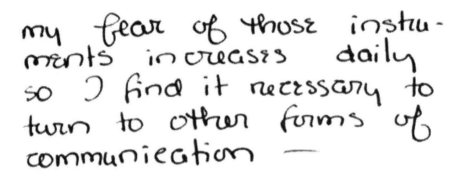

Short upper zone: Princess Grace of Monaco

Mix 'n match: variable upper loops

As you might guess, the writer whose upper loops are short or wide in one word or letter, tall or narrow the next, is inconsistent in his thinking. He doesn't have a steady opinion or point of view to offer on any subject. The same topic might be viewed from a totally opposite direction from one moment to the next.

> Variability of any kind points to someone who wants to be free
> to change their mind on a dime, especially when the variability
> is in the upper zone, the area specific to mental endeavor.

Down in the Boondocks – the lower zone

The area of physical activity, sexual and dreams, the lower zone contains one's attitudes towards the material and biological areas of life. An emphasis on lower-zone length and/or width reveals a strong interest in money, sex, and the material life. A de-emphasized lowers zone show a lack of interest in satisfying biological urges, an avoidance or them, or, possibly, little energy to invest in those areas.

While the lower loops are the place to look when you want to know about the writer's basic urges, remember to keep the whole picture in mind. Long or wide loops by themselves are not going to lead you to an accurate conclusion. Check the overall dynamism of the writing, the pressure, the speed, and the rhythm, areas that we have yet to cover.

Short Lower Loops

It doesn't take much determination or persistence to send short strokes into the lower zone. The writer of short lower loops probably should only take on projects that can be completed fairly quickly. Otherwise, he may lose interest or become discouraged over a period of time.

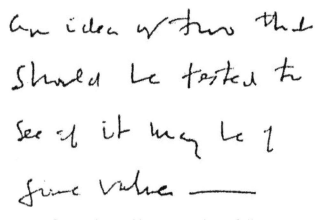

De-emphasized lower zone: Jonas Salk

With strong downstroke pressure, he works hard, but limited endurance and stamina make it hard to keep going. Staying close to the middle zone, he focuses his energy on the necessities of daily life.

On the other hand, with positive elements in the writing, there are highly productive people who have a short lower zone because they emphasize upper-zone activity, like Jonas Salk, who developed the polio vaccine. He apparently lived more in his head than in more earthy areas. His results speak for themselves.

Medium-long Lower Loops

The writer of a moderately long lower zone is active and productive, but also likes to relax and recharge his batteries. Where there is also moderate width in the lower loops, endurance and persistence increase as the increase in length.

Tales from the Script

Max Pulver, one of the most quoted early graphologists, said, "The dangers of intellectualism are lack of persistence, of perseverance with projects, and of attention to material, physical and sexual matters. Those who write in the opposite way remain to some extent imprisoned in the foundations." Here's my interpretation: people who live in their heads (too tall upper zone) are often impractical, but those who spend too much time in the lower zone (the foundation) tend to get stuck in material concerns.

> Slightly wide lower loops suggest a conventional lover who does what is expected and probably not much more. This is not the type you would expect to find scouring the Internet for websites featuring kinky sex.

Long Lower Loops

The longer the loops, the greater the interest in satisfying physical and material desires. The writer of long lower loops prefers to jump right into activities without a lot of planning (especially when she has short upper loops). She reacts on a physical level and enjoys sex. She is motivated by opportunities to acquire money.

> Plunging into the past (below the baseline) through long lower loops sometimes indicates an interest in family history research.

 When the lower loops are more than twice as long as the MZH, and especially if they are wide, the writer can't sit still. Constantly moving, you'll find him drumming his fingers on the table, tapping his toes, or pacing the room. He is anxious, can't relax, hates routine in anything. Sex may be used as a tranquilizer, with a list of partners to call on when he's feeling frisky. The trouble is, sex is only a temporary relief.

The two samples seen here both write with a very long lower zone, but are very different personalities. The top one makes wide loops in a released rhythm. The bottom is a slow arcade writing with a lot of control. Her lower zone is long, but varied. Some loops are like a cradle, song wide, some narrow. Always look at the gestalt—the whole writing.

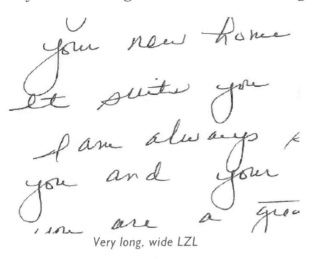

Very long, wide LZL

Very long lower zone

Narrow Lower Loops

Just as in the upper and middle zones, narrowness in the lower zone sig-nifies inhibition. If the lower zone is long and narrow or retraced, it will take some doing to get the writer to act on her desires. Because he's afraid he won't be able to perform adequately, he creates a self-fulfilling prophecy.

Moderately-Wide Lower Loops

Moderately wide loops when balanced with moderate length are made by the self-confident person who is not afraid to act spontaneously in intimate relationships.

Along with strong drives, resourcefulness and willing enough to branch out, he is willing to go where he hasn't gone before.

> Remember our mantra: always consider the whole handwriting before making an interpretation.

Extremely Wide Lower Loops

As the lower loops swell to more than twice the width of the MZH, there is a danger of fantasy overtaking reality. This writer overreacts to everything, exaggerating and distorting the facts to unrecognizable proportions.

One who brags about his sexual prowess, he may be unable to perform to the standards he set for himself. The writing below has extremely long and wide lower loops, but it also has some positive features that allow for a somewhat more positive interpretation.

Fine Points

Wide lower loops are called "money bags." They symbolize an emphasis on money and enjoyment of the "good things in life."

Extremely wide lower zone width of "moneybags"

Long after the honeymoon is over, the writer of wide lower loops will be finding new adventures to try with his lover. Imaginative and fun-loving, he's ready for anything. Now, if those loops are overly wide, he stays in fantasyland because there is not enough energy (or confidence) to act out the fantasy.

Extreme lower zone: Eric Idle of Monty Python's Flying Circus

Some Final Remarks About Zones

As in all other aspects of handwriting, extremes upset the balance and often are a sign of immaturity. Excessive size or lack of harmony in any zone is a negative indicator and intensifies the possibility of instability.

If you're interested in learning more about the lower zone, this subject is covered in greater depth in my book, *Advanced Studies in Handwriting Psychology.*

Last Words

Size of writing demonstrates the amount of space you feel you deserve. Middle zone height is about your ego needs; width shows how you get your ego needs met. Upper-zone height symbolizes aspirations, principles, and standards; width shows how open-minded you are. Lower-zone length and width reveal how active and productive you are.

Chapter 9

I've Got Rhythm:
Handwriting movement

In this chapter we explore rhythm in handwriting. This is probably the most complex aspect of handwriting. You will learn how to recognize the rhythms of space, form, and movement, and understand how they impact the writer's unique movement patterns.

Def·i·ni·tion
Rhythm: Characterized by regularly recurring elements or activities.

It may seem heavy going at first, but learning how to identify the rhythm of handwriting is an indispensable part of your graphological education. You will want to reviewing this chapter many times until you are confident that you have mastered the concepts found here. That might take a while, so don't be too hard on yourself if you don't get it right away.

Imagine that...

Learning how to unravel the complexities of rhythm will take you far along the road to becoming a good handwriting analyst.

Handwriting moves, as surely as you put one foot in front of the other to walk from here to there. The pen touches down on a sheet of paper and begins moving from the starting point to your goal, continuing to the end of the line. Without movement, there would nothing more than a dot of ink on the paper.

But more than just the hand is involved in writing movement. In chapter one we learned that handwriting, which is controlled by the central nervous system, is referred to in the field as "brainwriting." Every part of the brain is bound up in the act.

> Physiological and psychological factors affect the movement produced by pen on paper.

Both internal and external factors affect handwriting. **Internal** influences include illness. Whether you have the flu or a serious disease; if you have injured a finger, hand, arm, or shoulder, your handwriting will be affected in various ways. Likewise, some types of medications, as well as "recreational drugs" will show up as disturbances. Alcohol has been shown to affect handwriting, even after just one beer in some cases. Mental illness and situational or long-term depression, too, leave their mark.

External influences include writing materials—paper and pen or pencil; writing surface and conditions. If you are writing on a hard surface such as a table or desk, what you produce will look somewhat different than if you are sitting in bed with a magazine resting on your knees to provide a place to write, or in one of those cramped airline seats.

Fine Points

When a handwriting looks unusual in some way, always consider the internal and external factors. Ask for more information when you need it.

Different Strokes for Different Folks: rhythm

Calm or excitable, stilted or natural, the rhythm of movement expresses one's basic life force. There is a world of difference between a mechanical, dull temperament that functions like a robot, and an intense, vivacious one that treats life as a party.

The inherent rhythm in writing movement reveals, perhaps more than any other factor, how the writer adapts and functions in the world. The following chart illustrates different types of rhythm that exist along a continuum:

extremely irregular	weak	disturbed	strong	overcontrolled

Our discussion begins with the smallest element of writing movement, the stroke. Handwriting is composed of two basic types of stroke: curved and linear. As they thrust or slink or dance their way onto the paper, the various combinations arrange themselves into a pattern, a portrait of how the writer experiences the world and how he expresses those experiences.

Curved strokes are smooth and continuous. They move in two directions—centrifugal, or counterclockwise (outward and away from the center); and centripetal, or clockwise (inward and toward the center).

Linear strokes are straight and move in one direction at a time. To change the direction of a straight line, you have to make an abrupt stop and an acute turn. Balanced writing rhythm is produced through a combination of curves and straight lines.

Fine Points

Rhythm is one of the most important and one of the most difficult aspects of handwriting to learn. It demonstrates the ebb and flow of energy.

> A predominance of straight strokes draws one type of picture; a predominance of curved strokes draws another.

Energy Balancing: Contraction and Release

All living organisms have their own natural rhythms. The ebb and flow of energy that comprises rhythm involves two types of movement: one contracts, the other expands. In breathing, you inhale in a contracting movement; you exhale in an expanding movement. Ebb and flow, in and out, give and take, anticipation and realization, centripetal and centrifugal.

Def·i·ni·tion

Periodicity: a tendency to recur at intervals.

If you won the lottery, how would you react? Doesn't it make you want to leap out of your seat just to think of it! You even start breathing a little faster! When you're excited and happy (or excited and angry), you act expansively. Now, think back to a time when you were sad about something.

Even the memory makes your body contract, you seem to fold up and go inside yourself.

As energy expands and contracts it forms a pattern we call rhythm or "periodicity." That's a two-dollar word for doing the same thing over and over, but not in exactly the same way every time. The best example is seen in the ocean waves. You can count six smaller ones, then one big one, over and over again. A pattern, but not a

Fine Points

Don't mistake poor rhythm for a "bad" person. Rhythm shows how well-integrated the various parts of the writer's life are. In poor rhythm, something is out of whack.

machine. Each breath you take is similar to the others, but not identical. Some breaths are shorter, some are longer; some are ragged, some are smooth, but always, there is an in-and-out motion you can count on, unlike a hospital respirator, where the in-and-out would always be the same, or the steady tick-tock of a metronome, which is mechanistic, rather than rhythmic.

Handwriting with good rhythm suggests a more-or-less harmonious personality. The various elements, the physical, emotional, and spiritual, are working together to produce balance. Writing that is not rhythmic reveals a lack of unity within the personality. Something is out of whack, which implies that the writer's day-to-day functioning is impaired in some way.

Willpower or Won't Power?

A major factor that affects rhythm is one's strength of will. As defined for our purposes, "will" is the quality of mind that sets an activity in motion and also controls it. In other words, willpower provides the impetus to get things done and the self-control to call a halt at the appropriate time.

Handwriting that shows good willpower used in a positive way tends to be rhythmic. When the rhythm is too loose there is low willpower. When the rhythm is too tight, there is too much "won'tpower."

Def·i·ni·tion

> **Willpower:** restraint of impulses.

Rhythmic writing allows impressions from the outside world to impact the writer. She assimilates and expresses those impressions outwardly as appropriate and in a reasonable manner. There is a periodicity in her behavior and her handwriting, a sameness within a range, but not so much that the writing looks mechanical or machinelike. The will regulates natural impulses and inhibits some of the basic urges that might be harmful.

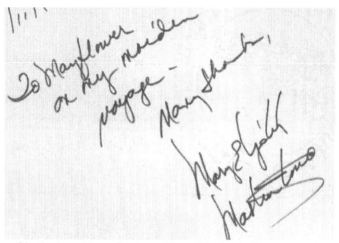

Rhythmic writing of actress Mary Elizabeth Masttrantonio

While the handwriting of director James Cameron (Avatar, Titanic, etc.) is printed, which doesn't show easily rhythm, there is a periodicity and dynamic rightward movement in the way he writes that suggests strong will.

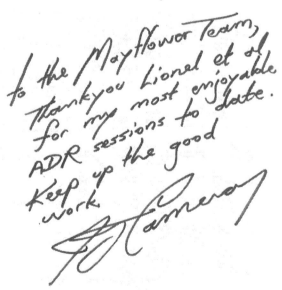

Strong willpower: James Cameron, Director

The Regularity Continuum

Socrates wrote, "In all of us, even in good men, there is a lawless wild-beast nature, which peers out in sleep."

One who feels compelled to control every impulse is inhibited, afraid to allow his emotions free reign, ever. He believes, deep in his psyche, that if he fails to keep every urge in check with the strictest controls at all times, he will become completely wild. Because this is unacceptable, he invests enormous amounts of energy in denying the very existence of the beast. This is what Swiss psychiatrist Carl Jung referred to as the "shadow" part of the personality that most of us do our best to keep hidden from public view.

The more **regularity** the handwriting displays, the greater force the will ex-

Fine Points

Willpower keeps us from doing things that are harmful (abusing drugs or alcohol, etc.). Someone weak-willed may not know how to quit. One who lets the world act upon him instead of being proactive has weaker will.

erts on the personality. The writing and the behavior are both stiff and overly formal, emotionally withholding (unbalanced). The energy returns to the self in a centrifugal, contracting movement that is reflected in the handwriting.

The contracted movement pattern of a person with extremely strong self-control tends to be highly regular, not rhythmic. Like a clock.

*me ,, let no one deceive me , be my Guide,
my Master and my Educator , let me learn*

Mechanical regularity

Too much regularity in handwriting is not considered good rhythm. It points to and inflexible person who is unable to adapt to the ups and downs of everyday life. Rather, he runs on a regimented schedule. To make changes is to produce anxiety.

At the other end of the continuum is the highly released movement pattern. When take to extremes, irregular rhythm can be wild and uncontrolled, which is just as problematic as the overcontrolled personality. The irregular writer is so impressionable that every input is immediately expressed in action.

Remember, movement comes in and goes out. Someone who only takes in and doesn't give out has no emotional growth. Someone who only gives out, but doesn't renew and refresh the spirit by taking in from the outside, depletes his energy and has nothing left to give.

The degree of balance between expansion and contraction in our own handwriting is what creates our own particular rhythm. It reveals how receptive we are to outside stimuli, how we assimilate it, and, finally, how we express it outwardly.

Released rhythm: Marianne Williamson, spiritual teacher

Balanced rhythm: Elizabeth George, author of the Inspector Lynley series.

Irregularity Breeds Contempt

When writing rhythm is too tight, too loose, or irregular, it points to difficulties. If you've ever seen a seismograph (the instrument that measures earthquakes) you will have an idea of what the irregular writer's emotional life is like: Magnificently soaring highs, profoundly plunging lows, with little uniformity to give it order. Some call personality type "high-strung."

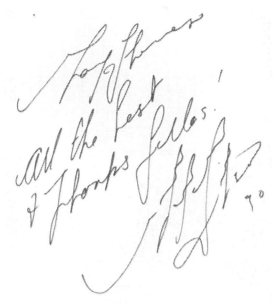

Irregular rhythm: Mel Gibson

The writer is never sure of how he feels, what he wants, or even who he is. He is deeply affected by external events. Every urge, every need, every desire is seen on his face, heard in his tone of voice, acted out in his body language. There is little or no restraint of emotion. Others experience him as superficial or shallow.

Irregularity in handwriting is seen in variable size, a wavering baseline, and changing slant. Strong rhythm is lacking, which negatively impacts the aesthetic quality of the handwriting and indicates a temperamental, capricious disposition.

Past, Present, or Future? Left and Right Trend

Carl Jung suggested that we can properly meet the demands of the outside world only if we have first developed inner harmony. Writing rhythm reveals a great deal about how well inner harmony has been achieved.

Jung spoke at length about the importance to personal growth of both pro-gression and regression. Psychic energy (life force) flows both backward and forward. When energy is regressive it reduces the impact of what is experienced when it is progressive.

If someone hits a tennis ball toward you at 70 miles an hour, you would be moving backward to allow some of the tremendous force to dissipate. That way, when the ball strikes, some of its impact will be lost.

Psychologically, we need to go backward to go forward. Like backing off from the tennis ball, stepping back to look at past experiences seems to lessen the impact of going full-bore into new experiences unprepared. It allows us to learn from our successes and our mistakes.

> In handwriting, the back-and-forth movement is seen in the
> contraction and release motion as we form our letters.

Any movement toward the left (the past) in handwriting is called left trend. Movement toward the right (the future) is right trend. Thus, any part of the writing movement—strokes, letters, words, margins, space——that travels in a leftward direction is considered left trend. Any writing movement that travels in a rightward direction is considered right trend. Both are funda-mental to writing. Without one or the other, all that's left is a straight line at the start of the page.

When the left-trending elements are stronger than the right-trending ones, the writer is seeking refuge in the past. For some reason, he fears the future and does everything he can to avoid going there. It's like a tug of war, with the past/left side winning.

Def·i·ni·tion
Left trend: movement toward the left side of the page.
Right trend: movement toward the right side of the page.

Writers with a great deal of right trend appear to be in a hurry to get to the right side of the paper. In that case, they may be running away from some-thing in the past, or are enthusiastically pursuing a future goal.

Def·i·ni·tion

Counterstrokes: strokes that move opposite to the direction they are meant to and contradict the original intention.

Western writing moves from left to right. Elements of the writing that migrate to the left when they should have gone right suggest either a rebellious personality or, perhaps, one that seeks comfort in the familiarity of the past. Or, there might be a sneaky intent.

Attorney General Jeff Sessions' handwriting contains numerous counterstrokes. See if you can spot them.

Counterstrokes: Jeff Sessions, US Attorney General

Rhythm and Blues

Rhythm in handwriting is an indicator of how well the writer controls his impulses. Good rhythm (reasonably balanced contraction/release patterns) is a sign of healthy impulses and impulse control. Disruptions in the rhythmic flow of energy suggest some sort of inner physical or mental imbalance that manifests in the writer's inner and outer life.

Although we judge the overall rhythm of writing, the chief aspects—spatial arrangement (the way the handwriting is arranged on the page); form (the chosen style); and movement (the writing rhythm)—each have their own functions. All three working together create balance and harmony.

The elements of *movement* include

- ✓ Left-right movement
- ✓ Slant
- ✓ Zonal proportions
- ✓ Flying beginning and ending strokes
- ✓ Degree of connectedness from one letter to another.

If several of these elements stand out from the page, the writing has a dominance of movement. Dominance of movement reveals an impulsive person whose emotions and instincts rule. He goes with his gut reactions, is spontaneous and unconventional, and lacks adequate impulse control.

The elements of *space* include

- ✓ Arrangement of the page
- ✓ Margins
- ✓ Alignment
- ✓ Space between letters, words, lines.

A dominance of space (the white area of the paper stands out more than the writing on it) indicates someone who has overdeveloped his intellect at the expense of his social life. He relates to the world through his rational mind and carefully filters every experience through his intellect before acting on it. He feels socially isolated and doesn't know how to close the gap.

Form is the most conscious part of handwriting. It consists of the writing style or letter design. You might call it the equivalent of font choice.

The basic elements of *form* include

- ✓ School type
- ✓ Simplified
- ✓ Elaborate
- ✓ Printed

Writing that has a strong dominance of form (you immediately notice the way the writing looks) reveals someone who is more concerned about the way things look than the substance of the message. It's "form over function." As you might guess, maintaining high social status is a priority.

Compensation

Someone who suffers a physical loss, such as eyesight, develops hearing or another sense to make up for the loss. The same thing happens psychologically. If one part of personality is weak or disturbed, another aspect may take over or compensate for it.

The person lacking social skills may compensate by exercising his intellect to make up for what he's missing socially. It's hard to generalize about these things, but the compensation will likely be reflected in his handwriting through a disturbed rhythm of Form (because it relates to the ego).

The compensated intellect will have a stronger rhythm of space (which relates to the intellect). If the compensation is expressed through physical activity rather than the intellect, it would be evident in a stronger rhythm of movement (which relates to the physical).

When you look at a handwriting sample and it's clear that "something is wrong with this picture," by zeroing in on whether it is space, form, or movement (or 2 or 3 of the elements) are weak or disturbed, we can determine which parts of personality are causing issues. In a case where problems exist in all three—space, form, *and* movement, a serious underlying disturbance is affecting the entire personality.

Tales from the Script

Surprising results came from a survey conducted on self-image and handwriting. In most cases, respondents whose handwriting was rhythmic and well-balanced stated in their self-assessment that they had a poor self-image, while those whose handwritings were less rhythmic felt they had a good self-image. A good demonstration that no single aspect of handwriting should be judged by itself. As important as rhythm is, like everything else, it must be evaluated as part of the whole picture.

Here's the bottom line:

Weak writing is too regular and conventional.

Disturbed writing has many irregularities.

Strong writing departs from copybook in positive ways.

The following tables use the "strong," "weak," and "disturbed" continuum to describe space, form, and movement as graphic expressions.

Space

Strong	Weak	Disturbed
Good proportions	Conventional	Awkwardly spaced
Well-arranged margins	Extra-wide spaces	Irregular gaps in word spacing
Balanced margins, lines	Poor distribution of space	size too large
Words clear and evenly spaced	Drifting margins	Overlapping lines
Good balance of zones	UZH or LZL over-emphasis	Zones not balanced
Initial/ending strokes missing	too narrow; long end strokes	Emphasis on white space

Form

Strong	Weak	Disturbed
Lively	Copybook	Exaggerations
Spontaneous	Conventional	Unnatural forms
Departs from school model	Monotonous	Distortions
Legible simplification	Narrow/retraced loops and ovals	Overly embellished
Original	Awkward	Inharmonious
Harmonious	Undeveloped	Highly angular
Some tasteful embellish-ments		ungraceful
Creative forms		Poorly developed

Movement

Strong	Weak	Disturbed
Rhythmic	Slack	Curved letters changed to angles
Sharp turning points	Sluggish	Straight strokes
Swinging	Listless	Angular
Curved	Dragging	Jerky
Elastic	Hesitant	Brittle
Fluid	Awkward	Stiff
Firm	Lacks pressure	Uncontrolled
Natural	Passive	Lacks harmony
Dynamic	Lethargic	Choppy strokes
Complex movements	Simple movements	Hesitations
Movement away from center	Movement toward center	Uneven tension
Moderate regularity	Emphasis on inner direction	Irregularity

Do You Wanna Dance?

Various types of rhythms make dance and music fun. The graceful 1-2-3 waltz rhythm is unlike the steady 1-2-3-4 of a military march. The brisk 1-2-1-2-3 of a cha-cha bears little resemblance to the laid-back beat of reggae, or the mercurial sound of acid rock. The following handwritings illustrate some different types of rhythms.

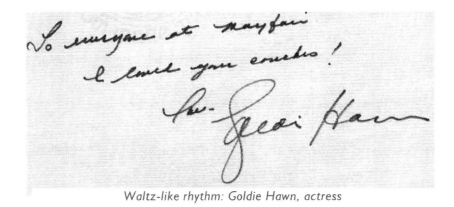

Waltz-like rhythm: Goldie Hawn, actress

Released rhythm: Judy Collins, singer

Marchlike rhythm: David Bowie, singer

Because I truly bue it. I spent my childhood in cinema thugues. Movies can be a medium that mixes all arts. But it all starts by a good screenplay so ? ...t.

Nervous rhythm – actress, screenwriter Julie Delpy

Extreme, Dude!

Extremes in handwriting hint at some form of compensation for a lack in one area or another. The writer prefers to deny what is really going on inside, so he tries to cover it up by distracting you with the exaggerations.

Until you are able to see the underlying picture of personality, try to ignore the exaggerations, as they may draw you away from the truth.

Extremes detract from good rhythm. Some handwritings have extremes that seem to jump off the page and hit you in the eye:

✓ Lower loops so long and wide they look like big, sad teardrops on the page

✓ Upper loops slanting so far to the right that the writing looks like it could fall over in a breeze

✓ Pressure so heavy it tears through the paper

✓ Ornaments that wouldn't even look good on a Christmas tree

✓ Extremes in writing.

IS I REMEMBER WHEN : TO THE POSITION I HAVE RELUCTANTLY. I FELT (H VERY DIFFERENT THAN

disturbed forms - extra strokes

Try to look beyond the strange eye-catching forms and see what is behind them. Is the space more disturbed? The form? The movement?

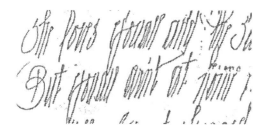

Strange forms, too narrow, leftward movement

Darkness is beginning to that they postpone the trip morning. Jack accuses him o,

Disturbed forms and too-wide space

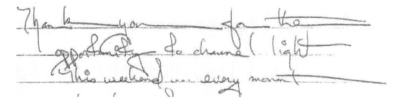

Disturbed forms and exaggerated rightward movement

Disturbed forms - too elaborate

As you can easily see, disturbances in the form (letter designs) are what cause you to stare and indicate problems in the development of the ego. Yet, the writers of the last five samples manage, somehow, to get along in the world. None of them are locked up; they appear to lead normal lives. This is a good time to remember that it's not our job to judge, just to describe the behavior we see on the page.

> Balance in rhythm is the desired state. However, "Perfect" balance can never be attained because humans experience continual input that requires adjustments and growth. "Good enough" balance, however, is absolutely attainable.

The disturbance of form creates issues in other areas, too. For example, the last writing in this group is extremely tall, which means it takes up too much vertical space. At the same time, it is extremely narrow, which keeps it from moving forward. And overall, for its size, it is too crowded. Figuring out behavior in cases like this presents quite a challenge. So, if you're having a hard time with it, don't feel bad. You will need a lot more experience before tackling a handwriting like these.

Last Words

Handwriting requires movement. Movement expands and contracts. Look for the degree of balance in how much the writing expands and contracts. Strong movement to the right is natural. In English, strong movement to the left is contrived. There are many different types of rhythms, which symbolize different types of temperaments. Extremes or exaggerations are never given a positive interpretation because they impede good rhythm and balance.

Chapter 10

Contents Under Pressure – the depth component

Pressure is the aspect of writing that best expresses the energy of the personality. Like blood pressure, which strongly influences physical energy, writing pressure regulates the flow of ink as it is expelled from the pen. In this chapter we'll cover which factors affect the stability and quality of the ink flow, and a few other items that it probably never occurred to you to ask.

Whether a task is physical, mental, social, emotional, it takes energy to complete. Since the human body is a closed system, what affects one part all the other parts. What happens on a physical level affects thoughts and feelings, and what happens on an emotional level affects thought and can also have a physiological impact.

Energy has been compared to many things: electricity, a horse and its rider, a body of water. Water is probably the metaphor that makes most sense because the ink flows through a channel onto the paper. Examine the ductus under magnification. Depending on the pen, the ink flow, like water, may be sluggish and slow moving, or a rapidly flowing river that is swollen to overflowing; a smooth, glassy lake; a swift stream; or a stagnant pond where nothing moves.

When the energy flow is smooth and the human system is working harmoniously, things get accomplished. When the flow is disrupted, the entire organism is impacted. The same is true of the ink flow, which is the depth component of handwriting. Figuring out this feature will help you understand the writer on a very basic level.

Ready for Action—Tensing and Flexing

We've already learned that tension and release creates a pattern in handwriting. For any part of the body to move muscular tension is required. Without tension, we would be as limp as the characters on cartoonist Gary Larson's boneless chicken ranch. It's tension that keeps the body in a constant state of readiness to act.

Too much tension is a sign that the body is always on high alert, which causes physical and mental fatigue. **Too much release** results in flabbiness and inability to react quickly when a response is called for. By now, you know what I'm going to say next. Say it along with me:

> a reasonable balance between the two extremes gets the most positive interpretation.

When writing, the physical movement of the hand involves two sets of muscles that allow it to tense and flex. Downstrokes use the tensing muscles and upstrokes use the flexing. The motion of the downstroke—the tensing, contracting movement—brings the pen back to the self. With that movement, the emphasis is on conserving energy and self-preservation. Therefore, if a handwriting demonstrates extra heavy emphasis on downstrokes, the writer is excessively concerned with the most basic of instincts, personal survival, more than other aspects of life.

Fine Points

Normally, upstrokes should be lighter than downstrokes because the upstrokes release the tension. It's easier to detect the secondary pressure pattern on a

The motion of the upstroke is the flexing, stretching movement, which takes the pen away from the self, toward others. During that movement the energy is expended on moving outward in releasing stress. If the writing emphasis is more on the flexing movement, the writer's focus is on outer concerns, such as altruistic or idealistic efforts or developing the spiritual side, more than satisfying basic instinctual needs.

Tension is created by a need (upstroke, moving outward). Release comes from satisfying the need (downstroke, toward self). Thus, the strength of the writer's needs and desires will be expressed in the output of energy.

Energy produces movement and affects both the writing pressure and the tension/release pattern.

Imagine that...

Some handwriting analysts insist on analyzing only samples written with ballpoint pen. This is a holdover from the old rules of the International GraphoAnalysis Society (IGAS) and with so many pens and inks available no longer applies.

External Influences

Several factors influence writing pressure. Some of these were mentioned in Chapter 9 and includes the type of writing instrument, pen hold, choice of paper, and writing surface. Here is additional detail.

Writing Instrument

One's choice of writing instrument can make a big difference to the writing trail it leaves behind. If forced to use an instrument he doesn't like, the writer with a strong preference for a particular type of pen may feel that his normal style is skewed, which could impact the accuracy of the analysis. Let the client use the instrument he likes best.

We'll make one exception and, in most cases, disallow pencils. Certainly, samples written in pencil can be analyzed, and sometimes that's the only sample available. But pencil is the least desirable because when it comes to pressure, the way the point wears down can be misleading and skew the results.

Pen Hold

The way you hold the pen influences the width of the stroke it creates. Try this experiment: hold your pen near the tip (called a short hold) and write a few words. You'll find the pen wants to stand almost upright, and the ink line it produces is thin and sharp with a very precise stroke.

Now, grasp the pen further back on the barrel (called a long hold), about 1 ½ inches from the tip. When you write, the ink flows more readily and spreads out in a thicker line. We'll talk about what these two types of line, or *ductus,* means a little further on.

Def·i·ni·tion

Ductus: the quality of the pen stroke produced by the flow of ink.

Choice of Paper

If the writing paper is thick and porous, the ink soaks into it like blotting paper and the ductus looks fuzzy or blurred under magnification. Very smooth or glossy paper leaves the ink sitting on the surface and may not give a true impression of pressure (pun intended). Twenty-pound bond seems to be the best paper for accurately estimating pen pressure.

Writing Surface

The surface on which you choose to write is another important factor. Here is another experiment: place your paper on a hard wood surface. Write a few words and check the pressure by running your fingers over the back of the paper. Next, put a magazine or other soft surface underneath the paper and write. See what a difference it makes. A hard writing surface allows little play on the paper, so the pressure leaves less of an impression. A softer surface allows too much play and makes the pressure appear heavier than it really is.

Fine Points

A shaky-looking handwriting might have been written on a rough surface. See something out of the ordinary? Get more information before analyzing.

Internal Influences

In addition to all the external influences on pressure, health and mood can have an effect.

When you're feeling ill, the pressure may be somewhat lighter because you don't have the energy to invest in the writing movement. The same is true of someone who is depressed. He just doesn't feel like making the effort. On the other hand, the angry person often tends to write heavier, digging into the paper.

Great physical strength, however, does not necessarily mean heavy-pressured writing. A big, burly football player may have very light writing pressure, while a tiny grandma's pressure may be very strong.

A Gripping Tale: 3 types of pressure

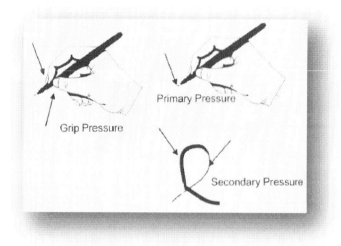

1. Grip pressure refers to how tightly you hold the pen. Do you cling to your pen like a limpet, leaving a dent in your finger? If you often get writer's cramp, your grip pressure is probably too strong.

2. Primary pressure. How hard do you press the pen into the paper. Primary pressure is a literal representation of the degree you assert yourself in the world.

3. Secondary pressure. Demonstrates the rhythm of tension and release in the pattern of light/dark strokes.

Pussycat or Storm Trooper?

Pressure is the third dimension of handwriting. The writing zones carry movement across, as well as up and down on the paper. That's the first and second dimension. Pressure moves *into* the paper and has been labeled the depth component. It reflects, in a very literal way, the *impression* that the writer makes on the world.

The timid, shy person tiptoes onto the paper in her house slippers without making a dent. The medium pressure writer has healthy self-confidence and isn't afraid to make her presence known. The angry, frustrated boy who rages at life storms onto the page in combat boots, leaving deep gouges in his wake, perhaps even ripping holes through the paper, like the sample below, written by a gang-banger.

Def·i·ni·tion

Depth component: Degree of pressure of the pen point into the paper; creates literal depth.

What Does It Weigh?

Pressure is not an indication of physical strength. As mentioned above, a 4'10 grandma might have much stronger writing pressure than a 300-pound fullback. The degree that the writer presses into the paper depends on the amount of *psychic,* not physical energy he expends.

Is there a heaven for a G?
Gangster/ Remember Me so
many Homies in the Cemetery.
Shed so many tears I
suffered thru the years and
shed so many tears. Just
Fuck The World 'Cause Im

Gang member

When it comes to pressure, don't worry about exact measurements. "Light," "medium, or "heavy" is close enough. How can you tell how heavy the pressure is? Turn the paper over and run your fingertips over the back. Can you feel the words pressing into the paper? Or is the paper totally smooth, the pen having left no impression at all?

If you cannot feel indentations, the pressure is light. If you can just feel it through the paper, the pressure is medium. If the paper is heavily scored, and the writing feels like Braille, the pressure is heavy.

A photocopy makes it impossible to detect absolute pressure (depth), is an important component of handwriting. This doesn't mean you cannot analyze scanned or photocopied handwritings, but it's better not to until you have some experience under your belt and are comfortable gauging the writing depth. Even then, it's necessary to be very careful. Scanning and photocopying can give a false impression of pressure.

Imagine that...

A photocopy can provide a better idea of the pressure *pattern* (but not the depth component) than the original. Set the copier or scanner on a "lighter" mode and often, the light/dark pattern will stand out.

Breaking the Surface: Medium Pressure

Medium is the most common pressure, so we start there. Medium pressured writing will be moderately dark, and you may feel a *slight* indentation on the reverse of the paper. In terms of need for physical contact, the writer is moderate and conventional.

As pressure is an expression of vitality, a pattern of lighter upstrokes/heavier downstrokes suggests someone with adequate willpower, stamina, and moderate sex drive.

If other characteristics support it, the writer is probably reliable and dependable, with sufficient backbone to help get through difficulties and the resilience to bounce back.

Running on Empty: Light Pressure

The pen dragging across the paper produces friction, which moderately light-pressure writers prefer to avoid. It may be that the writer had to face a lot of conflict in the past, and cannot stand the thought of dealing with any more. Consequently, he avoids obstacles whenever possible and takes the path of least resistance every chance he gets. This writer would rather fight than switch.

The light-pressure writer is often more spiritually than physically oriented. His sexual energies may be sublimated into the mental realm. He probably doesn't expend a lot of energy on sex or other activities requiring a lot of vitality and stamina. It's not that he doesn't work hard or doesn't like sex. In fact, he may work *very* hard, but in bursts of energy which can leave him exhausted.

The light pressure writer is very sensitive, sometimes (if the writing is also irregular) to the point of being temperamental. She cannot afford to let things touch her too deeply, and her feelings tend to stay on the surface. An emotional event may flatten her momentarily, but then she'll let it go and move on.

Blowin' in the Wind: Extremely Light Pressure

Extremely light pressure has a ghostly quality. The writing barely glides over the page, leaving almost no mark. Depression is often a factor, as the writer feels overwhelmed by life's stresses. For him, friction of any kind is like rubbing a towel over sunburn—unbearable! It may help the analyst to find out why his will to make an impact is so weak.

The extremely light writer is highly suggestible and doesn't have the inner strength to stand against someone with strong willpower. Because he has little interest or drive for experiencing life in all its fullness, he compensates by living in her mind. Anything that suggests power and vitality disturbs his sense of equilibrium, so he may choose a quiet environment with light colors and lightly seasoned foods.

Pressure Fades Away

Downstrokes that start strong but fade away before releasing the energy into the upstroke suggest the energy peters out before the effort is complete. If the pressure returns just before the end of the upstroke, a short rest may be all the writer needs to revitalize and complete what he started.

If your lover has this habit, give him a little break at strategic moments. You may find the results worth it.

Slightly Heavy Pressure

Moderately heavy pressure can be easily felt on the reverse side of the paper. The writer subconsciously experiences the writing surface as a force to be overcome, and he believes that he has the will to overcome anything. In general, the heavy-pressure writer is a hard worker who, if he also has a good contraction/release pattern, gets things done. When other people get tired and quit, he keeps on going.

His stamina takes him through a long day and he still has the energy to party at night. This is a sensual, hearty lover with a strong sex drive. Activities that call for bodily contact and physical strength attract him like the proverbial magnet. He enjoys pitting herself against difficulty and, especially with strong downstrokes, is determined to beat the odds. He is not afraid to demand what he wants.

> The moderately heavy pressure writer is the type who enjoys spicy foods, fine wine, bright colors, and rough textures.

Tales from the Script

Jennifer, a 26-year-old "California girl," works 9 hours a day in a busy county office as a secretary while she attends medical school 3 nights a week. On weekends and free evenings, she's haunting the nightclub scene with her friends or spending time with her boyfriend. Jennifer's stamina is evident in the moderately heavy pressure of her handwriting.

Playing the Heavy: Extremely Heavy Pressure

Extremely heavy pressure is a primary sign of frustration and anger. The increased tension on the pen results in deep scoring of the paper. If we believe that pressure reveals the degree to which the writer wants either to embrace or pummel the world at large, extremely heavy pressure would indicate frustration, hostility, and aggression.

Expect a ferocious drive for sensual gratification. This writer has little finesse and may be brutish in satisfying his needs. Everything is brought down to its basest level. When he wants something, he yells. If you disagree with him, he yells. If he is unhappy, he shouts. The term "Bull in a china shop" comes to mind.

Fine Points

Extreme pressure= stubborn, inflexible, nasty temper. Add strong right slant, slashing i-dots, heavy t-crosses; if this writer gets mad, run for cover.

If there is a positive side to the extremely heavy pressure, it is that the writer won't shirk away from doing the dirty work. When something unpleasant needs handling, he will do it.

Sudden Bursts of Pressure

When you see a sudden burst of pressure, check where it appears, as the word(s) themselves may be emotionally charged. Otherwise, the sudden pressure signifies a flare-up of suppressed emotion that has been smoldering for some time. If the pressure subsides right away, it simply reflects a quick burst of irritation that quickly passes.

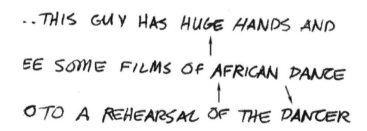

Musician David Byrne of the Talking Heads –
sudden pressure.

When the burst is on the horizontal axis, especially on an ending stroke, you can be sure the writer forces her will on the world. She must have the last word. If the horizontal stroke is in the lower zone (subconscious), she probably is not even aware of this tendency to be domineering. Certainly, she won't admit to it.

Life's Hard Enough—Displaced Pressure

For a balanced life it is just as important to take time out to play as it is to work. Without regular times out to relax and let go of the tension that builds up from day-to-day events, the body (and mind) eventually rebels. Tension without release can lead to stroke, heart attack, and other unpleasant health problems.

The Type-A personality finds it extremely difficult to relax and do nothing. They keep on pushing and don't know when to quit. The tension may be displaced or channeled into an area where it doesn't belong. When this happens, it may result in a phenomenon called **displaced pressure.**

Displaced pressure: Margaret Mitchell,
author of Gone With the Wind

Def·i·ni·tion

Displaced pressure: Instead of the upstrokes being lighter than the downstrokes, the pattern is reversed or is emphasized on the horizontal left-right movement.

Pressure Displaced on the Horizontal

When pressure is displaced onto the horizontal axis, as seen in heavy t-crosses, rather than the vertical (up/down) axis of handwriting, it signals excessive domination and force of will. Instead of directing the energy where it properly belongs, into the unconscious instincts of the lower zone, it gets hijacked.

Extra-long, Extra-heavy t-crosses are symbolic of aggressive willpower. The person whose pressure goes horizontal rules others with an iron fist. It may be camouflaged in a pretty velvet glove, but there is no doubt about who has the say-so. In the writing below, not only are the t-bars long and heavy,

Fine Points

If a left-hander displaces pressure on the vertical axis, give it less weight than a right-hander.

but some of the words show varying pressure on the horizontal axis, too.

When the horizontal pressure appears in underlining, it is a matter of emphasis. The writer is trying to exert her authority like an instructor who thinks you don't understand her.

Pressure on the horizontal axis

If the horizontal stroke is a long final stroke at the baseline and not done for the purpose of underlining, it suggests holding off and distrusting others.

Pressure Displaced onto Upstrokes

Very little is written about displaced pressure. It is usually not considered in a positive light, but can be a sign of successful adaptation. Dr. Klara Roman often found it in the handwritings of successful women who, for whatever reason, had sublimated their sex drive into their work.

The reversal of pressure means that when the writer should be releasing energy in light upstrokes, he is actually contracting (pressure on the upstrokes). He is, in effect, swimming against the tide of libidinal energy, making things much harder than need be. By forcing his will against the environment, he doesn't allow things to flow naturally.

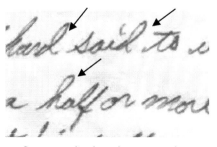

Pressure displaced on upstrokes
(vertical axis)

On the surface he may appear calm, but the lack of inner balance causes frustration. Like the writing above, the pressure moves away from the middle zone (day-to-day activities) where it belongs, and towards the upper zone, displacing energy into an area where it doesn't belong at that time. In other words, the writer is thinking when he should be feeling and feeling when he should be thinking.

When pressure is displaced in the lower zone with light downstrokes and heavy upstrokes, the sexual energy is displaced into the middle zone area of daily life. This doesn't mean the writer isn't interested in sex. Quite the opposite might be true, but there is no appropriate outlet for the sexual energy. The expenditure of energy into the middle zone is a compensation for it. According to Roman, if the displacement is carried out without loss of force or rhythm, the compensation is successful.

Manipulative behavior is a natural by-product of reversed pressure. The writer is determined to get done what she wants, by hook or by crook. If she can't get it by being nice, she'll force the issue. Insecurity generally is at the root. The writer's instinctual needs aren't being directly satisfied, so she exerts her will in some other area to make up for it.

Sometimes the pressure is the same on lower zone upstrokes and downstrokes. This happens when stress is unrelieved, the writer has no means of releasing his strong emotions.

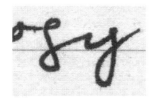

Unrelieved pressure on
up/downstrokes in lower zone

Directional Pressure

Directional pressure is not really pressure at all. It refers to a bend in a stroke that should be straight, and demonstrates a *feeling* of pressure that comes from the direction of the bend.

Directional pressure can come from any direction. If the bend is on tops of strokes, it represents stress from authority figures. Bent on the left, it is pressure from the past. From below, it comes from the instincts. From the right, the pressure is coming from the future.

Tales From the Script

Felix Klein, imprisoned in the concentration camps at Buchenwald and Dachau during WWII, discovered a surprising phenomenon in the handwritings of some prisoners. Those who survived had in common strokes on the right sides of letters that should be straight were bent. This indicated stress coming from the direction of the future. They never knew if they would be alive from one moment to the next, but they were able to adapt. Those whose handwritings were more rigid were killed more often. They didn't possess the same capacity to adapt or literally, to *bend* to life in the camps. We call it *directional pressure*.

Directional pressure: Princess Grace Kelly
bent downstroke = anxiety about the future

Directional pressure from the future

In the Zone

In this section we will be dealing with the parts of pressure that have to do with width of the stroke. Personality-wise, sensuousness and sensuality are viewed as different parts of the spectrum that have to do with the concrete senses.

Def·i·ni·tion
> **Sensuousness** has to do with gratifying the five physical senses: sight, sound, touch, taste, smell, but without a sexual component.
> **Sensuality** is the appeal to the senses and indulgence in erotic pleasures at its extreme. At least, that's the definition we'll use here.

Pastosity, No Marinara Sauce

Pastosity. What kind of word is that? A made-up one, actually, credited to early modern Hungarian graphologist, Klara Roman. Dr. Roman used the word "pastosity" to describe the broad flow of ink that was seen more in fountain pens in her day (20th century), but today is more likely to be from use of a felt tip pen.

Def·i·ni·tion
> **Pastosity:** from "pasta," representing a soft, doughy quality.

The pastose stroke is wide, both on upstrokes and downstrokes, and made with no real pressure. The stroke looks as if it were daubed on with a brush. The lack of release that comes from heavy pressure on both up- and downstrokes does not apply in this case because the pastose stroke is a released movement in itself. A load of ink is discharged onto the paper.

Pastose writing is produced by those who are physically in tune with their concrete senses. The things that turn them on are when they experience through touch, taste, smell, sight, and hearing. The scent of a rose might drive a pastose writer wild, or the sound of the birds singing early in the morning. Warm and earthy, he loves the tactile sensations of sexual activity. But the sensuous experience must be natural. Don't try to palm some knock-off perfume or fast food on this type of writer. She wants the real thing.

Because the pastose stroke is produced without pressure and is made by a long hold on the pen (further back on the barrel), it suggests someone who wants to enjoy creature comforts without expending a lot of energy to get them. If the "good things" come easily, fine. If not, that's okay, too. But sitting in the lap of luxury is much more pleasant than a cold dirt floor.

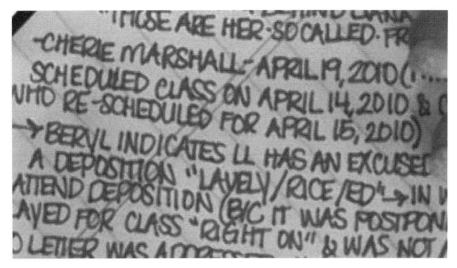

Pastose writing: Lindsay Lohan, actress

Unlike sharp writers, pastose writers tend not to be judgmental. They some more than fifty shades of gray between black and white, and the pastose writer usually is somewhere in the middle. On the negative side, in living mostly by her senses, the pastose writer expends far less energy developing the philosophical or spiritual side of life.

Mud Wrestling

Muddy handwriting, which is related to *blocked* pressure, is different from pastosity. It looks smeared and smudgy. The oval letters are flooded with ink, pressure suddenly billows, and/or there are numerous heavy cross outs. Unlike a healthy sexual appetite, muddiness comes from eroticism gone wild.

Fine Points

Signs of blocked pressure are muddiness, slow speed, lack of dynamic movement.

Muddiness is found in the handwritings of those whose sexuality may be linked to all sorts of unconventional practices frowned on by society. It suggests unbridled excesses and unbalanced discharge of energy. The flood of ink illustrates a flood of impulses which the writer makes little or no effort to curb. Guilt and anxiety are often a big part of the picture.

The only accurate way to study the pressure, pastosity, muddiness continuum is by looking at the writing under magnification. When the borders of the stroke are jagged and fuzzy-looking, more information is warranted. There may be serious illness. Father Anthony Becker reported that under 100X magnification, a stroke that looked like a caterpillar was found in the handwritings of people diagnosed with cancer.

Muddy writing: James Earl Ray, convicted assassin of Martin Luther King.

If the writer is in good health and there are supporting indications in the writing, there is a lack of control in the way he expresses his sensuality, indulging the senses indiscriminately.

> Take great care when judging muddy writing, keeping in mind that a *faulty pen* might be the cause. Always look for the simplest reason before jumping off the deep end and deciding the writer is a criminal or has a deadly disease.

Blocked Pressure

When pressure is blocked, the upstrokes and downstrokes are both dark and heavy pressured. This is different from pastosity, which is made without noticeable pressure.

Blocked pressure *looks* unhealthy. In fact, it may be time for the writer to go for a physical checkup. Circulatory problems, alcoholism, menopause, or heart disease are often a contributing factor.

If the cause is not physical, we can deduce that the writer feels stuck in a rut. What happens if you drive your car into a sandbank? You can't go forward and you can't go backward. You just sit there, spinning your wheels. And that's what life feels like for the writer of blocked pressure. Frank Victor likened this type of pressure to a dammed-up river.

Shading and Sharpness

Shading looks like the sculpted bas relief of an ancient temple. Writing in relief, otherwise known as shading, is produced by a fountain pen or calligraphy-type pen, sometimes with a chisel tip.

*Shaded writing: Elmore Leonard,
crime writer*

Shaded script is not spontaneous. Aesthetics are of paramount importance to the writer of shaded writing. Cultured and refined, he has socially polish and demands excellence in presentation.

Sharpness is different and is best identified under magnification. A sharp stroke is thin and has clean, clear edges. The aesthetic person enjoys the crispness of this type of stroke, and usually has a critical nature.

For the sharp writer everything is either black or white with no gray area in between. She enjoys an argument, but don't expect her to bend a millimeter. Her aggressive, dogmatic way of dealing with people and absolute refusal to adapt may push others away.

I am noticing

emotion alters my

I am feeling both

Sharp writing: Original "Catwoman" Julie Newmar

When combined with angles, which is usually the case, there is a certain coolness of personality. She likes others to see her as moral and righteous. However, the kindness and compassion that go with morality and righteousness appear to be somewhat lacking.

Last Words

Pressure reflects psychic energy, not physical strength. In handwriting, it symbolizes the energy available for the work of the personality. Extremely heavy pressure is a sign of frustration. Extremely light pressure is a sign of depression. Moderate pressure suggests physical health.

Chapter 11

Faster Than a Speeding Bullet: Speed

It's easy to gauge speed when driving your car. The flashing red lights behind you on the highway let you know were doing way more than 65 mph. Drive too slowly and the honking horns will be a reminder. Measuring speed on paper is another story. When you were not present to watch the writer's pen as it progressed across the page, it can be a challenge to figure out just how fast they wrote.

Speed is an important, but oft-neglected, factor to consider as part of any analysis. It relates to intelligence, spontaneity of thought, and dynamic action. Robert Saudek's experiments reduced writing to milliseconds in order to measure the time it took to write. You will find a table in this chapter that summarizes the indicators he selected to represent speed and slowness in handwriting.

Handwriting moves in two directions: forward and backward. In the forward movement we see how the writer approaches the world: enthusiastically, spontaneously, or hastily rushing forward, never quite having enough time to get everything done. When forward movement is inhibited, or there is too much movement to the left (backward), it signifies either caution and forethought, pre-meditation, or lack of ability and know-how. In this chapter we'll learn what impact speed has on handwriting and what it reveals about the writer's temperament.

The Age of Innocence

Many factors, both internal and external, influence writing speed. The most powerful of those is *graphic maturity,* which is an internal factor. Graphic maturity is a term coined in the early 1920s by Robert Saudek, who helped lay the scientific foundation for handwriting analysis.

Def·i·ni·tion

> **Graphic maturity**: the ability to write fluidly without having to con-
> sciously think about the act of writing.

Saudek wrote *Experiments with Handwriting* (George Allen & Unwin, 1922, reprinted by Books for Professionals, 1978), still considered the most important work on the subject, details his research on speed. Unless you have a particular interest in the physiological aspects of handwriting or are a masochist and want to wade through it yourself, I will summarize some of its basic tenets.

Before you learn how to write words, you first must learn how to form single letters. Graphic maturity is the point at which you can write fluently without having to stop and think how to form the letters and the words. Several checkpoints must be reached before a writer reaches that point:

- The writer has learned to control the writing instrument and feels comfortable with it.

- There is no physical or mental impairment that would affect the ability to write.

- The writer has become familiar enough with how to form an individual letter that when he hears the name of the letter, a mental picture of it appears in his head.

Before an entire sentence can be written automatically (that is, without thinking about each word before writing it), one more condition must be met: the writer must be able to focus on what he wants to write about and not be paying attention to the details related to the act of writing. He ignores or overlooks problems that may be directly related to the writing, such as:

- Poor legibility (possibly caused by faulty writing materials).

- Concern about how attractive the writing looks.

- Uncertainty about the spacing or other part of the writing pattern that makes the writer pay closer attention to the act of writing than the content. (Hesitancy of any kind impacts the flow of writing.)

The next checkpoint in the development of graphic maturity is familiarity with the language. The writer is considered familiar with the language if.

- He is comfortable speaking the language.

- A change of language mid-text does not disrupt the continuity.

- He is as comfortable with the written word as the spoken word.

Parlez-Vous Handwriting?

Even after a writer reaches graphic maturity, there are circumstances that may impact his ability to write without hesitating. Something in the text itself—a word or a thought that arouses painful memories—can cause him to falter or pause momentarily. Or, he may reach a word he is unsure of and be forced to stop and sound it out in his mind.

Fine Points

If a sample shows many stops and starts, ask about the writing instrument. Don't assume traits that might be the result of a bad pen or other external factor.

Content and purpose can make a big difference to writing appearance. If you are forced to write a check to the IRS, you might write slower because you don't want to do it. On the other hand, if you're send an enthusiastic postcard from Hawaii to a friend, the writing may be faster than your normal pace.

> Mood has an effect on speed. Angry or excited writing is faster than sad or tired writing.

Speed Bumps

Someone who is comfortable with the act of writing has a smooth, fluid writing movement. The writing comes naturally. But what contributes to fluidity, and what detracts from it? Speed in handwriting depends on many details and circumstances. Let's consider them one at a time:

Direction of movement. Fast writing moves to the right. Any interruption to the writing movement is like stepping on the brakes when you're driving your car.

Shapes of letters. Rounded movement is faster than angular movement. Angles require abrupt stops.

Size of letters. Medium-sized writing is faster than small or large writing. Exaggerations of any kind take longer to make and thus slow down the writing.

Extra strokes. Strokes that are unnecessarily retained or added take longer to make and slow down the writing.

Pressure. Heavy pressure creates friction on the paper and takes longer than medium or light pressure.

Quality of pen and paper. Ink clogging the tip of the pen impacts speed. Writing on poor-quality paper also creates pen drag.

Physical disability. Someone suffering from Parkinson's disease, multiple sclerosis, essential tremor or another illness that affects muscular control may be forced to write slowly out of necessity.

Mental illness. Chronic depression may slow down the writing. Other types of mental illness, such as the manic phase of bipolar disorder, speed it up.

Drugs. Prescribed, over-the-counter, or "recreational" drugs and medications may alter writing speed for obvious reasons.

Unfamiliarity with the language. If the person is writing in an unfamiliar language, the writing will be slower.

Self-consciousness about the appearance of writing. When the writer is more concerned about form than content, the need to write "beautifully" slows him down.

Dislike of writing. Someone who hates to write may have poorly developed script, which will slow it down. Or, he may be in a hurry to get the act of writing over with, which will speed it up.

Setting the Pace

The pace or speed of writing is affected by how rapidly the writer responds in emotional situations. The well-balanced person who expresses emotions appropriately writes at a fairly steady tempo most of the time. The tense and anxious person makes many starts and stops. One who lets it all hang out may write faster than he can control the pen.

Factors Affecting Tempo

We all have our own natural tempo. Some people are slow in everything they do. From rolling out of bed to getting around to making breakfast, the day moves at tortoise pace. They're even slow about going to bed. Others have energy to burn and never sit still. The day flies by in a whirlwind of activity without a second to spare between tasks.

Fine Points

 A fast thinker can slow down their writing, but a slow thinker cannot write

Environmental factors, such as the telephone ringing or someone walking into the room while the writer is in the act of putting his thoughts on paper, will temporarily affect speed. The disruption will appear as a hesitation in the writing speed.

Physical illness or an emotional crisis may cause temporary or permanent changes in writing speed. If normally you write fast, but you get the flu or you just smoked a joint (medicinal, of course!), the speed of your handwriting is apt to slow down, perhaps to the point that the words are an illegible slur.

Good news that excites you is likely to lead to faster writing.

Saudek's table of indicators for speed on the next page should help familiarize you with what to look for in determining the velocity of the handwriting you are analyzing.

> ### Def·i·ni·tion
> **Velocity (or Tempo):** the speed of something in a given direction.

Indicators for Fast and Slow Writing

Speed	Slowness
t crossed to right of the stem	t crossed to left of the stem
Long t bars	Short t bars
Loops balloon slightly to the right	Loops pull to the left
Increased right slant	Left-slanted loops
Left margin gets wider	Upright loops
Right margin gets narrower	Left margin gets narrower
No sudden stops or changes of direction	Right margin gets wider
Moderately connected	Very even margins
Light-medium pressure	Frequent change of direction
Clear ovals	Many breaks within words
Sharp strokes	Heavy pressure
Few covering strokes	Ink-filled ovals
Accents and i-dots look like dashes	Retouching or soldering
Fluent, smooth writing	Many covering strokes
Medium size	Accents and i-dots round, careful
Garlands, thread, mixed forms	Strong consistency
Illegibility	Large or small size
Words taper off	Angular forms
Simplifications	Slow arcade forms
Neglect of detail	Supported forms
Expansion	School-type writing
Short or missing initial strokes	Elaboration
End strokes to the right	Attention to detail
Slightly rising baseline	Narrowness
Loops moderate in width and length	Long end strokes
Final strokes decrease in size	Blunt, rolled-in, or leftward end strokes

Reading the Handwriting Speedometer

Speed in handwriting mimics the writer's personal pace in his day-to-day activities, and even reflects the way he speaks. Those who speak fast write fast. In conversation with someone who zooms along so fast you can hardly understand him, ask for some handwriting. Chances are you won't be able to read it because he thinks faster than he speaks or writes, which results in poor legibility.

Fine Points

A slow writer may be quiet and profound, or lazy and timid; a complete analysis will tell which it is.

The slower speaker is as deliberate in his writing as he is in his speech. Perhaps unsure and nervous in communicating, he tends to speak and write hesitantly, starting and stopping numerous times before being able to get out what is on his mind. Those who speak in short, staccato bursts write that way, too, like machine-gun fire.

Rarely will a handwriting sample be composed of either all fast or all slow elements. Some signs of slowness almost always appear in a faster script, though less often do signs of speed appear in a slow script (depending on the reason for the slowness).

It can be helpful to check the areas where the speed was arrested to find out what caused the slowness and vice versa.

> Neither speed, nor any other element of writing can provide a full picture of the writer's personality on its own.

Saudek's rule was that a sample containing at least two more indicators for speed than for slowness is primarily fast but has been slowed down. Conversely, if a sample has at least two more indicators for slowness than for speed, it is primarily slow but has been speeded up. The question is, what caused the writer to alter his normal tempo? We may not know the answer. Maybe the writer had a cold and stopped to blow his nose, or he saw something on the news that got him riled up. Sometimes it has to be enough just to make note of the difference.

As Slow as Molasses

Just how slow *is* molasses? Picture a stream of sticky syrup dribbling from the bottle, gathering in a lazy pool at the bottom of a bowl. That's the way the slow writer approaches life, enjoying the scenery along the way.

Assuming there are no mental or physical causes, slowness in writing assumes a reduction of emotional spontaneity. The moderately slow writer is apt to use school-model forms, which are less natural than a rapid, spontaneous script.

Moderately Slow Writing

Moderately slow writing is a sign of inhibition and self-control, as well as circumspection. The writer is most comfortable when he knows he has the time to thoroughly prepare and rehearse ahead of time; to follow a familiar routine where he knows what's coming up next.

Fine Points

A slow writer takes extra time to ensure correctness but is more likely to scratch out words or make corrections to the writing than the fast writer who cares less about making mistakes.

Less active but more thoughtful, the moderately slow writer cannot be hurried, nor will he be quick to change direction. If you demand quick changes he'll go even slower to prove that you don't control him. In fact, under time pressure, his stress level is apt to rise significantly. But when you need help with a project that requires patience dealing with others or involves a attention to lots of details, the slower writer is the one to call on.

P.s. Need your friendlip more than ever.

Moderately slow writing: former Secretary of State Madeleine Albright

The Tortoise: Very Slow Writing Speed

There is a vast difference between the careful deliberation of the moderately slow writer and the sluggish, plodding movement of one who is mentally impaired. In the case of very slow writing, there is a lack of graphic maturity and possible impairment.

Moderately slow

The moderately slow speed in the writing above is due to the careful, orna-mented writing of a very bright person who wants to make a good impres-sion. Below is the very slow writing by a woman with an IQ of 87. She was convicted in 2006 of second-degree murder in her child's death due to an overdose of antidepressants. Her conviction was overturned on appeal after she had served two years of a life sentence.

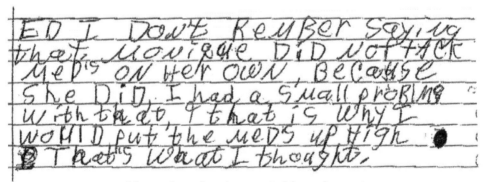

Very slow due to mental impairment

The extreme slowness of the unskilled hand will be obvious, as distin-guished from the writing of someone who has reached graphic maturity but has a careful, contemplative nature. Analyzing extremely slow, unskilled writing is beyond the training of the brand-new graphologist.

Sometimes a writer will intentionally slow down the writing pace. He is probably trying to hide information that could be detrimental to him. Fear of betraying what he wants to keep hidden makes him very careful and premeditate in how and what he writes. Underlying the deliberate slowing down of the writing act may be pathological anxiety or, possibly, criminal acts, such as in the next writing.

Tales from the Script

In a study of children who were performing lower than their grade level, it was found that their writing speeds were significantly slower than those of their higher-performing peers. This was not necessarily an indicator of lower intelligence, however. Stress may have been a factor, such as problems at home.

Steady as She Goes: Medium Writing Speed

Medium speed signifies a conventional approach and reasonable impulse control. The writer's personal tempo is moderate and restrained. He can handle delays without getting too upset (assuming other factors in the writing bear this out), and doesn't mind waiting for someone slower to catch up with him. He likes to process new ideas and thoughts, but isn't fanatical about making sure he has all the latest facts and data to support them. For him, good enough is good enough.

Medium-speed writing: Leslie Klinger, author of
The New Annotated Sherlock Holmes

Moderately Fast Writing Speed

Moderately fast writing requires a reasonably good measure of self-assurance. Unselfconscious, the writer puts the focus on the message more than the style. The fast writer is efficient, reacts quickly and wants to see things happen quickly. He takes the initiative when something needs to be done.

Fine Points

Faster writing speed is used by a normally rapid writer who is unimpaired physically, intellectually, and mechanically, or by a slower writer in a hurry.

His ability to comprehend the essence of a matter without waiting for all the details means he's a fast learner who can put new knowledge to use almost as soon as he assimilates it. It ticks him off when he has to wait for a slower thinker to catch up. He would like to put the words in the other guy's mouth for him! The moderately fast writer's interactions with others are smooth. He's never short of a quick answer.

Many Thanks for your patience + admire !

love Ralph Fiennes

Moderately fast writing: actor Ralph Fiennes ("Voldemort" in Harry Potter

Let's Play Jeopardy!

Legibility is an important factor to consider when judging fast writing. Since we write for the purpose of communicating, it should be legible enough for the reader to understand what the sender wanted to get across. When writing is so fast that it becomes illegible, the words lose their meaning and the basic purpose of writing—communication—fails.

Busy doctors are often accused of illegible writing due to being in a hurry. When the message affects a patient's well-being, deliberate slowing of the writing can be beneficial. Of course, as with a writer in any other career, doctors' handwriting reflects their personal style and temperament.

Haste Makes Waste

There's fast, and then there's *fast*. One is the ability to get things done quickly and efficiently. The other is rash and impetuous, always in a hurry.

The difference between the fast writer and the hasty writer is a sense of agitation in the latter. Borne along by the winds of necessity, he turns his attention to whatever is most urgent at the moment. Feeling the hot breath of Father Time on his neck, he fears he won't be able to accomplish all that he wants to do. Since the internal pressure to hurry up is unrelenting, it really doesn't matter how much time is available.

Impatient and impulsive, the very rapid writer's thoughts travel almost faster than his synapses can fire. Even when his body is at rest, his mind is moving at the speed of light. The knowledge he picks up is directly related to what he needs to know right now.

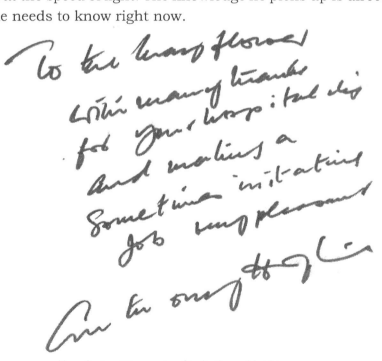

Very fast writing: actor Sir Anthony Hopkins

In his haste, he may leave out letters, diacritics (i-dots and t-crosses, for example), and punctuation, all of which contributes to illegibility. When he remembers to dot the i's and cross the t's, the dots and crossbars usually are made in a sharp, jabbing motion, symbolizing his irritability and a tendency to overreact.

If you want to start World War III, put a very fast and a very slow writer in a small room and lock the door. How long do you think it would take them to drive each other to distraction? All bets are off!

Last Words

Speed of writing depends on the graphic maturity and skill of the writer. Speed and spontaneity are closely related. Speed depends on the direction of the movement, shape of the letters, size, and pressure. Fast thinkers write fast. Deliberate thinkers write more slowly. Slow writing in a personal of normal intelligence is a primary factor in premeditated dishonesty.

Chapter 12

Keep it Simple Sweetheart: Writing Form

Handwriting is not like walking or breathing, acts that come naturally, it's a learned behavior, more like speech. The penmanship teacher used to spend many hours instructing her students in how to create the strokes and forms that make up the letters of the alphabet. These days, 80% of younger teachers admit they don't know how to write in cursive. Still, regardless of the system of handwriting (or printing) taught, everyone in the class starts out learning from the same model.

As you now know, graphic maturity is the point at which a young writer no longer needs to consciously think about the letter forms as he writes them; letters and words begin to flow naturally. At some point—the timing depends upon the child—something happens. Perhaps the margin begins to move away from the left side of the page. Or the writing size begins to shrink or grow beyond copybook size. The slant, baseline, and letter forms may look entirely different from what the school model dictates. What's going on here?

When the letter forms and their placement on the page have begun to deviate from what the young writer learned in school, a more personalized writing style is taking shape that mirrors the youngster's personality development. As he grows and matures, cultivating his own style and tastes along the way, his handwriting will gradually reflect the internal changes he experiences.

The element of handwriting that exhibits personal style is called "form," and is the focus of this chapter.

To Conform or Not to Conform, *That* is the Question!

Form is the most conscious aspect of handwriting. It represents a deliberate choice of writing style that reflects how the writer wants others to see him. He may choose to stick with copybook, or print. Or he may choose simplified or embellished styles that project his unique self-image.

For some reason, many people believe it's best to keep writing the way they learned in school. They don't know that prisons are filled with felons who write exactly the way they first learned. Not that most copybook writers are not felons, of course. It's a matter of wanting to conform. It's just that some people conform to the wrong crowd.

Follower or Leader?

Those who stick close to the school model tend to be followers more often than leaders. They are most comfortable when the rules are plainly stated and they have a good idea of their parameters. Rather than the maverick who is prone to go off on his own, adult copybook writers prefer to have a clear set of instructions and guidelines to follow, given to them by someone else. They like to do things the way they have always done them and feel threatened by major changes. Their motto is, "If it ain't broke, don't fix it."

Lest you jump to the conclusion that continuing to write copybook style is a "bad" thing, consider this: A wide swath of those who adhere to copybook style perform extremely important functions in society. Grade-school teachers, secretaries, and administrators most often choose copybook style, and where would we be without them?

Bottom line, though, teachers might be happy if their students all maintained copybook writing style, but the healthiest relationships, groups, and organizations embrace a variety of styles of being.

Pleasant copybook style writing: actress Marlo Thomas

Straying from the Straight and Narrow

Almost everything we do says something about us. We project our style in our body language, facial expressions, tone of voice, and handwriting. Some people feel more comfortable blending into the crowd. Others are more original and individualistic; they do things their own way. They care little about what people think of them. And, within that group of "original" people, there is a wide range of styles.

Dr. Martin Luther King Jr, civil rights leader

The form the writing takes on—the way it looks—demonstrates the writer's own personal style. Using copybook as a starting point, the degree to which the handwriting departs from the school model is the degree to which the writer feels compelled to express his own unique manner of being.

There are numerous ways to depart from the school model. The shapes of the letters may be different, or the size, slant, beginning and ending strokes, and margins. Or, the writer might strip away some of the nonessential strokes, change the basic form, or add ornamentation.

In preacher and activist Martin Luther King's writing the very tall, narrow upper zones are no surprise, given his legendary ability as an orator. Religious leaders (mostly men) frequently have upper zones that seem to be reaching to the heavens.

Originality can be expressed by simplifying the school model or elaborating on it. A tremendous number of possibilities fall between one end of the spectrum and the other. Starting with copybook as the midpoint, we work our way backward toward simplification.

Teachers have a strong influence on the young mind. An elderly woman reports remembering when her third-grade teacher very seriously informed the class, "You need to join up all your letters and write cursive—not printed—capitals, or else when you grow up, they won't let you vote, they won't let you have a job, they won't let you drive a car." Children tend to believe what adults tell them. A seemingly innocent remark such as this can have a long-range effect on an impressionable young mind.

The Simplification-Elaboration Spectrum.

Below, we see just six ways the capital letter g might be made along the spectrum from simplified to extremely elaborate. Apply this illustration to all of handwriting to get the idea of what it means to simplify or elaborate.

Just the Facts, Ma'am: simplified handwriting

Writing is done for the purpose of communicating, so it needs to be clear and readable. Lavish ornamentations are not necessary or desirable. To qualify as "simplified," a handwriting will be stripped of ornamentation and the less superfluous elements than copybook.

Fine Points

The beginning stroke is not an essential part of the letter. The ending stroke follows the end of a letter or word but is not an essential part of the letter, either.

For example, beginning strokes are dispensable. You don't need them to make a word understandable. The same is true of ending strokes. Upper loops are also optional. It's quite possible to make a downstroke that steers directly into the next letter without first moving into an upstroke.

The following handwriting sample is simplified down to the bare bones.

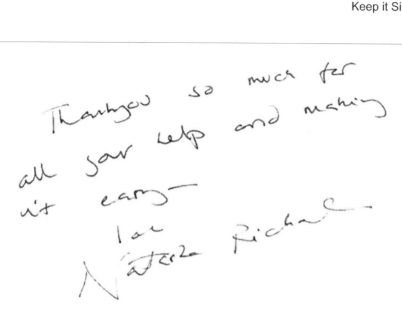

Highly implfied writing of actress Natasha Richardson
(late wife of actor Liam Neeson)

Simplifying copybook forms gets the message across faster through clever shortcuts. The writer who simplifies wants to be efficient and get down to basics. Don't bombard him with a lot of extraneous details or long explanations—he isn't listening.

In combination with an overall wide spatial arrangement (which is common in simplified writing), he tends to feel uncomfortable in a crowd. The simplified writer takes his time getting to know you before he will allow any type of emotional intimacy. Whenever possible, he elects to spend his free time with a few carefully chosen friends.

Writing that is low on loops signifies a direct personality that cannot stand verbosity and won't indulge in the kind of flowery speech that is liberally sprinkled with flattery. What you will get is the bare facts with little embellishment.

It takes a fast thinker to cut through all the irrelevant matter and get to the bottom line. The writer being more objective and realistic, puts more emphasis on the intellect than the emotions.

Below is the highly simplified writing of Jane Goodall, who has spent a lifetime working to protect chimpanzees and for the good of the planet.

Sometimes simplifying takes time. Writing a succinct letter, for example, isn't as easy as it sounds. Benjamin Franklin once wrote to an acquaintance, "I would have written you a shorter letter but I didn't have the time." It's easy to write at great length about a subject, but making the writing clear and concise takes much more effort.

Highly simplified writing: naturalist Jane Goodall

Ingenious Solutions

Because one of the aims of simplified writing is efficiency, writers who like to cut out the details often create very interesting shortcuts. The next sample illustrates some unique ways to get from one letter to the next. The writer, actress Miranda Richardson, certainly never learned these in penmanship class. She finds original, creative solutions to problems.

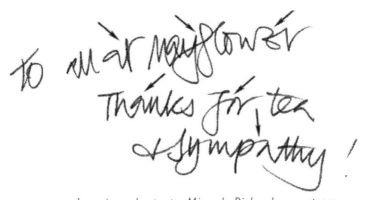

Ingenious shortcuts: Miranda Richardson, actress

The writer is proficient at constructing solutions to problems without relying on the standard, tried-and-true methods. Resourceful and innovative, she finds fresh, sometimes even revolutionary ways of doing the same old thing.

Fine Points

The extremely simplified writer lives at a high level of stress and is too impatient to put a little meat on the bones of his writing. He's as impatient and irritable as the writing.

There is, however, the danger of (as Nana used to say) "throwing the baby out with the bath water." In the need for efficiency and innovation, the simplified writer may reject what worked well in the past simply because it isn't new.

It is possible to achieve simplification without damaging the basic structures of the letters. To deserve a positive interpretation, the handwriting must be spontaneous, natural, and easy to read.

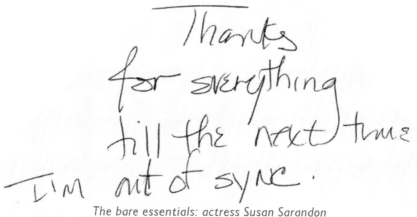

The bare essentials: actress Susan Sarandon

Skeletons in the Closet: Neglect of Form

When too many details are eliminated the writing may look emaciated, like someone who has been fasting too long. There is little meat on the bones. We say the form is neglected. Yet, if the downstrokes are present, the bare essentials are still there and the writer generally manages to function in the world.

The overly simplified writer is ascetic. He has little interest in form. Creature comforts and the extraneous trappings of life mean nothing to him. He views the world through objective eyes, sustained by purely intellectual interests. He doesn't consider other people's needs; in fact, he is probably barely aware of their existence. Reason and intellect are developed at the expense of his emotional life.

The next sample was written by a brilliant autistic man in his 60s. The writing is so simplified that it is difficult to read out of context.

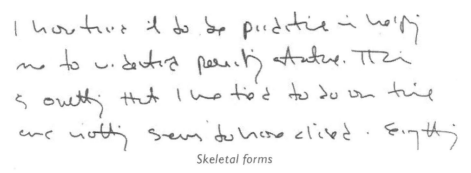

Skeletal forms

As in many other aspects of handwriting, "simplification" is a matter of degree. When the handwriting is so overly simplified that it has deteriorated to the most basic strokes and legibility is totally abandoned, it is called fragmented or skeletal writing. Whereas the writer of simplified writing wants to be clear and efficient, the skeletal writer achieves the opposite result—the writing becomes hard to read because it lacks some of the essential structure, the "backbone."

Extreme simplification may be a sign of emotional self-denial and an impoverished spirit. The writer may feel so profoundly stressed and unable to deal with the pressures of his daily existence that he is forced to divest himself of every emotion or experience that might add to the fullness of life.

Neglect of form can be a sign of narcissism or egocentric behavior. The person who is so consumed by his problems tends to become wrapped up in himself—to the point that he ignores the people and events around him. Emotional reactions are withheld and responses kept to the barest minimum. His emotional life is decaying, falling apart, and so is his handwriting. Communications with the outside world are impaired at best, nonexistent at worst.

Fine Points

Is the simplified style natural and spontaneous or does it look carefully drawn? Legibility is the key to interpretation.

Dressing Up Is Fun: Elaboration

At the other end of the spectrum from simplification is the enrichment/elaboration continuum. While simplification is fast, spontaneous, and unconscious, any type of ornamentation added to handwriting is done consciously and slows it down to some degree.

Again, we must ask: Is the writing legible, spontaneous and natural? If answers to both questions are yes, then the interpretation can be positive. If the elaboration detracts from the message or legibility in any way, a negative meaning is the result.

How elaborate is elaborate? The range is almost limitless. If handwriting was a sponge cake, simplified writing would be the plain, unadorned cake. Add a little frosting and you've got copybook writing. From there, let your imagination run wild. Birthday cake with flowers made of purple frosting? That would be embellished writing. How about wedding cake with bride and groom, sugar bells, and silver sprinkles? Now, that's elaborate!

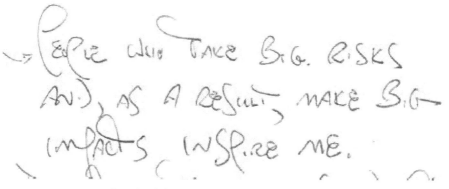

Simply elaborate! A combination of the two

Elaborated writing can run the gamut from richly enhanced to gaudy and overly dramatic. Writing decorated with many extra strokes, wide loops, and other embellishments is made by a visual person for whom form is often more significant than content. This is not a value judgment. It's a fact: The writer spends more time making the writing beautiful (beauty being in the eye of the beholder) than on what she writes.

The elaborate writer is likely to have a home filled with objets d'art—pictures and sculptures—with an emphasis on flamboyant, eye-catching, showy things. Her manner is dramatic, sometimes to the point of theatricality. You can bet she will make an entrance when she arrives at a meeting or party. When he describes an event, it's not a dry recitation of the facts, it's a full-blown story. In her life, everything is BIG and EXCITING.

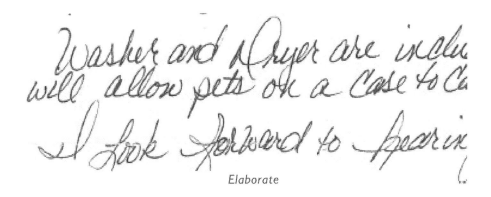

Elaborate

Artistic Additions

To be considered artistic, the ornamentation must add to the form picture, not detract from it. In other words, if the form stands out too much, it may reduce the positive meaning. Usually, positive ornamentation includes some type of flourish and original or unique letter forms.

Ornaments that are superfluous and overly complex become mere gaudy junk that serves no useful purpose. Always keep in mind that legibility is the first consideration. Below, Julie Andrews' simplified writing has some elaborations that draw the eye, but are not unattractive.

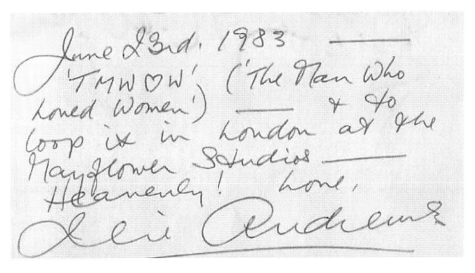

Artistic printed writing: singer, actress Julie Andrews

Distinctive Details

Writing that is full and round without being overly elaborated suggests full-ness of emotion and imagination. In a harmonious writing where the forms are balanced in a well-organized space, the interpretation could be an ex-uberant spirit with a zest for life.

Elaboration in disorganized, inharmonious writing, on the other hand, could signify one who overexaggerates or overestimates himself. Both types of writers have an abundance of ideas, but express them differently.

Elaborated writing of William Peter Blatty, author of The

Think of it as the difference between having a gift wrapped by a professional or by someone who is all thumbs. Either way, the gift is wrapped, but which would you rather give?

There's difference between enriching writing and over-embellishing it is an aesthetic one. Adornments in good taste that are not overdone, produces a more positive analysis than one where the handwriting is bedecked with a myriad of curlicues, inflated loops, and extra strokes. Both types of writers are attempting to beautify their scripts, but for different reasons. The enriched writer wants to enhance his writing and improve it. The embel-lished writer wants to impress others for his own self-aggrandizement.

The overly-embellished writer is apt to be ostentatious in presentation, drawing attention to himself. His

Fine Points

Writers of highly embel-lished handwriting devote hours to details that make their environment look im-pressive without leaving time to handle the mundane obligations that pay the bills.

need to be in the limelight is an overcompensation for a poor self-image. Believing that the only way to get the recognition he so desperately craves is to demand it, the over-ornamentation trivializes his efforts, and the attention he gets is likely to be of the negative variety.

The more extravagant the flourishes and ornaments, the more inflated the capital letters, the less the writer is in touch with reality. He may be conceited and narcissistic, boasting of his supposed accomplishments, which probably exist only in his mind. Such people are often social climbers who are impressed with other people's money.

In the case of the sample below, the elaborations draw the eye, so that the viewer is distracted from what is really going on.

Tales from the Script

Felix Klein suggested looking behind the elaborations and exaggerations to see what else there is in the writing. This is where the true self is hiding.

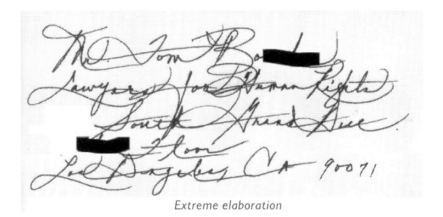

Extreme elaboration

The Icing on the Cake

We all use different faces or masks in different situations. Carl Jung called these masks our persona. We wear them to cover up the less desirable parts of ourselves (Jung's shadow side) to prevent others from seeing them. The mask changes according to circumstances. We probably don't wear the same face when dealing with the boss as the one we wear in bed with our lover (at least, one would hope not!). The mask we wear when a policeman pulls us over in traffic is probably not the one we wear at a party, and so on.

Def·i·ni·tion

> **Persona:** the outer self that masks the shadow side of personality. An
> overly strong persona is seen in carefully constructed handwriting
> called persona writing.

Some people are more concerned than others about controlling their
shadow side, and consequently develop a stronger persona (mask) to keep
it under wraps. One who is deeply afraid of his shadow peeking out and
giving him away develops a strong persona, which takes a lot of self-control.

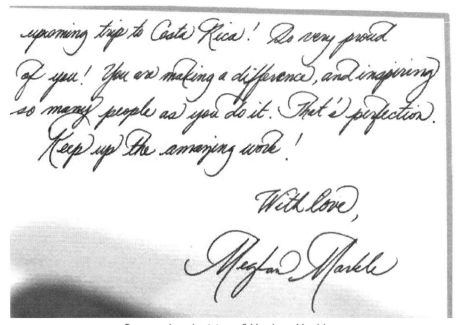

Persona handwriting of Meghan Markle

To maintain strong self-control all the time take energy, and is developed
at the expense of spontaneity. It shows up as a pictorial-style handwriting,
such as Meghan Markle's (now HRH The Duchess of Sussex) handwriting
seen here. She writes in calligraphy, so the writing looks more as if it were
drawn, rather than written naturally and spontaneously. It is more of a
work of art than communication.

Although the writing is elaborate and ornamented, it lacks spontaneity.
The Duchess' right-slant indicates that she is people-oriented, but the formality of the arcade forms (we'll cover these in the next chapter) suggests
that the formality covers up shyness (her acting career notwithstanding).

She has great charm, but the leftward arcades in the upper zone are self-protective.

"Persona writers" are often performers, artists, or orators who are careful to separate their private selves from the one they show to others. Generally polite and formal, sophisticated and charming, they give onlookers the sense that the smile is painted on (like a mask) and unchangeable, regardless of what is happening inside.

The important question to consider is: What is the purpose of the mask? Is it an attempt to deliberately disguise and obfuscate, or is it adopted out of a need to appear more beautiful, more sophisticated, more charming than the writer feels?

Persona handwriting can be somewhat more difficult to analyze than natural handwriting, but the careful analyst will be able to peek behind the mask and see what is lurking there.

The person who maintains individuality is courageous, independent, and driven to break away from the norm stands out from the rest. She insists on "doing it her way" and feel less of a need to adapt to the world than the copybook or persona writer does.

Last Words

Copybook style is the point of departure in analyzing handwriting. Communication is the most important thing. Whatever style the writer adopts, the handwriting needs to be legible and clear or there is no point in writing. Simplification means shaving off at least some of the unnecessary elements. Remember, though: *too much* simplification breaks down the ability to communicate clearly. Overelaboration is a sign of perfectionism called persona writing.

Chapter 13

Connective Forms

Are you flexible and quick to adjust to new environments, situations and people? Or do you insist on stubbornly sticking with the way you habitually do things and expect others to defer to your routines?

The answer can be found in your basic temperament, which is most clearly seen in the shapes of letters and the connections between them. These provide the next piece of the personality puzzle—how we relate to others— and are called connective forms. In this chapter we'll see how the connections between letters reflect the writer social relationships.

The Fab Four (Connective Forms)

There are four major forms: two rounded (arcade and garland), one angular, and one thready (indefinite), which is a combination of the two rounded ones.

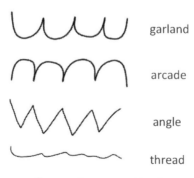

garland

arcade

angle

thread

Four major connective forms

The easiest way to determine the form is to check the tops of the lowercase letters m and n. The **arcade** has a rounded top and is open at the bottom. The **garland** is the opposite: open at the top, rounded at the bottom. **Angles** are closed at both the top and the bottom. **Thread** is flattened, open on all sides.

Fine Points

If m's and n's look more like a w or u, the primary form is garland.

The school model teaches a combination of the garland, arcade, and angle forms, and most adults adopt one of these three types as a primary way of forming letters and linking them together. To the school model, we add thread, which is a flattened combination of the garland and arcade.

A writer who uses a mixture of all the connective forms suggests an innate ability to relate to many different types of people on their own level. One who adopts a single type of connective form is a one-dimensional personality whose behavior is regimented and premeditated, lacking the capacity to act spontaneously.

Swiss graphologist Max Pulver describes the connective form as defining the way the writer adapts, both to his inner and his outer world. For instance, the choice of mostly rounded forms is made by the more passive individual (the more rounded the form, the more passive the person), mostly angular forms are chosen by resistant people (the more angular, the more resistance), and mostly thready forms are adopted by those who refuse to make any choice at all.

Changing the form that is natural to you is extremely difficult. Here's an exercise for you: the following figure shows the four major connective forms. Pick one that is unlike your own writing and copy it for several lines. How did that feel? Probably pretty uncomfortable, since you were imitating a form that reflects something other than the way you naturally function.

Let's All Be Friends: Garlands

Outside of handwriting, a garland is a decorative wreath of flowers worn on the head. It's pretty, draws compliments. A garland in handwriting comes in several varieties. The basic form has firm pressure and a natural, easy flow of left-right movement.

Although both sexes use all the connective forms, the garland is viewed as having more feminine qualities. Rounded on the bottom and open at the top, it is formed like a cup or bowl, ready to receive whatever you are prepared to give.

As the writing movement goes from me (left) to you (right), you'll recognize the basic garland as a spontaneous movement outward, opening itself up, extending toward others like an outstretched hand. Sociability, warmth and a willingness to please are implied in this movement.

Being open from the top, the garland writer is influenced by outside forces. Trusting and open, she reaches out to others with a smile and expects them to smile back. When they don't, it hurts her feelings.

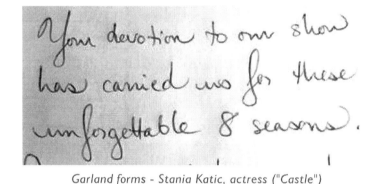

Garland forms - Stania Katic, actress ("Castle")

The garland writer can be sentimental, frequently tying her basic needs to home and hearth. When the garlands are combined with arcades, they become circles. This writer won't argue or fight about anything else, but when it comes to defending her home and family, she can be a tiger.

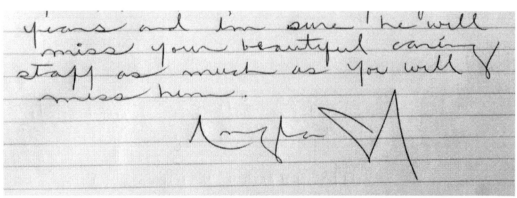

Flat garlands with arcades - actress Angelina Jolie

Def·i·ni·tion

> **Flat garland:** the connecting strokes hug the baseline. In the shallow
> garland, the connecting strokes droop. Strokes of the weak garland
> are made without pressure.

Garland forms: thriller writer Elmore Leonard has surprising garlands in his text, but an angular signature, which tells us that what he presents to the world is tougher than he feels inside.

Garlands: Elmore Leonard, author

Wilting Garlands

When the garland form lacks firm pressure and rightward trend, the positive interpretation is lost. Instead of being merely receptive, flat, shallow or weak garlands are a sign of extreme susceptibility and dependency.

> The shallow or weak garland implies weakness of character. In
> some cases, it might be plain old laziness.

Made by those who talk much but say little, the writer is easily influenced and goes overboard in self-indulgence. Lacking the energy to resist outside pressure, he allows others to propel him in a direction he might not be eager to go.

Gullible and naive, the wilting garland writer is ready to believe anything he hears, so if he happens to fall in with the wrong crowd is likely to find himself in hot water, right along with them.

Fake It Til You Make It—Sham Garlands

Another negatively interpreted garland form, the sham garland (sometimes called "clothesline garland") is made without the free flow of movement of the genuine garland. The letter connections are rounded on the bottom but the movement is restricted, slow, and careful. Upstrokes are partially concealed by downstrokes, which implies a need to hide something. Connecting strokes generally occur at or near the baseline, so whatever is being concealed is taking place in the middle zone, the zone of relationships, emotions, and day-to-day life.

Fine Points

The shallow garland writer goes with the flow to avoid having to fight for what she wants.

The sham garland writer wants to appear affable and adaptable, but something has him worried and afraid to act naturally. Consequently, he covers his fear with a veneer of congeniality. The friendliness of the normal garland has become a mask.

Musician Lionel Hampton's garlands are balanced with other

Occasionally you will come across looped garlands. Since the loop is made by a slight turn to the left, it is regressive or a counterstroke. In other words, it's going the wrong direction.

> Klara Roman says the looped garland is a case of balancing tension and release by momentarily going inward. Trait-oriented graphologists call it the "worry stroke," and say it is made by those who carry the woes of the world on their shoulders.

Garlands: Rochelle Krich, author

Above, Rochelle Krich, author of the Molly Blume mystery series, makes a perfect garland form in the "n" of enjoy.

Cover Me, I'm Going In: Arcades

The second type of rounded major connective form is the arcade, named for its archlike shape.

Fine Points

The arcade writer is an emotional person who doesn't like to show it. Emotional responses are kept under the arches.

The arch is a superstrong structure that may be used as a bridge to travel over; an aqueduct to carry life-sustaining water under; or a means of protection under which to hide from a variety of hazardous conditions. It becomes an impenetrable bulwark against the outside world.

No matter the pressure, and the stress of being under the microscope - she's humble, loving, and sincere.
She builds and nurtures her family, while also looking out for so many millions in so many ways

Arcade forms - singer, Beyonce

Consider the Marble Arch in London, or the Arc d' Triomphe in Paris, the India Gate in Delhi, or the Gateway Arch in St. Louis. Some of this very impressive architecture has stood for eons and weathered all sorts of assaults, including WWI and WWII.

In the sample above, note the careful writing and rounded tops on the h and n, which indicate a certain formality and self-protectiveness. While the arcade writer may be very friendly and appear outgoing, it will take some time before she allows you to get close.

Imagine that...

In classical graphological literature, the arcade is listed as a major sign of dishonesty. While that may be true in some slow handwriting samples, it isn't the case in faster ones. Speed is the modifying factor.

The arcade form turns the bowl of the garland upside down, making it rounded on the top instead of the bottom. While the garland is open to influences from the outside, the arcade closes off at the baseline, making it inaccessible from any direction except within.

If you were to place an apple on the kitchen counter and cover it with a bowl, how accessible would the apple be? That's the effect of the fast arcade form in handwriting—the sense of impenetrability.

The inner need of the arcade writer to be strong and conceal his emotions sometimes gives others the impression that he is cold or unfeeling, but nothing could be further from the truth. With rounded forms, he is just as emotional as the garland writer. However, he would never want to be forced into having to explain or expose his inner feelings.

> An arcade in fast writing is interpreted differently from an arcade in slow writing—they even look different.

Fast Arcades

The fast arcade begins with a releasing movement pushing toward the upper zone, which shows the writer's interest in achieving great things. Driven toward success and accomplishment, he is driven to ever-greater heights.

The arcade ends with a downstroke that returns toward the self and the lower zone. Especially when the pressure is displaced onto the upstroke, the energy is sublimated from other areas and the writer drives himself, not allowing obstacles to deter him. Because the arcade is closed at the top, the writer is able to shut out distractions and single-mindedly pursue his objectives until he has achieved his goal.

The negative side of the fast arcade writer's one-track mind is that others may see him as pushy and overbearing.

When the arch is tall and comes at the beginning of a word, the writer has a strong desire to make an impact, to be seen as impressive and imposing without having to say a word.

Fine Points

The fast arcade writer is interested in the past. Open at the bottom, toward the past and the subconscious, he wants to know where he came from.

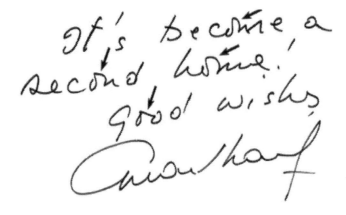

Arcade forms: actor Omar Sharif (Dr. Zhivago) made perfect fast arcades

Fast arcades are seen in the handwritings of highly creative people. Those who work in the arts, as well as architects ("arch"-i-tects—get it?!) tend to use the arcade form because the structural appearance appeals to them. Similarly, structure and form are important to the fast arcade writer. In fact, he may be quite attracted to architecture on one level or another.

Especially when combined with a long lower zone, digging for his roots and genealogy attract this writer. As something of a traditionalist, he would like to maintain life the way it was. It takes some time and effort on his part to accept "progress."

> The arcade writer has a more formal approach than the garland writer, so is less spontaneous. Some fast arcade writers are reserved or shy, others are snobbish and class conscious. Look at the whole picture to determine which is true.

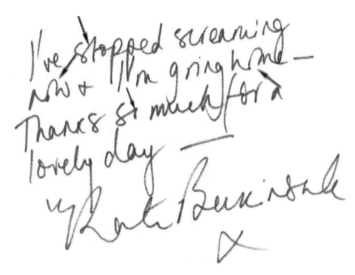

Actress Kate Beckinsale combines fast arcades with garlands

Slow Arcades

In a handwriting made up of slow arcades, the statuesque arch is now more
like a baseball cap, pulled down low over
the forehead to conceal the wearer's
identity. Or a turtle who has retreated
inside his shell. The maker of the slow
arcade is self-oriented and defensive.

Fine Points

Narrow arcades signify
secretiveness and inhi-
bition, the wolf in
sheep's clothing, a
hypocrite.

Not waiting to be attacked, he barricades himself behind the walls of the
arch, just in case. The slow arcade is a controlled form, unlike the free and
easy movement of the garland or the grace of the *fast* arcade.

An arcade at the end of a word is a deliberate, inhibiting movement. The
writer withdraws the outgoing gesture and returns it to himself. This may
indicate defensiveness, embarrassment, or insincerity.

The sample below, written by Lyle Menedez, who along with his brother
Eric was convicted of killing their parents, are an example of the slow, cov-
ering-up arcade as noted by the arrows.

Tales from the Script

When the last stroke of a word returns leftward in an arcade, it is a sign of deliberate secretiveness and withholding of information. Pulver, who was big into symbolism, likened the final arcade to the writer biting his lip to keep from saying something that he doesn't want you to know. The return to self also suggests selfishly keeping things to himself for his own ends.

Convicted murderer Lyle Menendez: slow arcade forms

No More Mr. Nice Guy: Angles

Okay, I've got my boxing gloves on. Now we can move on to discuss the angular writer. Why the gloves? Because the angular writer is always looking for a fight or argument. Friction is part of his daily diet. The garland writer seeks peace and harmony; the arcade writer wants to be left to his own devices. When things are going too smoothly for the angle writer it unsettles him and he feels the urge to make waves.

To form an angle, the hand is required to make an abrupt stop and change direction. There is little room for flexibility in the writing movement or in the angle writer's nature. He is not interested in adapting to the needs or desires of others, but expects, even insists, that they should accommodate him. He sees every situation as an opportunity to exert his will.

The angle writer doesn't sit around, waiting for something to happen. He makes decisions and acts, especially when acting provokes a power struggle. With the addition of heavy pressure, the writer may treat people with a ruthless heavy hand.

The handwriting of Heinrich Himmler, filled with angry angles, is an extreme case in point. Architect of the Nazi concentration camps, Himmler led the brutal Nazi SS in World War II.

Angular forms: Heinrich Himmler

Fine Points

Some German copybooks at the time of WWII teach angular writing. But not *this* angular!

Assuming no major negatives like we see above, one of the angular writer's affirmative characteristics is that when he uses his power for good, he can be extremely effective. When he needs to stand firm, there is no shaking him. He will never give up, no matter how high the odds are stacked against him. Some call it stubbornness, but he sees it as persistence.

Your Guardian "Angle" Is Watching

When the angle is slightly rounded rather than making a completely sharp point, it's called a soft angle. The softness mitigates some of the more difficult aspects of the angular form and allows the angular writer some moderation. His obstinacy becomes a gentler persistence, and inflexibility becomes just plain firmness.

Having developed some tolerance and adaptability, the soft-angle writer is easier to get along with than the sharp-angle writer. He still has strong opinions but are not be expressed so directly and severely. The better nature of the angle is allowed to shine through.

Def·i·ni·tion
Shark's tooth: what should be an angle is made with a curve (easy to see on final stroke of m, n, h); signifies a cunning, shrewd personality.

Biting with the Shark's Tooth

So-named because it looks like one, the shark's tooth form is an angle with a curve in it, which you can see in the following illustration. The stroke bends inward, as if being pushed from the left side. That makes it a counterstroke (going in the opposite direction to the way it should go).

The shark's tooth is a smooth-looking stroke that hides cunning, crafty behavior under a courteous exterior. The writer smiles at you while calmly stabbing you in the back. If this form is seen only once or twice in an otherwise positive script, the inference is that the writer can be pretty nasty when pushed, but that the trait pops out only under duress.

Don't Pin Me Down: Thread

You will not find the thread form in any copybook. It combines the arcade and garland but breaks them down, making it hard to identify which is which. The result is a flat, wavy form that is at once ambiguous, indefinite, and equivocal.

Like the arcade, the thread form is often treated negatively in graphology texts. It is assumed that all thread forms should be treated equal. Not so!

There are two distinct types of thready formations—primary and secondary.

It is impossible to make thread forms slowly. The mind that makes it thinks fast. In **primary** thread, legibility remains unimpaired and the form helps the writing movement progress to the right because it accelerates the speed.

Fine Points

The thread writer is avoidant, evasive, twisting away from unpleasantness like a slippery eel even faster than the garland writer (who also avoids conflict).

Secondary thread is illegible because the writing thins out, in many instances, to a mere wavy line.

Primary Thread

Primary thread is made with light-moderate (never strong) pressure and is often seen at the ends of words where the last letter breaks down and to some extent thins out. Some letters (most notably the m's and n's) lose their definition and become slightly wavy-looking. Overall though, the letters retain their basic shape.

Primary thread: Chris Darden, OJ Simpson prosecutor and author

The primary thread writer thinks and acts fast. Plumbing the depths is of little interest. He prefers to skim the surface. At his best when handling complex matters, he tends to get impatient when someone tries to feed him too many details.

> The thready writer is the King of Adaptability. He's the chameleon who, wherever he is, has the ability to take on the shape of his environment and blend in. The thready form is able to penetrate the defenses of others and get under their facade. When this talent is not used for good the writer can become manipulative and exploitative, as is the case with secondary thread.

The thready writer lives by his instincts and goes with his gut reactions. Jumping to conclusions without the benefit of logic, his basic assumption may be correct but due to a lack of supporting information, the final judgment can be flawed.

Thread forms suggest tact and diplomacy. A master equivocator, the writer hopes to avoid having to take a stand and promote a particular viewpoint.

avoid friction at all cost, he is unlikely to expend the energy to fight. When forced into a corner with no other way out, though, he comes out swinging.

Secondary Thread

Secondary thread is made without much pressure, resulting in a formless scrawl in the middle of words. It is a sign of inner hysteria, where the writer feels crushed by life's burdens and feels as if he can handle no more.

The secondary thread writer is like a rubber band, stretched so many times it has lost its resilience. His basic motivation is self-preservation. Since he won't fight, he takes flight, always leaving a back door open so he can wriggle out in case of trouble.

President Richard Nixon used secondary thread forms

When the writing is illegible (and assuming no mental or vision problems), there is a total lack of concern for others. If this writer doesn't even care whether the recipient can read his message, what does that say about his level of compassion and fellow-feeling? His only concern is to stay afloat.

Secondary thread is the connective form of choice by the con artist, the person who refuses to make a commitment of any kind, and one who feels unable to take a stand.

The truth is, it's a waste of time for these people to make a choice, because once they do, they are just as likely to abandon it for something more attractive five minutes later. Their favorite road is the path of least resistance.

Felix Klein's list of personality characteristics for the secondary thread writer include poor self-esteem, avoidance of reality, opportunistic, poor discrimination, lack of restraint, sly.

The Double Bow

The double bow is the rarest of all the forms. Like the thread, it combines the arcade and the garland, but it retains more of their shape. There is greater emphasis in the double bow on the up/down movement than left-right.

The writer can't seem to find his niche. He wants to appear conventional and sincere, but doesn't want to have to make a choice. He is always working at maintaining equilibrium, hopping from one foot to the other, changing sides as need be. Having no opinion of his own, he won't give you his point of view because it depends on who he is with at the moment. Upon finding himself in a position where he could be taken to task for his actions, he simply slides over to the other side. His main objective is to avoid the complications and responsibility that comes with having an opinion.

Combining Forms

Some combinations of forms are particularly desirable, such as the garland/angle combination. The softness of the garland derives strength and support from the angle, so the writer is not a complete pushover, driven by his emotions. The angle is made softer by the garland, showing a greater willingness to adapt.

Combination of forms with high angles: Margaret Mitchell, author

Some garlands in arcade writing temper the arcade writer's reserve and allow for greater spontaneity. Likewise, some fast arcades in a generally garland writing bring a little more reserve and caution to the more gullible garland writer.

See the handwriting of Margaret Mitchell, author of *Gone with the Wind*, on the previous page. She used a combination of forms with many angles.

The most negative combination is angle/thread, a primary sign of the exploiter who capitalizes on the weaknesses of others. He is sneaky and undependable. Don't trust him with your kitchen trash!

Last Words

The shape of connections between letters and within letters reveal the writer's style of relating to other people. Rounded forms are made by more passive, accepting types. Angular forms are made by active, self-assertive types. Thready forms are made by avoidant types. A combination of the four major forms is used by the healthiest personality types. The least desirable combination is the thread and angle.

Chapter 14

Reach Out and Touch Someone: Connections

Can you imagine a conversation where there were no pauses between the words?

Itwouldbereallyfrustratingtryingtofigureoutwhatthemessageis.

See what I mean? Pauses in conversation give both the speaker and the listener a chance to catch their breath and contemplate for a moment what was just said. Without pauses, information floods in, obscuring the meaning of the message. Pauses that are too long are no better. They impair continuity, so that ideas are chopped into discrete bits of information without any means of linking them together:

h o w   c a n   y o u   r e m e m b e r t h e   l a   s t   t h o u g h t   w h e n s o   m u c h   t i m e   h a s   e l a p s e d ?

Impulse Patterns

Handwriting consists of a series of impulses echoed on paper. The spaces

Fine Points

Collect samples from people with varying speaking styles and chart the impulse patterns of slow, smooth speakers compared to rapid, uneven speakers.

between them are like pauses in conversation. Some pauses are short, some are long; some are smooth, some are choppy.

The smallest writing impulse is found in a single stroke, which proceeds to the next impulse, the letter, then the word, and finally, the sentence impulse. A writing impulse begins when the pen starts moving on the paper and ends when it is lifted.

Writing impulses mimic speech. Some people speak rapidly, rushing to get their thoughts out, while others are more deliberate and careful in delivering their message. One who speaks with many starts and stops creates a considerably different impulse pattern on paper than another who speaks smoothly and expresses herself well.

Tales from the Script

Klara Roman discovered that poor writing impulses had a relationship to problems in speech. Those who spoke fluently and articulately wrote with smooth, continuous writing impulses. The handwritings of those who stuttered or stammered or had other difficulties in communicating also matched the way they spoke.

Using handwriting movement as therapy, Dr. Roman helped many speech-impaired people improve their ability to speak. As a result of her research, clinics in Europe began using handwriting analysis to help diagnose and treat speech-impaired patients.

Unquestionably, different impulse patterns reflect behavioral styles unique to each individual. These patterns tell us about the writer's ability to function in the world, intellectually/spiritually, socially, emotionally, and physically. The degree and type of linkage from one letter to the next is symbolic of how well the writer…

- Connects thoughts.
- Functions in social relationships.
- Coordinates activities.

I Might Be Psychic: Airstrokes

Handwriting exists in several dimensions. One of those dimensions is "above" the paper. Yes, writing actually starts in the air. Like an airplane on final approach to the runway, the hand hovers briefly above the paper as the writer decides where to bring the pen in for a landing. In between writing impulses, too, the pen rises off the paper momentarily before moving into the next writing impulse.

Ideally, while the pen is raised, the hand keeps moving in the same direction through the air as it was on the writing surface below. When the pen touches down again, the flow of ink resumes as if there had been no inter-ruption.

Def·i·ni·tion
Airstroke: the movement of the hand in the air, which continues in the same direction as the writing on the paper.

Smooth airstrokes are created when the writing picks up in the same di-rection when it lands on the page. When the writing movement stops ab-ruptly or makes infinitesimal changes of direction, it creates a pattern of abrupt strokes. The hesitant writer who is unsure of his next move stops suddenly to reconsider or adjust his path.

Imagine that...

Abrupt stops and starts are often seen in forgeries where the forger has to stop every few strokes to think about the signature he is simulating

The confident writer creates a continuous, smooth airstroke that advances in the same direction along the graphic path. Use a stylus (or work on a photocopy) to trace the movement along the graphic path from the end of one writing impulse to the next. If you can't trace the movement in a smooth line from one stroke to the next, the airstrokes are abrupt.

Def·i·ni·tion
Graphic path: the trail of ink made by the writing movement as it proceeds from left to right.

You'll need your magnifying glass to examine the starting and ending strokes to determine whether an airstroke is smooth or abrupt. Under mag-nification, the point at which the movement tapers off as the pen was raised will show a lightening in the trail of ink. Stopping to change direction cre-ates an abrupt airstroke where the ink does not taper off.

Disruption of the writing movement affects the rhythm. Frequent stopping and starting is like walking along a dark street at night, breaking stride every few yards to look back and see if anyone is following. It suggests a lack of self-assuredness, unlike someone who has a strong command pres-ence and moves forward with a sense of purpose and self-confidence.

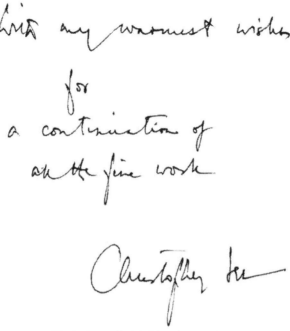

Airstrokes: Christopher Lee, actor

Smooth (above) and abrupt (below) airstrokes.

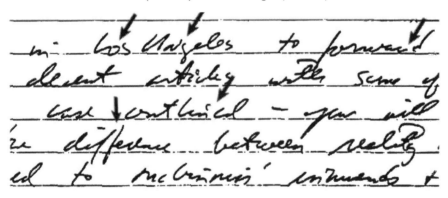

Green Beret Dr. Jeffrey MacDonald, convicted of murdering his family

A handwriting with smooth airstrokes is produced by a mind that makes leaps of logic faster than a speeding bullet and grasps whole concepts at a single bound. The writer spends a lot of time "in the air," which, in graphology, symbolizes the mind. He seeks efficient solutions to problems, avoiding the friction caused by contact with the paper.

Ties That Bind: Connectedness

Connectedness refers to the degree to which a group of writing impulses join together to form words. The correct term for the connecting strokes is ligature. (Yes, that's the same word referred to in crime stories where the victim was tied up or strangled.) The friendlier meaning in handwriting is to unite two or more letters into a single unit.

Def·i·ni·tion

Ligature: something that ties or binds.

A handwriting is considered connected if shorter words—about six or eight letters long—are joined together. If there are breaks, they should be after syllables or in other expected places, such as breaks to dot the i's or cross the t's. When the connections are broken in unexpected places, or the connections in a short word are mostly or all broken, the writing is considered disconnected. This refers to cursive writing. Printed writing is a different style with some (but not all) different rules.

Connections between letters are made by joining upstrokes and downstrokes. Downstrokes are the spine or backbone of writing. Without them there is nothing to support the body. Legibility may be impaired somewhat, but you can still decipher the message. When the downstrokes are removed and you are left with only upstrokes, it is impossible to read what the writer is trying to get across.

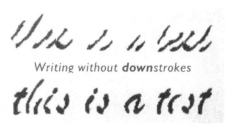

*Writing without **down**strokes*

*writing without **up**strokes*

Connectedness shows how well the writer strings her thoughts together, and how comfortable she is dealing with the outside world and adapting to her present circumstances.

Let's Stay in Touch: Connected Writing

"Connected" doesn't mean that every single element in every single word is linked together. Pausing after syllables or for diacritics doesn't count as breaking the impulse. Where the breaks occur is important. If they come at the beginnings of words it signifies something different than if they are made at the ends. If they occur in the middle zone, it affects a different area of behavior than in the upper or lower zone.

> ### Def·i·ni·tion
> **Diacritics:** also called diacritical marks, are t-crosses and i-dots and other marks added to words to help with pronunciation, such as accents.

Moderately Connected Writing

Moderately connected writing, (except letters after syllables and diacritics), is made by the moderately adaptable person. Provided the airstrokes are smooth, he is able to use either logic or intuition, whichever is appropriate to the situation. His thoughts flow smoothly using deductive thinking, and he strings together series of ideas into whole concepts. He needs to be able to relate the small details to the bigger picture for it to make sense.

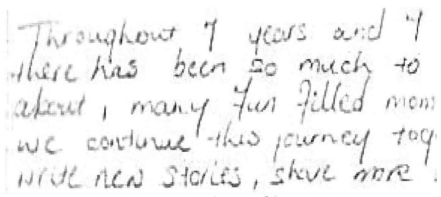

Moderately connected writing: Rihanna, singer

Socially, the moderately connected writer wants to relate to others in some way. The writer is attracted to group activities and (with supporting evidence, such as a well-developed lower zone) welcomes other people into her life. Feeling connected to a circle of friends she can count on makes her feel emotionally supported and comfortable.

Highly Connected

The highly connected writer links most of his letters. He may pause occasionally after capitals but, for the most part, he connects everything else.

Although he has a good memory for facts, he may not be as quick to associate them with the events they represent. For instance, he might remember that November 9 is an important day for some reason, but not that it's my birthday (well, it's important to me!).

He enjoys handling details, putting things where they belong, and dealing with the practical necessities of life. Once he has started a project, don't bother to interrupt; he keeps going until it's finished, the same way she finishes writing a word before taking a break.

Linking letters is a progression from left to right, from me to you. The highly connected writer feels a strong need for involvement with others. Her behavior and attitudes are consistent from one day to the next, and she can be counted on to respond similarly in like situations.

Overconnected

The overconnected writer makes no breaks at all, even after capital letters. If the writing is also narrow or crowded, what was seem as consistency in the moderate to highly-connected writer has burgeoned into obsession. The unrelieved effort reflected in overconnected handwriting is the hallmark of a refusal or inability to let up, even for a moment. The persistent connections at the baseline are made by someone who needs to feel her feet firmly in contact with the ground. This is someone who expends the bulk of his energy taking care of the practical, material aspects of life. Not one to trust his intuition, he feels compelled to gather as much logical data and as many facts as possible before making any kind of change.

Fine Points

The overconnected writer can be overwhelming. The need for contact, if combined with close word spacing, suggests poor social boundaries.

In discussing the overconnected writer, Klara Roman said, "Overconnected configurations are produced by rhetoricians, verbose persons, time wasters, individuals who make much ado about nothing."

The writer discharges an avalanche of thoughts and ideas without giving his listener a chance to assimilate them. Just as he can't seem to relinquish the writing impulse, he goes on and on, whether you want to listen or not. He may give lip service to allowing others to have their say, but doesn't really hear them. He is too focused on his own thoughts.

Overconnected writing: convicted serial killer Robert Long

In extreme cases, the emotional excitation implied in overconnected writing is sometimes a sign of a psychological disturbance. The writer's refusal to give anyone else any space suggests some sort of paranoia. She doesn't trust anyone else, so she feels compelled to control as much of her environment as possible.

I Need My Space: Moderately Disconnected Writing

Writing with many smooth breaks in simplified, original (that is, simpler than copybook) writing is the sign of a quick, facile mind. The writer leaps nimbly from one thought to the next without waiting for all the data. Especially if the connections are smooth, with airstrokes in the upper zone, there is an ability to proliferate a series of ideas and combine them into a workable system.

With a propensity for sailing off the page with many airstrokes, the moderately disconnected writer tends to be more mentally than socially oriented. She is generally more comfortable in the theoretical world than in the company of others. Although she may have plenty of friendships, it isn't quite as easy for her to connect with others as it is for the connected writer.

> *One of my favorite quotes is by Schopenhauer - It reads; "all Truth passes Through Three Stages. First, it is ridiculed.*

Mixed connectedness, abrupt - Steve Hodel, author of Black Dahlia Avenger

If the airstrokes are choppy and abrupt, you know that the writer's emotions are less controlled and more erratic. His behavior is not always consistent, and he may surprise you by suddenly changing attitudes. You may think you're having a very pleasant conversation, when all of a sudden, he abruptly gets up and walks off. He abruptly disconnects his written words in the same manner.

The next sample, written by the late world chess champion Bobby Fischer proceeds in abrupt stops and starts. Known as a troubled genius, he won a $5 million rematch against his Russian nemesis, Boris Spassky, but he had a reputation for not always being rational.

> *Dear Mr. Vattuone this is to inform You that as of today March 26, 2005 You are hereby dismissed as my attorney. You may no longe...*

Disconnected: chess master Bobby Fischer

Gimme A Break: Extreme Disconnectedness

Extreme disconnectedness is different from printed writing. Here, we're talking about cursive writing that has been chopped into small writing impulses. You will not find smooth airstrokes in totally disconnected writing. The nervous activity and constant restless movement in many directions are the order of the day for the extremely disconnected writer.

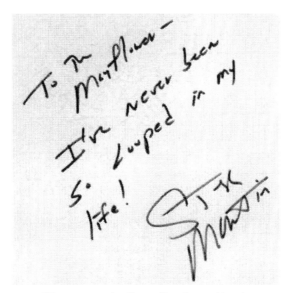

Disconnected - Comedian Steve Martin

Often highly creative, the challenge for this writer is consistently putting that creativity to work productively. The ideas gush out, spattering in all directions like paint from an aerosol can. Some of them may be pure genius, but others are just flights of fancy. Being able to clearly define which is which can be a challenge.

Moody and inconsistent, you never know how the writer will react from one minute to the next. Establishing close relationships is difficult for this individual. The breaks between letters suggest a breaking of the bonds between self and the outside world. It's easier to stand alone than to bother cooperating with others.

I Want to Break It Off

Do you know someone who has trouble making and keeping commitments? Chances are, the last letter of some words will be separated from the rest (especially when the last letter is "g").

The writer rushes headlong into a new relationship or makes a major decision, but as the time draws closer to put his money where his mouth is, he gets cold feet and pulls back. After getting some space, he reconsiders and may move forward and fulfill the commitment. First, though he is likely to do this push-pull cha-cha several times.

Fine Points

When the disconnected final letter is g, the writer has trouble making *emotional* commitments in intimate relationships. Such a writer might marry but continues emotionally withholding.

Some handwritings are generally connected, but the writing impulse breaks consistently in one particular spot, perhaps always after the first letter, or always after the last letter. What does that mean?

Let's say you start to write a word, but after the first letter you pause and reevaluate. Is that what I really wanted to say? Yes, it is. Then, having broken the connection, you go on to finish the word. Art is imitating life. When the writer pauses after the first letter of a word, it mirrors a tendency to reconsider after having made a decision. The writer feels he needs to step back and take a deep breath, or to wind himself up before carrying on.

Disconnected final and initial letters: President George W. Bush

This tendency is seen above in the handwriting of President George W. Bush.

Bring Me My Soldering Iron

Sometimes a writer will realize that breaks have crept in where she didn't intend, or doesn't want them. So, she goes back and tries to connect them after the fact.

Def·i·ni·tion

Soldering: an attempt to fix a break by mending, retouching (going back over the strokes), or soldering.

A soldering iron, such as you'd find in a machine shop, is used to melt and apply solder to two pieces of metal in order to join them together. In effect, that's what happens when the writer wants to connect a "hole" in her writing, only the soldering material in this case is ink.

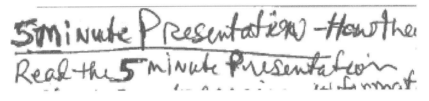

Extreme retouching

In some cases, soldering and overwriting may be an indicator of heroin use or petit mal seizures. Always get more information when you see a feature of this type.

The significance of mending and soldering is that the writer is anxious to make things look better than they really are. She doesn't want to be seen as wrong, so she makes an effort to correct and improve herself. Some writers use this method to hide something they don't want seen, so it may be a form of dishonesty. As usual, it all depends on the whole configuration of the writing. Often, the retouching (in the form of mending or soldering) just makes matters worse, as the following example illustrates.

Viva Variety! Printscript

Some people combine printing and writing. Graphologists call this style printscript. Depending upon whether the overall graphic picture is harmonious or not, the writer may be wonderfully creative, or merely impulsive and erratic.

The best day of my life. Nine hours synching & I LOVED EVERY MINUTE OF IT!

Creative Printscript: actress Emma Thompson

The Fine Print: Printed Writing

There are several types of printed writing, block printing and manuscript printing being among the most common. Block printing is made in all capital letters, while manuscript printing uses upper and lowercase letters. Manuscript printing used to be taught as a lead-in to learning cursive writing.

Using the principles of gestalt graphology, it is almost as easy to analyze printing as cursive writing. As with any graphic movement, printing utilizes space, form, and movement just like any other style of writing.

Some people (notably police officers, architects, and engineers) block print because it's a requirement of their type of work. If they print only at work, but write cursive at home, we would analyze the cursive. However, if they print in social settings too, such as writing personal letters, the printing will reflect the true personality.

Interestingly, many printers, while breaking the connections between their letters, place the letters close enough to touch. This suggests that while there is a conscious desire is to keep a distance, the inner need is for closeness. You can analyze it as connected writing.

With manuscript printing, like cursive, the writer can go into all three zones (upper, middle, lower). Block printing is viewed in the same manner as writing with an emphasis on the middle zone. The writer's energies are concentrated in the day-to-day area of routine and social interaction.

Like other middle-zone writers, the block printer's ego is central to all aspects of his life. He is preoccupied with his own affairs and while he is probably outgoing and friendly, like an onion, you will have to peel back many layers to really get to know him. Not averse to sharing his opinions, he expects you to agree with him. But if you don't, it won't change his mind.

Here are examples of three very different print styles.

THIS REPORT COMPARES ALL CU
MONTH DATA TO A REFERENCE M
YOUR CHOICE (AS LAST MONTH, 1
MONTH LAST YEAR). EXCEPTION
VARIABLE SO THAT ANYTIME EXP1

Block printing of an architect

to sell, date parties
und recruit. Have fun
meeting the challenges

Printscript: mixed cursive/print in a sales person

fight, but my spirits are high,
Considering the circumstances. I've
gotten 2 traffic tickets (really

Upper/lowercase printing – career unknown

The Bare Bones: Skeletal & Disintegrated Writing

Skeletal, fragmented, or disintegrated writing is stripped down to its absolute bare minimum, but still retains legibility. That is, the downstrokes are still present, but not the upstrokes. The writer is ascetic and stingy in attitude and manner. There is no flesh on the bones of her writing—no loops or flourishes to enrich it. Her emotional detachment hints at little or no connection between herself and the world. If she is not just plain eccentric, mental illness (impending or present) is a possibility.

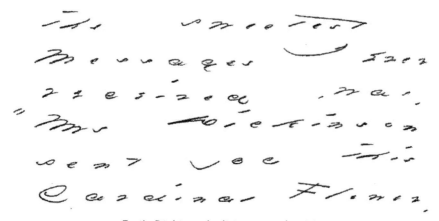

Emily Dickinson's disintegrated writing

Tales from the Script

In her later years, the handwriting of American poet Emily Dickinson disintegrated to near-illegibility. As she became more reclusive, the letter forms became more difficult to read. Emily created her own original forms, but the positive interpretation that normally comes from originality is lost due to their eccentric, even hieroglyphic appearance. Readability is the key.

In cases of severe mental illness or distress where the mind begins to break down, it is manifested on paper. As the mind deteriorates, the writing regresses through the various stages, all the way back to the basic stroke impulse.

At that point, regression to an infantile stage is complete. The next writing, of a Down's syndrome adult, is a stunning example of her ability to organize the page, while being unable to go beyond the basic stroke in communicating with others.

Printed writing of adult with Down Syndrome

I Don't Know How I Know It, but I Do: Intuition

Everyone has it, but not everyone uses it. Some people develop it to an astounding degree, while others prefer to shun it altogether. What is it? Intuition. What can handwriting uncover about this special means of perceiving?

For our purposes, intuition is an instinctive, unconscious process that begins in the lower zone, the area of the unconscious. It is quite unlike the deliberate theorizing, measuring, and computing of a series of ideas in conscious thought. But neither is it stuff just popping into your head out of the blue.

Intuition seems to have some relationship to previous knowledge. When the unconscious (lower zone) recognizes a truth about something within the realm of your experience, the perception quietly germinates, unfettered by logical thought processes.

An insight ready to manifest erupts into the conscious mind above the baseline and blossoms in that "Aha!" sensation. If the perception happens to come mid-word, a smooth break or an airstroke results.

But what if the airstrokes are not smooth; isn't that also intuition? Well, sort of. Abrupt breaks can signify a torrent of ideas popping into consciousness, but more on the order of sudden hunches that are not connected to anything in particular.

Imagine that...

Some psychics have highly connected writing, others highly *disconnected*. Their information comes, not from intuition, but from outside themselves.

Experiment: It is extremely difficult to force a change in the degree of connectedness in an individual's handwriting. Try to print for an extended period if you normally write cursive; or try writing cursive if you only print. It feels yucky (that's the technical term). Once a writer has reached graphic maturity, the tendency to connect or disconnect comes naturally.

Last Words

The disconnections (airstrokes) between letters are just as important as the connections. Connected writing shows an ability to connect thoughts. Overconnected writing is a sign of argumentativeness. Disconnected writing shows a break in the flow of thought. Printed writing is not the same as disconnected cursive writing.

Chapter 15

In the Mood: Slant

When you are really interested in what someone is saying, you probably bend forward toward them so you can hear better and pay closer attention. If the message is one you don't like or approve of, you may lean backwards as a show of resistance. With a so-so attitude your posture might be upright—you feel neutral about the topic. As you will see in this chapter, slant is a lot like body language.

As you already know, in handwriting symbolism, the left represents the self (the personal "me"), and the right represents other people (the global "you"). The degree to which handwriting slants to the right or left reveals whether and how much the writer wants to be involved with "you," the world at large.

> A feature that changes with mood, slant is one of the more superficial aspects of handwriting analysis.

Slant records the writer's emotional reactions and receptivity to outside influences, the moment-to-moment flow of feelings and responses. Thus, it as can be used to measure reaction and response to internal and external stimuli: is it quick and spontaneous or controlled and measured?

Culturally Speaking

Nationality and culture exert some influence on slant. United Kingdom school models teach an upright writing position. Historically, the British have a reputation for generally cooler responses to emotional events, which is one characteristic of the neutral slant. The key word is "generally." Of course, "your experience may vary."

In the United States, the learned slant is moderately rightward, but there is a far wider range of variation in the handwritings of Americans than other cultures, which, in itself, is an indicator of independence, a well-known American trait.

At some periods in history, writing had a far greater right slant than now; at other times, it was more upright. In his book, *The Psychology of Handwriting* (George Allen & Unwin, 1926; reprinted, Books for Professionals, 1978), Saudek describes some of the changes in handwriting slant in various European countries over time. That is one more reason why knowledge of the school model is important if you are analyzing writing done by someone who learned to write in another country. How much they deviate from their school model is as significant as if school-model style is retained.

Tales From the Script

Graphology pioneer Alfred Mendel wrote that slant indicates the writer's position between the mother (left) and father (right), or, according to Klara Roman, between male and female leadership. The more left-slanted, the more inclined the writer is toward females. The greater the right slant, the more the writer is influenced by males.

Gauging Slant

There are two types of slants in handwriting, and both are found in all three zones: **Upslant**, made by a stroke moving upward, away from the self, and **downslant**, made by strokes moving downward, back toward the self. Upslant demonstrates surface reaction but not the deeper emotional expression found in some other areas of handwriting, such as rhythm and pressure. Downslant shows how well the writer controls the immediate gut reactions.

You don't need an expensive caliper to take the slant measurement; a plastic protractor will do. The flat side of the protractor should line up with the baseline of the writing you want to measure. Slide the gauge along the upper loops until one of the slanted lines passes directly through the middle of the loop (or close to it), from the apex (top) to where the downstroke

crosses the upstroke at the baseline. This allows you to find the angle between the upslant and the baseline. to see where the slant falls.

In measuring upper zone upslant, we draw a line (on a copy, not the origi-

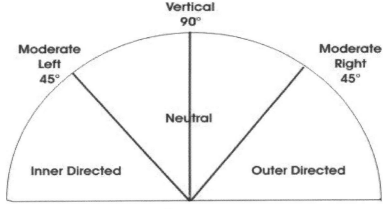

Slant gauge

nal sample) from where the upstrokes and the downstrokes of an upper
loop cross at the baseline, to the top of the loop. The angle is now determined between the line we've drawn and the baseline.

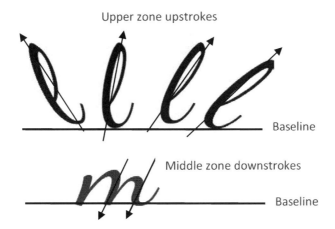

Measuring upslant (above) and downslant (below)

The letter l is used here for clarity, but b and h are also used in measuring
upslant.

To measure the downslant in the middle zone, find the slanted line that most closely approximates the final downstroke on the m's, n's, and h's. This allows you to find the angle between the downstroke and the baseline.

A 90° angle is vertical, or upright. Slants between 90° and 45° in either direction are

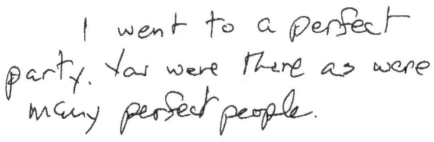

Variable slant - film critic Roger Ebert

moderate. Any slant leaning further than 45° to the baseline is extreme. Writers who can't make up their minds adopt a variable slant.

Feeling It in the Heart: The Right Slants

If your spouse brought home a new friend to meet you and you wanted that person to feel welcome, what would you do? You might reach out, maybe even with both hands, to grasp her hands in a warm clasp and tell her how glad you are to meet her. The act of reaching forward and extending yourself is reflected in right-slanted handwriting.

Moderate Right Slant

The writer with a moderate right slant is sociable and affectionate. A stronger right slant, however, suggests someone who might impulsively throw herself on you and give you a big hug and kiss. She is expressive and enthusiastic, a bit sentimental, finds it easy to love others and show it.

Def·i·ni·tion

Upslant: a moderate right slant is where the upslant in the upper zone measures between 120° and 130°, and in the middle zone, between 110° and 130°. These numbers are approximate, not absolute.

Right-slant indicates some degree of subjectivity. The writer doesn't care so much about logic and reason, he just knows how he feels. A moderate slant shows some restraint and doesn't get totally carried away with his feelings. He may share his opinions and viewpoints, not afraid to allow someone else to influence him. Emotions are involved, though, so the writer's decisions may be colored by his feelings about the subject matter.

> The *consistency* of writing slant shows the degree of stability in emotional equilibrium.

Actress Juliette Binoche has a warm and friendly handwriting with a slight

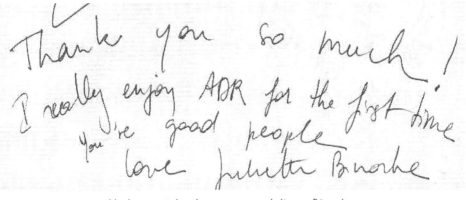

Moderate right slant - actress Juliette Binoche

right slant (we won't talk about her convex baseline!). Her adaptability and flexibility are strong, but interesting to note the long, extended final strokes on a couple of words. This is something to revisit in a later chapter.

The kind of warmth and sincerity found in a moderate right slant are desirable characteristics. As the slant moves further to the right, the emotional controls begin to weaken.

Strong-Extreme Right Slant

The stronger the slant, the more subjective the writer. When the slant becomes extreme, he is responding on a purely gut level, seeing things only from his own point of view. His attitude says "How will this affect me?" He is too impatient to put the brakes on and examine the facts before acting, so it doesn't take long to reach a decision. He is more reactive than responsive, consequences be damned.

The very strong right-slanted writer is quick to jump to conclusions and overreact. He makes assumptions and proceeds accordingly. There are times when his rash, reckless responses might put others at risk, but when things go wrong, it never occurs to him that he might be responsible. Taking time to check things out before hurtling into headlong into a situation could save everyone affected a lot of grief.

Strong right slant: Vice President Dick Cheney

With supporting evidence, such as narrow word and line spacing (and in the sample above, a high degree of thread forms), the extreme right-slant reveals a writer who responds at the drop of a hat. Especially when letters and words become progressively more slanted to the right, real emotional problems are a strong possibility. Whatever he experiences is expressed in an instant. Expect him to broadcast his feelings openly and extravagantly. When he is angry, he is explosively angry. When he is loving, he is passionately loving.

Upright, Uptight?

A vertical or upright slant is midway between left and right slant. Self-control and self-discipline are needed to maintain such a neutral posture. Try standing up straight for an hour and see what a strain it can be! If handwriting is like body language, the vertical writer is standing very straight and projecting an austere demeanor.

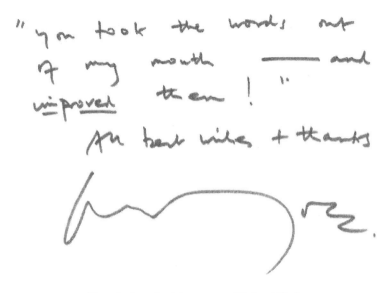

Upright handwriting: actor Michael York

The unsentimental, levelheaded demeanor of the upright "slanter" may make him appear as cool and detached as James Bond, but the apparent lack of emotion is not because he isn't emotional; he would simply prefer to deny that he is. Above all concerned with controlling his behavior, he weighs his words before speaking and thinks before acting. The closer the slant is to upright, the more the writer curbs his initial impulses.

This is what most graphologists refer to as a "head before heart" person. Thus, he won't blindly go where fools rush in; he listens to his inner voice, which speaks the language of logic, not emotion. Being fair is very important to the vertical writer. He takes pains to stay impartial and carefully weigh the facts, balancing all the pros and cons, before reaching a decision and acting on it.

Tales from the Script

Graphologist Marcel Matley says of women who choose a left slant, "she says in her heart, if not out loud, to the father figure who threatens her, 'I'll show you, you bastard, I will become a better man than you are.' So she tends to become the kind of male he is, out-drinks him if he drinks, out-sexes him if he is a sex addict, outperforms him in business if he is a businessman, etc."

You'll Never Know How Much I Really Love You:
The Left Slants

When you have a real aversion to someone and unexpectedly run into her on the street, what do you do? You might turn away, give her the cold shoulder. In effect, that's what left-slanted handwriting does. The left slant is a formal rejection of the world at large; a literal turning away; a slap in the face to anyone who wants to approach the writer with social overtures.

Even a moderate slant to the left shows an oppositional attitude toward the world in general. When the writer needs encouragement and emotional feeding, to whom does he turn? Himself. The writer is leaning away from "you." He feels uncomfortable asking anyone else for anything important. It would be too much of a risk—he might be rejected.

Rejection is something he's felt before and prefers not to repeat the experience. It might not be childhood experiences that prompt the left slant, though in one case, an individual said she switched her slant after her parents divorced; in another, when his wife left him for another man. And another after he discovered his lover had an abortion without discussing it with him. Slanting to the left is a trust deficit manifest on paper.

Def·i·ni·tion
> A moderate left slant is where the upslant in the upper zone measures between 80° and 90°, and the downslant in the middle zone measures between 80° and 90°. These numbers are approximate, not absolute.

The left-slanter is every bit as impressionable and emotional as the right-slanter, but he keeps his responses to himself. Like the right-slanter, the greater the degree of left slant, the more emotional, this person is likely to be. The difference is, he is that much more self-contained. In fact, if you mentally flip the angle of left slant to the same angle of right slant, the emotions indicated are doubly strong, yet doubly inhibited.

Such a writer may appear friendly and outgoing, yet, even after a long acquaintance, if you think about it, you will realize you know very little beyond what you see on the surface. You are left to guess at what the left-slanter is thinking and feeling.

They are almost always pleasant to work with and make an effort to do a good job. When things start going wrong, however, they take refuge in an "everyone for themselves" attitude. They'll watch their own backs before covering for someone else.

Teenagers who are feeling rebellious about knuckling under to their parents' and teachers' influence often use left-slanted writing. Since the right symbolizes authority, one who deliberately turns to the left is defying authority and convention. Think of it as "thumbing their nose" at the rest of the world, saying, "I'll do what I want, regardless of how you feel about it."

Imagine That...

Left slant is never taught in school models. When someone adopts a left slant, it is a conscious choice to reject the norm. To preserve a left slant over a long period of time takes sustained effort. Thus, while a moderate right slant is considered spontaneous, a left one is always viewed as unnatural.

Moderate Left Slant

Chances are, the person with a moderate left slant has been the victim of some pretty unpleasant experiences and feels compelled to protect herself at all costs. The left-slanting male experienced early conflicts with his father, stepfather, an older brother, or some other influential male. He may never have been acknowledged by his male role model, or worse, been abused.

A boy's response to the disappointing relationship may be to repudiate any behavior or attitude that approximates anything close to that person. Sometimes he will compensate by growing into an especially sensitive or refined young man. More aggressive boys may even accuse him of being a "mama's boy."

Being in control is all-important to the moderate left-slanter. Consequently, he takes the time to screen his emotional reactions through the fine mesh of logic, believing that he can think his way through life. Some will use a chemical substance as a substitute for experiencing their feelings.

I know how you must feel — so long on the path — so closely missing the greatest prize — and now for you, all the question comes up again —

Moderate left slant: Jacqueline Kennedy before she became Mrs. Onassis

Extreme Left Slant

Alfred Mendel conducted a study of famous authors who wrote with a strong left slant. It turns out that they shared a common background: a very unhappy childhood and parents who were out of harmony with each other. Mendel concluded that left slant is an indicator of unresolved difficulties very early in life, resulting in a generally negative atti-

Fine Points

The extreme left-slan-ter is paralyzed by ina-bility to trust. If some-one is "acting nice," there must be an ulte-rior motive.

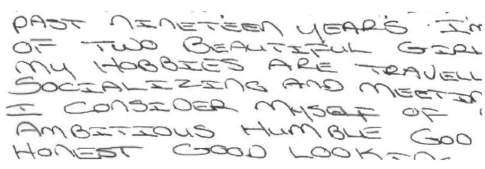

PAST NINETEEN YEARS. I'm OF TWO BEAUTIFUL GIRL MY HOBBIES ARE TRAVELL SOCIALIZING AND MEETING I CONSIDER MYSELF OF AMBITIOUS HUMBLE GOO HONEST GOOD LOOKIN

Strong left slant in rounded writing

tude.

He desperately wants to avoid being susceptible to any more emotional damage than she already has experienced. This self-protective attitude is like a turtle refusing to come out of his shell.

Remaining aloof this way saps energy. The extreme left-slanted writer is exhausted by the conscious need to repress his reactions, and his lack of energy may lead others to wrongly conclude that he is passive and lazy. If he is able to find some way to successfully compensate for the disappoint-ments he has experienced even with a left slant, there will be signs of strength, such as good pressure and vitality, and a well-formed middle zone.

The extreme left-slanter is preoccupied with the past, where mothering and nurturing were supposed to be. Looking for something to hang on to, some stability, this writer failed to get what she needed in the past. He returns there again and again (leftward movement), hoping to find some way to make up for what was lacking.

Convicted Oklahoma City bomber Timothy McVeigh's handwriting below reveals a strong left slant in combination with a tiny middle zone (poor contact with reality); wide letter and word spacing and printing (isolation). The writing resembles a sling shot, pulled back, taut, ready for launching.

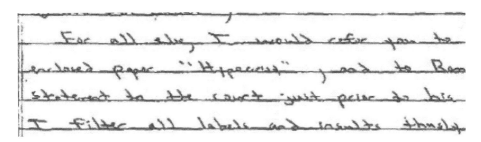

Left slant: Timother McVeigh, bomber

Every Which Way but Loops: Variable Slant

What happens to a computer without a surge protector when the electrical current spikes? The motherboard is fried. No more computer. When elec-tricity doesn't flow smoothly it leaves a lot of damage in its wake. The per-son whose loops slant in every direction is like someone being zapped with electrical current every 5 seconds or so.

The variable slant writer turns indecisiveness into an art form. Consumed with ambivalence, it is close to impossible for her to make up her mind and stick with it. She can't even decide which way to write, for heaven's sake! She might try to control her responses, but constant excitement and rest-lessness subject her to the capricious waves of emotional input which fling her in every direction.

Which way to go? What to do? Who to believe? An inner battle rages. What's worse, it's not a war she has a chance of winning because the enemy is within. She finally makes up her mind, then someone with a better argument comes along and she switches to their side. Of course, she may just as quickly switch back, and for those counting on a firm decision, this can be crazymaking. Of course, if you want her on your side, you're in luck, as she willingly explores all sides and is on all of them.

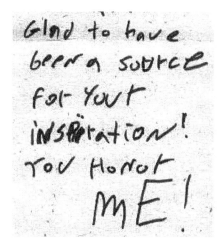

Variable slant (and everything else!) of director Quentin Tarrantino

Lefties Are in Their Write Minds

I remember how much harder it was for my two left-handed kids to learn how to write than my right-hander. The left-handed writer has many more challenges in the graphic field.

There is a myth that left-handed people use left-slanted writing. I did an informal study to test this theory. I compared 120 handwritings, were 60 of the writers were left-handed and 60 right-handed. Each group was comprised of 30 males and 30 females. Of the entire sample, only two wrote with a left slant. Those two were right-handed.

We've already established that left-*slanters* are rebellious, but Roman takes it further and opines that when a left-*handed* person adopts a left slant, he is protesting the pattern that is imposed on him by the outside world. For a lefty to be able to write with a right slant, he is forced to turn her paper in a counter-clockwise direction. When the paper is absolutely straight to the edge of the writing surface it is nearly impossible for him to write correctly because he would be dragging her hand across what he had just written. Try it. You won't like it.

Tales From the Script

According to Klara Roman and other graphological trailblazers, the natural mode of the left-hander is to write upside down or backwards (mirror writing), which goes against the grain in the right-handed world we live in, where supposedly, about 15 percent are left-handed.

When a left-hander adopts a right slant, give her credit for having made the adaptation. The same goes for when she makes rounded forms, which are more difficult for the lefty to make than angular ones.

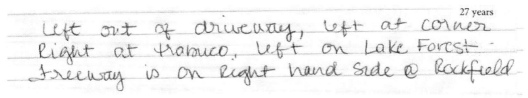

Left-handed female writer with upright slant, rounded forms

Left Slant and the Sexes

Women who use a left slant seem to find it especially difficult to relate to men and, even more so, male authority figures. They can be highly competitive with men, either directly or indirectly challenging male leadership. The pull to the left says that any close relationships they develop are likely to be with mother substitutes.

Women whose writing slants left except for the **lower** zone, which pulls to the right, as below, are also rebelling against male authority. They probably won't rebel openly, but find more passive ways to express defiance. Additionally, the right-slanted lower zone in both men and women pulls away from the left, the mother influence. Therefore, conflict exists in the

Lower zone pulls right in upright-slight left slanted writing (female)

Fine Points

Rounded writers with a left slant tend to be possessive and have trouble letting go of a relationship once it's over.

relationship with the mother or some other close female role model, such as a sister, aunt, or other mother substitute.

A left-slanted **upper** zone in men's writing is fairly uncommon. It suggests a strong attachment to ideas about women, particularly the mother. The writer prefers to steer clear of situations where other men can dominate him. Such men are often eager to please and work hard to make relationships succeed. However, when the left slant is in the lower zone, it implies disappointment in his intimate relationships and he may have doubts about his ability to satisfy a lover.

Stuff About Slant That Doesn't Fit Anywhere Else

When the upper zone slants in a different direction from the lower zone, it indicates conflict between the way the writer thinks and acts. If the upper zone slant conflicts with the middle zone slant, there is disagreement between thoughts and feelings.

An unvarying slant, like any other mechanical-looking handwriting, is a sign of overcontrol. The writer is predictable and consistent, but also emotionally inhibited and passive. She is afraid to let go and respond to her feelings.

Sometimes one letter in a word will unexpectedly tip over toward the baseline. Some handwriting analysts call these "maniac" letters because they're a mini-volcano of emotion. This is a pretty common characteristic, and certainly not always the sign of a maniac (I even make them myself, once in a while).

Left-slanted PPI in variable slanted writing

The personal pronoun "I" that slants to the left in a normally right-slanted writing suggests feelings of guilt. The writer is pulling away from others, and since the single letter I represents the self, she wants to hide something from the world.

Last Words

Slant is a gauge of emotional responsiveness. Upstroke slant shows your gut reaction. Downstroke slant shows how quickly you respond to your gut reactions. Left-slanted writing is never natural. Slant is one of the easiest elements of handwriting to deliberately change.

Chapter 16

A Rose by Any Other Name: Signatures, PPI, Capitals

We've just completed a discussion of the most conscious aspect of handwriting, its overall form. In this chapter, we'll delve into some very specific form choices—capital letters, the signature, and that extra-special letter, the personal pronoun I.

When someone discovers that you are a handwriting analyst, very often they will thrust their signature at you and expect an instant analysis. Would the same person go to the doctor's office and expect to get a diagnosis based on a quick peek down her throat? Yet, they think a handwriting analyst should be able to draw a full personality portrait from just a signature—the equivalent of a cursory glance at her tonsils. The doctor can see that those tonsils are enlarged, but must do some tests to find out the all-important *why?*

Tales from the Script

A woman who stayed through a long, difficult marriage finally got a divorce. She completely changed her signature and got a call from the bank, asking if she had written a particular check since the signature was so different from the one they had on file. Her public image had changed in the divorce and the change was reflected in her new signature.

Like the cover on a book, your signature is how you want to be seen; it's your public image and represents the personality on its best behavior. Some graphologists are willing to make an analysis based on the signature alone, but the old masters cautioned against it. It doesn't tell what goes on behind closed doors.

A signature that is congruent with the rest of the writing is a primary sign of a genuine, up-front person who has nothing to hide. When the rest of the writing is entirely different from the signature there is a duality. Either the writer has a strong need for privacy, may have something to hide, or else is hiding from something. The body of writing will uncover the true story.

> Some European graphologists teach that the signature is what tells the greatest truth about the writer. Experience will tell the truth. Do your own experiments.

How Do I Look?

In the days before modern handwriting, pictographic drawings transmitted information. These symbols represented the message they wanted to get across. When you sign your name to a document, whether it's a legal contract or a personal letter, you are leaving a symbolic representation of who you are, not unlike those early pictographs.

Developing a signature is a highly individual and personal matter, like choosing clothing. Someone whose body is covered with terrible blemishes might select a heavy overcoat as a covering. Or perhaps he feels the need for a suit of armor as protection from a world that seems threatening. On the other hand, maybe the writer is a nudist who isn't bothered if others see all.

Imagine That...

According to Roman, sometimes the signature is symbolic of a wish, rather than the reality. When one's self-image is tied strongly to their profession, or there is some other significant life event, a symbol may appear in the signature.

In the group of signatures below, the symbol of a ship sailing on the high seas is clear in a cruise-ship captain's signature. Liberace drew a little piano beside his name, complete with candelabra. News anchor Peter Jennings, who died of lung cancer, seems to have made a lung in his signature, but he was also an artist, so it might be a palette.

Then George Foreman's signature has its boxing glove, and the knife in the signature of John Bobbitt, famous for having suffered the unkindest cut of all at the hands of his wife. It's probably safe to assume that the knife was added to his signature after the event. It would take an entire book to explore the fascinating symbols people make in their signature to represent who they are.

Symbols in signatures: 1. Liberace. 2. Peter Jennings.
3. John Wayne Bobbitt. 4. George Foreman 5. Cruise ship captain

Changes in the signatures of world leaders

One's signature is crafted to project what we want others to know about who we are. It identifies you as you. Once you've chosen a signature you like, it tends to remain constant, at least most of the time.

That notwithstanding, there are times, after undergoing major life changes, that a signature may alter in a significant way. Sometimes a woman who has taken her husband's last name will make a change to her signature following a divorce. Traumatic events that result in a blow to a person's self-image might cause a change in signature.

Some compelling examples are seen in the signatures of Napoleon, Hitler, and Richard Nixon. Their signatures underwent dramatic changes as their power declined.

Changes over time in signatures of Nixon, Napoleon, Hitler

Do You Read Me?

Makeup, dentures, hair dye, high-heeled shoes—the methods we use to change our outer appearance are many and varied. There's nothing wrong with wanting to improve on the basic model, unless it's for the purpose of deliberate deception. An illegible signature may result from someone who is in a hurry and has to sign many documents. On the other hand, maybe the writer doesn't want others to know the truth. Desire for privacy, or something more ominous? Examine and compare the body of writing.

The legibility of a signature speaks volumes about the writer's willingness to be known. Following are some of the ways people commonly present themselves in their choice of signature:

Clear and legible. What you see is what you get, warts and all.

Illegible. Nobody gets a look inside (we have to look at the body of writing).

Illegible signature of President Barack Obama

Some people, especially those in public life, have two entirely different signatures. The public one is the gift wrap on a package. What's inside may not look exactly like what the wrapping implies. The one chosen for private correspondence is more revealing of the real person. Grammy winner Paula Cole has a very private side that is seen in her illegible signature. The legible signature is much more like her handwriting.

Singer Paula Cole's handwriting and her two different signatures

Middle name or initial included. Including the middle name or initial is a sign of pride. It's a formal, official way of presenting oneself; Hillary Rodham Clinton, or George W. Bush, for example.

All in the Family

The family name represents one's ability to interact on a social level. The given name symbolizes one's personal ego. If the person behind the signature is balanced and harmonious in both roles, the first and last names will be compatible and congruent. Sometimes they're not, as we'll see next:

Surname larger. Pulver spoke of one's surname as being their history or trademark. In the case of a man, it reveals his regard for his family (or, for a woman who takes her husband's name, her husband's family). If the initial letter of the surname or the whole name is made larger than the given name, it denotes great respect for tradition and pride in the family name, perhaps the writer's father.

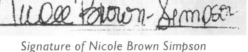

Signature of Nicole Brown Simpson
larger surname capital

Given name larger. The person who writes her given name larger than the family name may not be too enamored of her family. He may have suffered some disappointment at the hands of his father or other male family member and devalues the name by making it smaller. A woman who hates her husband may symbolize her animosity by shriveling up his name. A larger first name suggests that the following writer would rather be known as "Bill" than "Mr. Clinton," for example.

Fine Points

The height of capitals shows the drive to achieve. Extra- large initials in a signature are frequently a compensation for low self-esteem.

Signature of President Bill Clinton.

Signature Slant

If the given name and the surname slant in different directions, it's a good bet that there is an inner conflict being waged between the writer's ego and her social life. Check the body of writing for the cause of the conflict.

Surname-only illegible. If the given name is written clearly but the family name is illegible, the writer has "issues that call for tissues" with her father.

Given name-only illegible. An illegible given name with a clear surname points to an insecure ego.

All the Trimmings

Some people enjoy ornamenting their signatures, much like sewing fancy buttons and beads onto a garment. It makes them feel important, or it's just fun to dress things up. The question for the graphologist is, is the writer choosing to do it for fun or because she feels compelled to do it? The

The autographs of actor Brad Pitt(1) and rapper Eminem (2) look like logos

answer will be seen in how natural and genuine the embellishments are. A free and easy movement that adds attractive swirls is interpreted differently than carefully drawn ornamentation.

The Wrapping on the Package

Anything that goes beyond the plain and simple writing of one's name is considered an embellishment. From ornate capitals to flourishes and swirls, there are countless ways to elaborate a signature. When placed underneath the signature, these decorations are called paraphs. Commonly used in bygone days, the paraph is rare in the United States today. It is still used in some Middle Eastern and South American countries.

Def·i·ni·tion

Paraph: a flourish appended to the signature. May be an underscore, wavy line, scroll, or other decorative form (see John Bobbitt's knife). In "olden days," it was used as a means of preventing forgery.

Signature **embellished**. Embellishments represent a need to draw attention to oneself in some way. The writer feels his accomplishments deserve recognition.

Flamboyant signature of actor and former California Governor Arnold Schwarzenegger

Signature **underlined.** Underlining the signature is a way to emphasize it. The writer is proud of the poise and confidence he projects. It may be either a bold statement or a defiant, compensatory gesture for a low self-image.

Signature **crossed through.** When the final stroke of the signature goes back to the left and lines through it (or an intended underline slashes through it), it is canceling oneself out. A wife who detests her husband might unconsciously cross right through her married name, or a man who hates his father might cross through his own name.

Signature with **period or dot** at the end is a sign of caution, backing off, inhibition, and mistrust.

Signature with a **covering stroke/encircling.** This extra encircling stroke is used to cover over or protect the ego and cover up some part of the writer's life.

Ups and Downs

The position of the signature and its size are also significant.

Signature **smaller than text**. Either the writer underestimates herself or wishes to appear more modest than she really is. The text will tell the truth.

Signature **larger than text**. This is a show of bravado. The writer wants to appear supremely poised and self-confident, even though she really feels quite small inside. She needs to impress others with her competence and stature.

Ascending signature. The writer whose signature soars is ambitious, hopeful, and goal-oriented, especially if she also makes tall capitals with strong rhythm.

Descending signature. This indicates extreme discouragement, fatigue, or illness. The writer may have lost all hope and is simply giving in to depression.

Fine Points

A signature at the far-left side of the page *could be* a red flag. If the writing is also small and narrow, the writer may be contemplating suicide. *Look for other signs.*

Memories

The placement of the signature on the page has its own story to tell. Normally, we expect to see the signature toward the **right-hand** side. The writer who exceeds that expectation and goes all the way to the right drives herself mercilessly.

The nearer the signature is to the **center** of the page, the stronger the inhibiting movement.

Since the right side represents the future, the more the signature hangs back, the greater the writer's fear of the future.

Leftward tending strokes suggest a return to past memories. When the leftward stroke is in the upper zone, the emphasis is on cultural or philosophical recollections.

A final stroke that gets larger in a rightward direction, on the other hand, is an emphasis on the self and outer life. The writer is pleased with himself and wants others to know it.

John F. Kerry

Right-tending strokes in the signature of Secretary of State John Kerry

The Man/Woman Behind the Curtain

In the Wizard of Oz, when Dorothy and her companions finally made it to Emerald City, they stood quaking in front of a frightful image with a booming voice. That is, until Toto the dog revealed the little man behind the curtain. Capital letters are the big scary voice the writer projects, and the small letters are the reality behind the curtain: the ideal self and the real self.

School models call for capital letters to be two to three times the height of the middle zone. Some writers exaggerate their capital letters to extremes. Others shrink them to barely copybook height. Capitals may also be more elaborate or simpler than copybook. The next list covers what various styles may mean:

Capitals **copybook**. Conventional and conservative, the writer has little interest in breaking away from what she was taught and going out on a limb.

Capitals **plain and simple**. The writer has no illusions about who and what she is. Her manner is direct and up front.

Capitals **ornate**. The writer may be overly impressed with herself, and thinks others should be, too. Attracted by status, wealth, and social prominence, some degree of narcissism is evident in this showy display.

Capitals **very small**. Modesty and constraint are indicated here. The writer wants to shrink into the woodwork, rather than be swept into the limelight. She may be submissive and pliable, or just plain spineless.

Capitals **large**. The person whose capitals are large but not extreme has self-confidence, pride, and ambition. He believes in his ability to accomplish what he sets out to do.

Capitals **well-formed**. With a sense of pride and dignity, the writer presents herself well.

Abraham Lincoln's modest signature

Capitals **extremely large**. This is the self-aggrandizing person who comes on strong. He makes himself the center of attention and exaggerates her accomplishments to anyone who will listen. Whether what she says is based on reality or is mostly in her mind is another story. One can't help but think of Donald Trump's showy signature with its extremely high capitals.

Capitals **poorly formed**. The self-concept is not well developed. If this is the writer's "ideal self," she may need some help in improving her image.

A graphologist was shown the handwriting of a young radio announcer who wrote with extremely tall capital letters. "You're looking for bigger and better things," the graphologist told the announcer, who announcer laughed and shared that she had just accepted a more prestigious job at a much larger station.

Let's Get Personal: the PPI

Besides Russian Cyrillic, English is the only language where a single letter represents the personal pronoun. In French it is Je, in German Ich, but in English, I stands on its own as the personal symbol. That makes it a highly significant letter.

Entire books have been written on the subject of the personal pronoun I, which will be referred to as PPI from here on. Jane Nugent Green's *You & Your Private I* (Llewelyn, 1975) goes into great detail to describe the various aspects of the self in relation to the PPI. My personal favorite on this subject, *The Freudian I*, by Terry Henley, uses Freudian concepts to explain the complexities of this single letter.

A sampling of various forms of the PPI

The school model calls for a PPI of about twice the height of the middle zone. Anything higher than that is considered tall; anything shorter is short. Besides the height, the width, or scope of the letter is important. So is the pressure, placement, and most telling of all, the shape of the I. Of course, these aspects of the PPI must always be considered within the gestalt of the handwriting you are analyzing.

Copybook PPI

According to Henley, the downstroke (the backbone) of the PPI represents the self. The straighter the downstroke, the more independent the writer. Conversely, the more curvature there is, the more dependent the writer is on others for emotional support.

As in all parts of handwriting, the initial writing impulse represents mother, and the final stroke represents father. In the Palmer copybook, the first stroke starts at the baseline and moves into an upstroke, which turns at the apex, returns to the baseline, moves left into a curve, and finally ends to the right. Thus, when made this way, the upper loop (the sail)

Fine Points

Find a word in the text that begins with a capital I, e.g., Indiana. If it connects to the word, you can trace the writing movement to see whether the writer began at the top or the bottom of the PPI.

represents mother and other females, and the bottom loop (the boat) represents father and other males.

In some schools, children are taught to write the PPI in the reverse of what was described earlier. Also, some writers who were not taught to reverse it, do it that way. "In reverse" means that the bottom part of the I is made first, then the top. It's not always possible to tell which way the I was made unless you check the pressure pattern under a magnifying glass. The heavier pressure will usually be on the downstroke.

Common Types of PPI.

Copybook PPI. The writer has conventional attitudes. She probably had a "normal" family life in a two-parent home. Whatever issues she had with her parents as she grew up did not do any long-term damage to her ego.

Reversed PPI. Henley says the reversed PPI (when not taught) is a sign of rebellion. Others define it as the writer seeing herself differently from how others see her.

Def·i·ni·tion

> **Stick figure PPI**: PPI is made in a single downstroke.
>
> **Roman I**: PPI has a crossbar at the top and bottom added to the downstroke, like a Roman numeral I.

Printed or Stick figure PPI. A sign of independence, making yourself number one. With crossbars, some support is needed.

PPI with **upper loop only**. The writer was strongly influenced by mother (or another female figure). The father may have been missing, physically or emotionally or both.

PPI with **lower loop only**. The writer's mother image is missing from her life. She may not have been present for her, either physically or emotionally. The male image was a stronger influence.

PPI **very small**. The writer is modest and unassuming. She doesn't like to draw attention to herself. She may have been devalued at home, and hasn't developed a strong self-image.

Lowercase PPI. This may be an affectation, as in the writing of e. e. cummings, who wrote almost everything in lowercase. Or, if other signs in the writing bear it out, the writer's self-concept may be poor. He feels he doesn't deserve to give herself the reward of a capital I.

Large and wide PPI. The writer takes up a lot of personal space. When the upper loop is wide it suggests that the writer has an expansive, open view of women in her life. The same would be true in reverse if the lower loop were wide—men are given a lot of latitude.

Lower loop turns left. When the final stroke of the PPI ends toward the left, it is a gesture of rejection. The writer's father has disappointed or hurt her and she can't deal with it.

Angular PPI. Angles are not prescribed by the school model PPI; therefore, there are significant ramifications when they are added. The angle is a sign of inflexibility. In the upper loop of the PPI it signifies anger and resentment toward the mother/females. Angles in the lower loop show aggression directed toward the father.

Retraced PPI. Sometimes you'll find a retraced upper loop in the PPI, which suggests that the writer squeezes his feelings about his mother into tight little packages that he doesn't want to look at. In some cases, the writer who blames mother for a separation from father retraces the PPI's upper loop.

Very round PPI. The soft, bloated PPI looks like a fetus, and the behavior of the writer may be babyish. She needs a lot of mothering and may have come from a home where she was pampered and overindulged. As a result, she has a hard time standing up for herself. This type of PPI is often found in dependent women and some gay men.

PPI with a **figure eight**. A figure eight lying on the baseline is a counter-stroke and indicates unresolved issues or conflicts with the father/males.

PPI looks **like a number 2**. The writer sees herself as a second-class citizen in her own life. She puts everyone else first, herself second, third, or last.

PPI **leans left**. In handwriting that otherwise is right-slanted, this is an indicator of guilt feelings. The guilt usually has something to do with sex or religion.

Fine Points

Interpret separated d's the same as the separated PPI.

Top and bottom **loops are separated**. The upper and lower loops are made separately. Frequently, if you question the writer, you'll find that her parents were separated, either physically or philosophically, maybe both.

PPI is **isolated**. When the PPI stands away from the other words with an island of space around it, the writer either feels alone or needs to be alone.

PPI **lies on the baseline**. If you see a PPI that looks like it's fallen over on its side, chances are the writer is disappointed in her father but has decided to accept her for who and what she is.

These are only a few of many more possibilities. Do your own research, question as many people as you can about their history and try to see how it fits in with the PPI they choose to represent themselves.

In 1989 an informal study was undertaken to see what could be gleaned from the PPI. To receive a copy of the questionnaire that was distributed and collect your own data, send an email to sheila@sheilalowe.com

Last Words

Your signature is your public image. It's what you want the world to know about you. Capital letters represent your ideal self, while lower case letters represent your real self. The personal pronoun I tells about your self-concept and your attitudes toward your parents. The PPI should be examined for size, shape and placement relative to the words that come before and after.

Chapter **17**

Details, Details

Finally, we've come to a discussion of beginning and ending strokes. You had to learn about the important concepts of space, form, and movement before we could get to the fine points. But now, here we are, going from the general to the specific.

As in all the other areas of handwriting, depending on where they start and finish, beginning and ending strokes can be interpreted on several levels: the physical (lower zone), social/emotional (middle zone), and intellectual (upper zone). And, always, the movement from left to right symbolizes going from me to you.

Def·i·ni·tion

> **Beginning/Ending strokes:** In copybook writing, all letters have a beginning stroke that leads into the letter. It's also sometimes called an "initial" or "lead-in stroke" or "entry stroke." All letters also have an ending stroke that leads into the next letter. It is sometimes called a "final stroke" or "exit stroke."

Beginning strokes show how the writer moves from within himself out into the world. On a physical level, the type of beginning stroke provides clues about how eager he is to get going on a new project or activity; on a social/emotional level, his sense of independence; on an intellectual level, how much preparation he needs before starting out, and how well he understands the basics.

Ending strokes show how the writer relates to the outside world. On a physical level they indicate his eagerness to move forward; on a social/emotional level, his attitude toward his fellow man; on an intellectual level, his ability to think progressively.

The variety of beginning and ending strokes is astonishing and diverse. They come in all shapes and sizes, and, as small an element as they are in the overall writing sample, they can fill in some very important details about the writer's personality.

In the Beginning: Initial Strokes

Remember when you got your first bicycle? Your dad attached training wheels so you wouldn't fall over and hurt yourself. You needed that extra support to help keep your balance until you learned how to stay on the seat and ride in a straight line by yourself. Before long, though, you wanted to be rid of the training wheels because you felt all grown up and could now ride without help.

Initial strokes are the training wheels of handwriting. When you are first learning to form your letters, the initial strokes provide you with the support you need to steady your hand as you proceed into each word. Once graphic maturity is reached, however, most initial strokes become superfluous and can be discarded without losing legibility.

Fine Points

Long, curved initial strokes show strong attachment to family. Being babied too long has impacted the ability to act independently. The longer and the more curved the stroke, the more sheltered the writer.

There is a second aspect to retaining or rejecting those lead-in strokes. As part of the original handwriting training, keeping them might signify one's willingness or desire to follow the rules. Once one understands the reasons behind the rules, he can choose his own path and follow them, or not. No one will be harmed should the writer choose to discard this particular rule, and he can prove his spirit of independence by omitting the expendable initial stroke.

Jettisoning the initial strokes reveals a self-confident, independent writer who relies on himself. With the capacity to act quickly, he doesn't have to spend a lot of time on the preliminaries. He understands what is important and what is not. He no longer wants or needs training wheels to guide him along his chosen path.

But what about people who retain the initial strokes? That's where we are going next.

Can't Let Go

The writer who retains the initial stroke is either unable or unwilling to remove the training wheels. He believes he needs a crutch, and has difficulty letting go and "riding" on his own. It's hard for him to get started, either with a new project or activity, or making a social connection.

Let's Get in Shape

The shape of the initial stroke will tell us whether the inability of the writer to let go of the past and move from me to you is because the past was a comfortable place where he would like to stay, or because he's afraid to leave it and move forward.

> Any type of long initial stroke indicates that the writer feels compelled to think about it for a while before starting anything new. He uncomfortable going into unfamiliar territory unprepared.

Extremely long, straight initial strokes that start well below the baseline is known as the "springboard stroke," and hints at difficulty in the past.

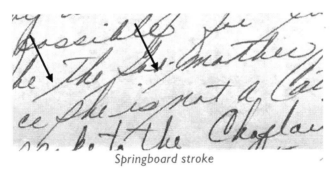
Springboard stroke

However, the stroke is made with great energy going into the middle zone, which reflects a strong desire to take past difficulties and turn them into achievement. The longer the stroke, the greater the obstacles the writer has had to overcome in order to feel successful.

The shorter, **straight** stroke has been called, by the trait-stroke school, the "resentment stroke." Whether the writer is actually resentful or not, theory tells us that this type of stroke forms an angle with the following stroke, and is a sign of tension and aggression. The aggressive acts take place in the middle zone, and the writer's behavior is quarrelsome and contentious. He is on the defensive, always on guard against criticism, seeing himself as a victim, rather than as someone who is powerful in his own right.

An example of a straight initial stroke in author
Mary Higgins Clark's handwriting

A **long, curved** initial stroke has a friendlier implication, but is still a sign of immaturity. Chances are, the writer was babied at home, which can be a very seductive memory when things aren't going well. So, he returns to old friends and/or family for support and encouragement, rather than standing on his own and trying to sort things out for himself.

long curved initial strokes

Curved initial strokes that start high in the upper zone look like a smiley, and the writer has the demeanor to match. You'll find that people who begin with a curved or wavy initial stroke smile a lot and are generally cheery folk. They have a good sense of humor and prefer to look on the bright side.

Felix Klein said that the person who retained the long initial stroke needed a second cup of coffee before he could get going in the morning. He would have to wind himself up before he could face the day. The long extra stroke symbolizes the need of the writer to put a little distance between himself and the new activity. He has to think about it for a while before getting going.

The **small, cramped loop** on an initial stroke has been called the "jealousy loop." I'm not sure of the reason for that one, but the definition offered by the trait-stroke schools is "jealousy focused on one person."

A special case is the **large initial** letter. When the first letter of a word (not a capital letter) is larger than the rest, it shows a need for recognition and superiority. The writer comes on strong at first, to make his presence known. After the initial burst of energy he backs off.

Large first letter (male writer)

The End: Final Strokes

The last stroke of a word signals the end of an effort. The project is done and it's time to rest. What does the writer do? Does he want to reach out and socialize? Or does he put up a wall between himself and others?

Where there is **no final stroke** and the last letter is abruptly cut off, the writer is likewise often abrupt or sometimes even rude in his social transactions. He hates "wasting time" on the polite amenities. You may be speaking with him, when suddenly he turns on his heel and walks off without a word.

No final strokes - actor Tim Roth

The **long garland** final stroke is like a hand reaching out generously, in friendship. The writer wants to move forward and take others along with him. She is kindly and empathetic, willing to share resources and time. In the same gesture, she is holding her hands out to be filled, showing readiness to receive, as well as to give.

*Curved initial and final strokes in novelist
Nora Roberts's handwriting*

When the long final stroke is not garlanded, but is **straight**, the meaning is entirely different. It is a holding-off gesture, as if the writer were putting out a stiff arm to keep others away. He doesn't trust people and doesn't want them getting close enough to hurt him, as seen in the next sample.

Fairly uncommon, but in some samples, you will find the **long final stroke made only at the end of lines.** It fills up the space between the last word and the edge of the paper. In this case, it signifies a superstitious sort of "touching the wall" for safety, as we did as children. Similar is what Helena Bonham Carter does below. Her final strokes are not long, but she adds a long horizontal stroke to fill in the space.

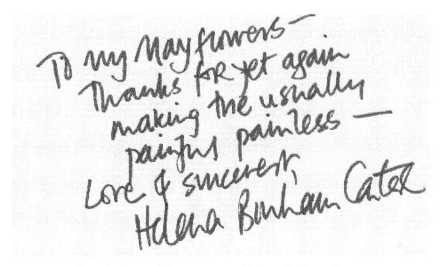

Long horizontal lines - actress Helena Bonham Carter

A final stroke that returns to the left, **arching back over the word** like an umbrella, is a self-protective gesture. Think of someone crossing their arms over their head to fend off a blow. This type of ending stroke also effectively builds a wall between the writer and others who might like to become friends with him.

Covering return strokes: Canadian novelist and poet Margaret Atwood

When the final stroke **returns to the left under the word**, below the baseline, it is a way for the writer to emphasize himself. He wants to draw attention to his achievements and have others applaud him for his contribu-

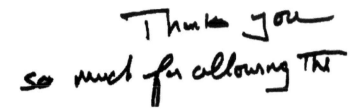

Former California Governor Gray Davis's long straight final

tions.

Final strokes that **rise into the upper zone** may denote someone with a tendency to worship. It is also a seeking for higher truths. The writer who goes into the upper zone when he doesn't need to is interested in philosophy and exercises his intellect every chance he gets. He may also be ambitious and optimistic, especially if the baseline also rises. *However,* when the stroke turns back to the left, throw that interpretation out the window. In this case, it either strongly self-protective or attention-drawing, as in the following sample.

Phone:

Time:

A final stroke that **ends abruptly with pressure** on the downstroke is self-assertive; the writer can be dogmatic in defending his point of view. Add to that an increase in the pressure and you get belligerence.

Final strokes that tend to **turn down** show a pragmatic, matter-of-fact way of dealing with the world. There is a certain ponderousness in this seeking of the baseline or below. If other signs support it, pessimism is possible.

Heavy-pressured final strokes suggest that the writer experiences unbearable surges of emotion. If the final stroke is in the middle zone, the writer will have unexpected outbursts of temper and aggressiveness. If it is in the

lower zone, he may turn the aggression inward in depression and self-sab-
otage.

A final letter that **grows suddenly larger** than the rest of the word is made
by one who blurts out whatever is on his mind. He has a childish, immature
way of demanding what he wants, using no finesse or tact.

Most handwriting samples will have more than one type of initial and final
strokes, with one standing out more than another. Look for a preponder-
ance.

Heavy down-tending finals of muralist Diego Rivera

I Love You, Period: Punctuation

Not much is said in the classical texts about punctuation, and we're not
going to say much about it here. However, there are a few things to be
aware of when considering those seemingly insignificant exclamation
points and question marks!?

Some writers use excessive punctuation, adding heavy underlining, quotation marks, and exclamation points. Some add asterisks or smiley faces
here, there, and everywhere. The effect on the page is often confusing and
disturbing. The person who turns punctuation into ornamentation doesn't
understand where things properly belong. Theatrical and melodramatic, he
is the type to overdo everything and simply does not know when to quit.

Overdone punctuation is used by someone who needs to draw attention to himself in some way. Always on the move, looking for action, he craves excitement and can't sit still. When making a period or a comma, he goes over and over the same spot, grinding the pen into the paper. Dot grinding

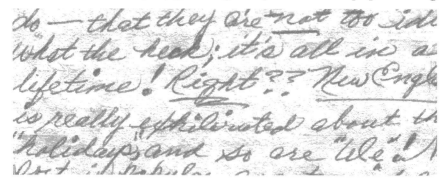

Excessive punctuation in the writing of a mentally ill person

is a form of compulsion and frustration, often seen in the handwritings of both abusers and victims of abuse.

Round, careful commas and periods suggest a careful, meticulous mind. The writer is a methodical thinker who wants to take the time to do things properly. More often than not, this type of punctuation is found in copy-book writing and is a sign of the conventional personality.

Tales from the Script

People suffering from some types of mental illness often use excessive punctuation. Particularly those diagnosed with paranoid disorders write with extremely heavy punctuation of all types: periods, commas, quotation marks, exclamation points, and question marks. They also tend to underline more than normal, and, in some cases, write all around the edges of the page. They feel compelled to control all space on the paper.

Periods that look like commas, with the final stroke fading into a tail thanks to a fast pen, denote impatience. The writer may have a quick temper and an irritable nature. He can't stand to wait, and wants to get on with it. His rather careless attitude implies that it's okay with him if some of the details fall through the cracks. He has more important things to do than hang around, trying to get it right. Thready connective forms usually will also be found in the sample.

Yoo-Hoo! Here I Am!

Inappropriate, lavish underlining is done for emphasis and signals someone who wants to feel important. He draws attention to his own words, as if to say, "Here I am! Listen to me!"

Very heavy underscores that almost (or actually) tear through the paper are a sign of a strong negative emotions, most often anger or frustration. If the writer makes a habit of using this form of punctuation, he probably has an explosive temper.

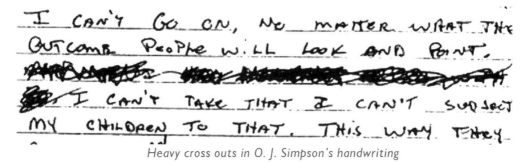

Heavy cross outs in O. J. Simpson's handwriting

Heavy crossing out demonstrates a need to be right. The writer can't stand for anyone to see that he's made a mistake, so he completely blacks out the error. To be told he's wrong or take criticism is unbearable, which is part of narcissistic behavior. This is someone who always demands his own way, no matter what. As long as everyone is doing what he wants and things are going according to his wishes, all is well. Push him or expose his weaknesses, and you can expect an unpleasant eruption of anger and hostility. If this person is in a position of responsibility, many people can be hurt as a result of his actions.

Don't Let Go! Hooks and Ties

You may use a plastic or metal hook to hang your bathrobe on the back of the bathroom door. You use hooks if you go fishing. Grappling hooks are used by those who like to climb mountains. Hooks are made for many different situations, but they all have the same basic purpose: holding onto something.

Fine Points

 Beware of sneaky little hook at ends of words. They appear generous but at the last minute, the hook keeps hold of what was offered and pulls it back.

In handwriting, too, hooks symbolize holding on. Some hooks are large and round, such as the garland initial or final strokes discussed earlier. Others are tiny, seen only under magnification. Each type has its own significance. Where they appear, their shape and size, add yet another piece to the personality puzzle.

In the next section, we'll talk about hooks and ties (another form of holding on). Hooks are more often found in angular writings more often than they're found in garland writings, but depending on the type of hook, they may be present in fast or slow writing. Ties are seen in more rounded handwritings, and may serve the purpose of lending some strength to the overly-flexible writer.

Hooked on Handwriting

Hooks have two basic meanings: tenacity and acquisitiveness. They can be made on initial or final strokes, or both. In the upper zone a hook means grabbing onto an idea and holding it. In the middle zone it could represent a refusal to let go of a social attachment. In the lower zone, it usually has to do with sexual attitudes.

Hooks at the beginning of a letter or word suggest holding on to what is past, while hooks at the ends of letters or words imply reaching out and actively attempting to acquire something new. Because hooks are superfluous appendages, they are not usually considered a positive sign.

Lots of hooks in the handwriting of actor

Small initial hooks are made with speed and express impatience and irritability. Large initial hooks represent holding on to past experiences. Large final hooks may be a sign of greed and a desire to acquire as many possessions as possible.

> Hooks can appear in any part of handwriting. They may be large, such as the kind of hook that you hang your bicycle on; or they may be tiny tics that are barely seen.

Writing with many hooks is done by someone who can't let go—of the past, of relationships, of anything. It's even hard to take the trash out on pickup day. If the writing is also narrow and cramped, you can bet the writer's a packrat whose home is filled with all sorts of miscellaneous stuff.

An easy place to spot a hook is on t-bars, as well as initial and final letters. Use your magnifying glass.

The Old School Tie

Like the hook, a knot or a tie holds something together. In handwriting, knots are a sign of persistence. It's not enough that this writer forms the stroke or letter, he has to tie it up with a neat bow, too.

Ties in the handwriting of actress Kirstie Alley

One who stubbornly persists in his beliefs, once he gets hold of an idea, he will not let it go. There is a tendency to get caught up in the small details and miss the importance of the big picture. By wasting energy on trivia, he has less time for important considerations.

Another, slightly more sinister interpretation for knots and ties is secretiveness. When the tie is in the form of a double looped oval in the middle
zone, the writer is locking his lips and hiding the key. We know he's got
something to hide, but we don't know what it is.

Last Words

Initial strokes reveal how comfortable the writer is in leaving the past behind, as well as how he deals with essentials. Final strokes tell about social
attitudes and whether the writer is interested in extending himself on be-
half of others. Punctuation plays an important part in handwriting analysis. Some hooks may be seen only under a magnifying glass, but their significance should not be underplayed.

Chapter **18**

Making it in the Minors: trait strokes

If you learned to play a few chords on the piano rather than studying the theory behind the music, you might not be able to play Chopin's Ballade in G Minor, but you could probably make Mary Had a Little Lamb sound pretty good. This chapter is for those who would rather learn the "easy stuff" of trait-stroke empirical elements than the underlying theory it takes to understand the more complex gestalt aspects of handwriting analysis.

Important note: like everything else in handwriting, the "this-means-that" indicators should always be analyzed within the context of the whole writing sample.

Def·i·ni·tion
> **Trait-stroke:** the school of handwriting analysis assigns personality-trait names to individual writing forms. This method builds a picture of personality as if using bricks, laying one atop the other, and seeing what results at the end.

Use the individual letter interpretations that follow, taught by the atomistic or trait-stroke schools of handwriting analysis, for fun and to "amuse your friends and amaze your neighbors." The serious analyst should use them only as *secondary* information to round out the analysis. Always look at the big picture first, and then see where these "small signs" fit in. For some reason, the interpretations, applied to lowercase letters, seem to work.

Don't t's Me: letter "t"

According to *Tattletale t's*, by Geri Stuparich (available through the American Handwriting Analysis Foundation: www.ahafhandwriting.org), there are more than 400 ways to make the letter t. We will cover only a handful of the more common forms.

The letter t has two parts, a stem and a crossbar. The crossbar requires a dynamic left-right action (or right-left in some left-handers). In the trait-stroke school, the t-cross represents the ability to set and meet goals.

Stem Height

The height of the t stem is a clue to how strong the writer's self-image is in regard to work life. If the stem is moderately tall, about twice the height of the middle zone, the writer has a good self-image and independence.

Very tall (more than 2.5 times higher than the middle-zone height): pride that has grown to the extreme of vanity. The writer of a very tall t stem had a strict, demanding father (or other male authority figure) who was never satisfied with the writer's accomplishments. Consequently, whether he realizes it or not, he continually tries to impress her father, but is afraid he can never quite measure up.

Short: the independent person who follows a different drummer. Self-approval is more important than what anyone else thinks. The approbation of others is not necessary for him to feel good about his successes.

Copybook: more comfortable following than leading. Conservative, conventional, content to go along with the crowd, don't expect this writer to branch out independently.

Looped: sensitive to criticism about work.

> Any wide loop is a sign of emotionalism and sensitivity because loops are containers for emotions.

t-Bar Height

The height at which the t is crossed is a literal demonstration of how high the writer sets goals. Copybook height is around two-thirds up the stem. Most of the t-bars need to actually cross the stem to keep in touch with reality—the baseline—where the t sits.

The person whose t's cross at copybook height sets his goals at practical levels that he knows he can accomplish, not reach for attainment greater than he believe he can reasonably meet.

There are two possibilities for a t crossed very low on the stem. It may denote depression and a lack of energy for creating new goals. The writer sets his sights on easily attainable aims to ensure that he won't fail. The second possibility is that the writer has recently achieved a goal and is content to rest on his laurels for a while.

A t crossed higher than what copybook demands indicates someone with high goals. The writer seizes opportunities to advance herself and is willing to work long and hard to get what she wants out of life.

Some t-bars fly high above the stem into the graphological stratosphere, like JFK, whose writing appears below. If it's just a few, this is the visionary who looks ahead and sees the possibilities of tomorrow. If none of the t-bars connect, the writer is out of touch with reality. "Visionary t's" need to balance with others that stay in touch with the stem.

President John F. Kennedy's "visionary t's."

t-Bar Length

The t-bar length reveals how much willpower the writer puts into attaining goals. **Copybook** t has a short bar, which reveals a conventional, conservative attitude. The writer pursues goals with a practical outlook and, with other supporting signs, can be counted on to finish what she starts.

Very short t-bar: an insecure person whose willpower is only so-so. Sticks to what he knows and does his best not to annoy anyone by pursuing his goals too heartily.

Long t-bar: dynamic will. The left-right thrust distinguishes the writer as someone who knows what she wants and is not afraid to push herself forward to get it. Forceful and with an ability to direct other people, her enthusiasm and excitement help get things moving.

An **extremely long** t-bar that crosses entire words: an extremely controlling and forceful person who tends to bully others into doing things her way.

t-Bar Pressure

The pressure exerted on the bar as it moves from left to right is an important indicator of stamina. It tells whether the writer has the sustained energy to meet her objectives.

Strong pressure throughout the t-bar indicates that the writer has the stamina and vitality to withstand pressure in the pursuit of her goals.

A **weak-pressured** t-bar is made by one who runs out of steam and gives up too easily.

Pressure that **starts out strong and fades** away before the end of the effort symbolizes the same behavior in reality. The writer starts out strong, but the energy peters out before the job is complete.

All sorts of t-Bars

The form of the cross bar has to do with ideas, attitudes, and theories, since it is in the upper zone. t-bars come in an amazing variety. Here are just a few:

Slants downward (especially with heavy pressure): known as the "domineering t." Another descriptive word: bossy.

Points upward: optimism, ambition, hopefulness. Looking forward with excitement to moving ahead and succeeding.

Concave t-bar (bows downward, as if someone were pressing down on it): is easily persuaded to change course and often allows others to take advantage.

Convex t-bar (an arcade): self-protection. The writer stands alone and rejects help. Isn't about to become vulnerable by accepting a helping hand.

t-bar **connects to the next letter**, or is connected to its own stem: quick intellect. Makes easy mental connections and is resourceful when dealing with problems.

various types of t's

"Different" forms of t-bars.

Lassolike t-bars that swing to the left before returning to the right. Often found where a violent death (murder or suicide) occurred close to the writer and the writer suffers guilt feelings. He mentally returns to the past, trying to figure out why he didn't handle things better.

Uncrossed t's or **crossed to the left:** procrastination. The writer has a hard time crossing through the t, so you can imagine what it's like for her to make a decision and follow through on it!

t **crossed to the right**: The writer is eager to get going on a new project. Enthusiasm and excitement.

t made in **one stroke at the end of a word**, with the bar coming up from the baseline in an arcade movement called an "initiative t": doesn't wait to be told what to do. Jumps right in and gets started without a blueprint or instructions.

Fine Points

Bizarre forms of t-crosses are found in some convicted criminals who see the world differently from the rest of us. Ignoring the norms, they make their own rules.

Pointed t-bars: The sharp point on the end of the bar is used like a dagger to cut others down to size. Ridicules others with sarcasm and make them feel "less than." Makes cruel and cutting remarks as a defense against insecurity.

t **crossed twice**: compulsive, insecure, anxious. The type who goes back into the house several times to make sure she turned off the gas. Takes on a sinister cast when combined with other negative indicators, such as heavy pressure and strong right slant.

Unconventional t-bars

Although it is normal and acceptable to include a moderate variety of t's, when one handwriting contains an wide spectrum of t forms, it suggests that the writer is uncertain about where he wants to go and what he wants to do. As always, look for balance.

Fine Points

In trait-stroke, the closer the i-dot is to the stem and the rounder the dot, the greater attention the writer pays to details.

Seeing i to i: lowercase "i"

The difference between an i-dot and an idiot is i. The small letter i may seem insignificant, but it has a place in handwriting analysis. The style and placement of the i-dot add valuable information about the writer.

The **careful, precise,** round dot placed close to the stem is said to mean that the writer is loyal.

A dot **flying high** and to the right is made by an impatient, adventurous person who is interested in the future.

Missing i-dots are an indication of a poor memory and a tendency to procrastinate. In some cases it is an act of rebellion—"I'm not going to do what I'm supposed to do!"

A **circular** dot is sometimes part of a picture of originality and creativity. More often, it is used by someone who has not yet reached maturity. The circle i-dot writer is often gullible and naïve, presenting a paradox: she wants to stand out from the crowd but she needs the crowd's acceptance.

Tales from the Script

A notable exception is Walt Disney, whose signature was created for him by the art department (and it's said that he hated it!). It appears to be a symbol of a train.

Walt Disney art department signature

By contrast, the circle i dots in the next handwriting were made by a killer.

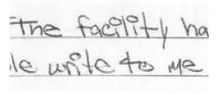

Circle i dot of a convicted killer

If you saw the circle i dot of the killer in the context of the whole handwriting (the gestalt), you would see that in this case, the circle dot is a red flag for pathological, attention-drawing behavior. An excellent illustration of why "trait stroke" interpretations should never be made outside the context of the sample you are analyzing. Always look at the big picture.

When the i-dot takes the form of a **heavy slash**, brutality is often the cause. It may be that writer has a mean mouth, or worse.

There is an ironic sense of humor behind i-dots formed like a **dash or a comma**. When there's also a little hook, it's a sign of irritability.

Let's Get Organized: lowercase "f"

The letter f is the only tri-zonal letter in handwriting. That is, it passes through all three zones. The top and bottom of the f should theoretically, be approximately the same length and height.

The f can be used as a gauge for the writer's sense of organization. If the top and bottom loops are the same height and length, he is said to be well organized. An emphasis on the upper loop suggests someone who plans better than he executes. Conversely, with an emphasis on the lower loop, he is more interested in getting going and doing, rather than planning.

Louise Rice (the newspaperwoman who originally brought graphology to the United States) believed the fluid f typified altruism, possibly because of its graceful rightward movement.

A **fluid** f is made in one smooth stroke, and signifies efficiency and effortless movement.

The f with a **large knot** around the stem means pride in family—perhaps because f stands for family? Of course, it stands for lots of other things, too, like food. Some graphologists believe that an inflated lower loop on the f is an indicator of a particular love for food.

Tales from the Script

The letter f also stands for **father**. Shirl Solomon, *Knowing Your Children Through Their Handwriting and Drawings* (Crown Publishers, 1978), teaches that the lower loop of the letter f represents father, even though it is in the lower zone (area of "mother"), because it is where the letter ends up (Remember, in graphological symbolism, everything starts with mother, ends with father). So, the shape of the lower loop of the f may tell you how the writer feels about her father.

Various forms of the letter f

The x-Files: lowercase "x"

The letter x has an important place in history. Those who could not write their name could at least make their mark, their x, to sign a legal document.

To analyze the x, determine whether the cross bars are straight or bowed, and whether the pressure is heavier on one side or the other. Even its placement in the check box on a form will reveal information about the writer. Is it on the left side of the box or the right side? That will tell you something about how the writer feels about the past and the future. If he makes only one diagonal line without a cross-bar, consider it carelessness.

You can also check the pressure. For such a simple structure there is an amazing number of forms of the letter x.

Tales from the Script

Richard Kokochak, who specializes in jury screening using handwriting analysis, has turned analyzing the letter x into a science on its own merits. Richard analyzes the direction the cross bars are made, where they are placed on the jury questionnaire, the pressure, style, and several other aspects of this deceptively simple letter. He has helped select dozens of juries using handwriting analysis.

It's OK: lowercase "k"

The small letter k looks like a person. The stem is the spine, the cross-bars are the arms. That opens up several possibilities.

A warm, affectionate person who loves to hug and hold her partner close frequently **loops the arms** of the cross bar around the stem.

Cross bars that **don't touch** the stem show less comfort with physical contact.

Cross bars that **slash through** the stem suggests hostility, which may be directed at the self, since the movement is toward the left.

Rebellious

Angry

Standoffish

The letter k

k with a **"buckle"** instead of a cross bar is actually closer to copybook style. The trait graphologists call a large buckled k the "defiant k" or the "rebellious k," presumably because it bursts out above the middle zone and makes its presence known.

Mmm Mmm Good: lowercase "m, n"

The m's and n's are used by the trait school to determine thinking style. The theory is that **rounded tops** on these letters signify "cumulative" thinking. Since the rounded top is an arcade form, it follows that cumulative in this context means successively building one idea on top of another. So, a cumulative

Fine Points

Copybook m has three humps: me, you, the world at large. First hump higher, the writer relies on her own opinions. Second or third hump is higher, other people's opinions are taken more seriously.

thinker would be one who remembers and uses what she has learned in the past. He "accumulates" ideas.

Sharply **pointed tops** are made by the "investigative" thinker who wants to know the reasons why for everything.

Sharply **pointed bottoms** are made by the "analytical" thinker. Analytical means to analyze, so the pointed m and n writer digs for facts and then carefully examines them.

The m and n with a **thready, wavy** top is called the "superficial" thinker. His mind skims along the surface, picking up what it needs along the way and discarding the rest.

An assortment of m's and n's appear in most handwritings because we use all the different types of thinking for different purposes. However, in most cases, one will be dominant.

Mind Your p's and q's: lowercase "p"

Okay, forget the q's, but the letter p has some interesting messages. As a mostly lower-zone letter, the p is often referred to as the "physical p." Thus, a **long loop** on the p would show an interest in physical activity. However, the reverse is not necessarily true. Someone with short p's could be the captain of the football team.

The **"peaceful p"** has a rounded top. This can apply to any letter that is rounded because the writer who shies away from angles is more of a peace lover.

The **"argumentative p"** is the copybook form, which requires a tall, straight stroke that moves high into the upper zone. The writer loves to engage others in a debate, if not a downright argument, just for fun.

The **"bluffing p"** has a large lower loop and may be used by flirts who don't back up their implicit sexual promises. It also appear in the handwritings of sales people.

Bluffer

Easily influenced

Argumentative

Lowercase p

r You Still with Me?: lowercase "r"

For some reason, the small letter r is connected to the writer's dress sense. An r that looks like a **backwards 3** is said to be a sign of the natty dresser, someone who pays special attention to her appearance and the image she projects. Maybe it's because it takes more time and effort to make this letter form?

Mechanical

Sharp thinker

Dress-conscious

The letter r

The **flat-top r** is made by those who work well with their hands and enjoy using tools. The theory behind this interpretation may be that the flat top is an arcade, which is favored by people who are interested in building.

The **needle point r** has a sharp top and those writers live by their intellect. Sharp-minded and curious, they love learning new facts.

The **rounded top r** is a sign of someone who is more susceptible to outside influence.

The **printed r** or any printed letter *in a generally cursive writing* is often a sign of creativity. The printed r is also called the **parochial r,** because it is taught in Catholic schools.

Oh, My Dear! Signs of Culture

The so-called "signs of culture" in handwriting include the **Greek E**. Even though this is actually a capital letter, it is sometimes used in the lower-case. The trait school defines it as someone who has an interest in literature and likes to read.

Lyrical d

appreciated and

Greek e

Nine

Greek g

Change

"Cultural" letters

The **lyrical d,** another Greek letter, is also said to indicate cultural leanings. Some graphologists believe it is mostly adopted by poets. Interestingly, you won't find it in the writings of Dickinson, Milay, or Whitman. Prince Charles uses it, though. That's his handwriting below.

Finally, the **figure-eight g** is considered a sign of literary talent. Made in one smooth, fluid stroke it presumes a quick, facile mind. According to Huntington Hartford, *You Are What You Write* (Macmillan, 1973), add to that interpretation a philosophical bent and a sense of humor.

The trait-stroke schools talk about "cultural letters," but many highly cultured people, including brilliant scholars and literary giants, make no cultural letters in their scripts at all. Moreover, the Greek E is seen in the handwritings of prison inmates! That's why it's a bad idea to generalize. *Always* look at the context in which those letters appear.

L. A. Confidential: The Communication Letters

The middle zone, the area of daily life and relationships, is where we communicate. Therefore, the middle zone letters are where we look to find out how the writer communicates. The middle zone encompasses all the vowel letters and the parts of other letters that don't rise above or sink below the middles zone. The round letters, o and a, lend themselves especially well for the purpose.

Think of o's and a's as little mouths. How many of those little mouths are open and how many are closed? If all the o's and a's are **closed**, the writer is close-mouthed and careful in what she reveals. She may talk a lot, but says little of consequence. Look for a balance

Fine Points

When hooks, loops, or black marks appear inside middle-zone letters, check for other signs of sexual abuse.

of open and closed forms. If the writing is crowded and covers the paper, you can bet that the writer is quite chatty. When the o's and a's are wide open at the top, it's a sign of loose lips. Gossip is probably a favorite sport.

In many instances, the lowercase a that looks like this **typographical** letter a, with a covering stroke over the top is made by those who have something they'd rather not discuss. Often, there is childhood sexual abuse in their background. However, please note that this is a creative form of the letter a, and many artistic types use it (you know I have to say it: look at the big picture).

Typographical form of "a"

The type of a or o where the writer makes a **full circle** before actually forming the letter is a sign of "talking around" a subject, never directly addressing family problems. This is often the case in families where alcohol abuse
or other addiction was a problem. Religious fanaticism could be at the root.

Intrusions

Clear communication calls for direct, simple speech. One who proliferates
an overabundance of technical jargon or multifarious, meandering dis-
course ends up only obfuscating the essential underlying connotation. See
what I mean? In handwriting, anything beyond the plain facts is fluff or
intent to distract and distort the information.

Doug tells me that you are one of t
top handwriting analysts in the country
I would really appreciate it if you.

The "double-joined" oval

Extra strokes in communication letters effectively tamper with clear communication. One way to interfere with the free flow of information in handwriting is to add extra loops to the o's and a's, as in the next sample.

Extra loops in the ovals are the equivalent of zipping your mouth shut and
putting a lock on it. An extra loop on the left side of the letter, since the left
side represents the self, suggests a form of denial or, in effect, keeping secrets from yourself. When the loop is on the right side, the secrets are kept

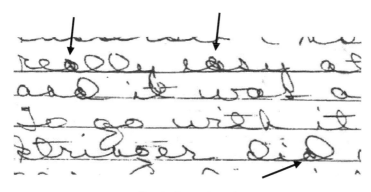

Triple-looped ovals

from others. Some writers make loops on both sides of the letter. That can mean a real Sneaky Pete. But she's probably only fooling herself. When extra loops or hooks appear inside o's, a's, or other round letters, they are called "contaminated ovals."

Secrets and Lies: more "o's and a's"

Tiny loops that hang down inside o's and a's are a fairly uncommon phenomenon, but they show up often enough to deserve a mention. Remember: loops are containers for emotion. That means extra loops inside the o's and a's are evidence of unreleased emotion about some experience or event. We don't know what the event was, but you can be it was unpleasant. The writer might desperately want to talk about what is troubling her, but just can't get the words out.

Hooks inside o's and a's are a bad sign. Some graphologists call them "stingers," as they represent sneaky, nasty ways of communicating. Others say it is the sign of one who speaks with a forked tongue. One author goes so far as to call it the indisputable sign of a pathological liar. That may or may not be true, but be sure to check on the facts before believing anything such a writer tells you.

e Is for Ear

Part of communication is listening, as well as speaking. The trait school uses the small letter e to determine whether a writer is a good listener or not. Think of the e as an ear. If the letter e is wide open, the writer listens well. If the letter e is squeezed shut, the writer has her hands over her ears. She isn't a good listener. This may be extrapolated to any other letters.

I'll Believe Anything You Say

Like the oval letters, the lowercase b, when left open wide, is akin to a mouth naively hanging open with the writer ready to believe anything you tell her. Innocent or just plain clueless? The overall writing will reveal the writer's level of maturity.

Last Words

Some individual letter forms can help you interpret personality. Use them judiciously in the context of the whole picture. The small t relates to goals. Check the stem height, cross-bar length and placement, and overall pressure. Beware of bizarre t-crosses. Communication letters are like little mouths. Check to see if they're open, closed, or have a forked tongue! Extra loops, hooks, or other intrusions into the oval letters are known as "contaminated ovals," and can mean problems in communication. Greek letters are viewed by some as a sign of culture.

Chapter 19

Waving the Red Flag: Danger Signs

There is probably truth in the saying, there's a little bit of larceny in us all. Bottom line, no-one is all bad or all good. The human animal is a conglomeration of attributes, mannerisms, and characteristics that run the gamut from almost 100 percent honest to dirty rotten scoundrel. The many shades of gray along the honesty/dishonesty continuum are buffered by the development of the conscience.

> How do you feel about the employee who makes personal photocopies on the company copy machine or spends hours on the Internet at work, e-mailing memes to friends? Your view of integrity and dishonesty may be very different from someone else's. There is no such thing as a "criminal handwriting." When identifying signs of potential for dishonesty or violence in handwriting, the key word is *"potential."*

For the scrupulously honest individual, taking so much as a paperclip home would be unthinkable. Yet, someone else might feel justified in handling personal business on company time, with an attitude that says "the company can afford it," or even "they owe me!" Few people, if they hit the jackpot at the out-of-order snacks machine, would walk away and leave the pile of change or packages of Oreos for the next guy.

Fine Points

One red flag appearing a few times shows a tendency. When present consistently, the behavior is part of the overall personality pattern.

In every chapter so far, we've covered the positive and negative aspects of each element of handwriting, using "natural and spontaneous" as a benchmark. Now, however, we are going down a different path, beyond "ordinary" negative behavior into the realm of red flags of pathology.

Def·i·ni·tion

Honesty: not deceiving, stealing, or taking advantage of one's trust.

Integrity: staying true to a set of principles and beliefs.

What follows here is merely an introduction to some of the more noticeable and significant red flags that can be found in handwriting. It would take an entire book to fully discuss pathology in handwriting. If you are interested in pursuing this topic, my book, *Advanced Studies in Handwriting Psychology* may be of interest.

One True Thing: Honesty and Integrity

The two big problems in determining dishonesty and integrity in handwriting are these:

1. Honesty is subjective. The way the writer feels about his behavior, even when it positively stinks, will affect how it manifests in his handwriting. If he doesn't feel guilty, it may not clearly show up.

2. Handwriting reveals only attitudes and potential for behavior. Predicting whether the writer will act on his potential or not should be left up to psychics.

What is dishonesty? Clearly, it runs the gamut, from deliberate lying to concealing information to bending the truth slightly to save someone's feelings. Even those little white lies are a form of dishonesty that some feel are necessary and important in our society.

> One whose handwriting is filled with signs of dishonesty may never act on his potential for bad behavior. That makes it no less useful to recognize that the potential is present.

Some graphologists believe that groups of four or more graphological red flags are needed before reaching a conclusion of probable dishonesty. In gestalt graphology, the overall pattern is always the most important clue.

> Just one characteristic *may* be enough to identify pathology in a particular sample; much depends upon the quality of the rhythm, pressure, and speed.

Dishonest acts can be spontaneous or premeditated. There are those who suffer absolutely no qualms about stealing, lying, or cheating on a daily basis. Then there are those who, in normal circumstances, would be horrified at the thought of committing a dishonest act, yet, under extreme stress, might cave in and do something dishonest that is completely out of character. Is the impoverished parent who sneaks a carton of milk to feed her baby in the same category as the teenager who shoplifts an Xbox? Both stole, but with very different psychological motivations. The signs in handwriting will be different for both types.

> Our job is to interpret, not to judge.

Read the Road Signs: clues to pathology

Some of the following red flags for dishonest behavior have been covered in previous chapters because they are part of the range of normal behaviors. However, outside the context of their "normal" meaning, and when combined with other negative traits, they take on a more menacing significance.

Cover stroke. This is a stroke that literally covers another stroke, making it look like a single line. To produce a cover stroke the writer makes a sudden change of direction. An inappropriate change of direction in handwriting symbolizes a change of direction in the writer's thinking. He has second thoughts about revealing something.

Cover strokes and extreme t-bars:
handwriting of convicted serial killer/rapist Bobby Joe Long

When the cover stroke is in the lower zone, which is somewhat less common, the writer may have something embarrassing to hide about his sex life. A cover stroke on a circular letter in the middle zone, such as a or o, is more difficult to execute than on a straight letter. It often indicates avoidance or denial of the truth. Again, embarrassment may be a factor.

Slow arcade. The slow arcade writer is highly aware of the way things look. She is image-conscious and has a "do as I say, not as I do" attitude. An arcade at the end of a word which curls back to the left suggests a deliberate concealing of the truth, perhaps by evasion. Thus, it may not be an overt lie, but a sin of omission.

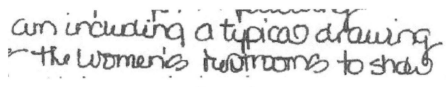

Slow arcades

Secondary thread. The writer is evasive in another way. Determined to avoid taking sides or committing to a specific course of action, he is opportunistic, manipulating and exploiting any situation he can to suit his own needs. In the worst case, the writer is a con artist who uses all kinds of chicanery and deception. He bends the truth the way he bends the middle zone. By remaining ambiguous, he dodges responsibility. If he can't be pinned down to a particular statement, he can't be blamed for the outcome. Look back at Richard Nixon's handwriting in chapter 5.

Extremely wavy baseline. This is less a sign of direct dishonesty than one of plain old unreliability. The writer may tell you he'll do something, but it never gets done because he is easily sidetracked. He'll say he's going to be somewhere, but never shows up. His passive-aggressive behavior keeps on edge anyone who is counting on him. First, make sure there is not a physical problem, such as hypoglycemia, before assuming pathology.

Counterstrokes. Strokes that turn in the direction opposite to what is normal and expected. One example is an ending stroke that should move to the right, but instead returns to the left. It's another form of evasiveness and covering up. Marcus Wesson, next, whose counterstrokes appear in the upper-zone, which turns in the wrong direction.

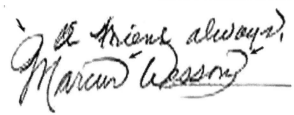

Coiled forms: Marcus Wesson, incestuous father
convicted of killing nine of his children

Extremely long t-bars. When the t-bars cover entire words, in combination with signs of rigidity (many angles, heavy pressure, cover strokes, etc.), they suggest a highly controlling nature.

Fragmented strokes. Bent, or broken and patched-up, or soldered strokes suggest the writer wants to make himself look better than he is. Usually, however, he just ends up looking worse. See the bent strokes in serial killer Westley Dodd's writing.

Westley Allan Dodd, serial killer

Coiled forms. Strokes that curl into shapes like a snail's shell are a sign of extreme self-centeredness. The coiled stroke goes into the center in a leftward motion, bringing everything back to the self. This is a form of elaboration that suggests vanity and a need to protect the ego. The writer draws attention to herself, but when things go wrong she makes excuses and will say anything to make herself look good.

Excessively complicated strokes. These strokes reduce clarity and can come from a need to cover up information with excessive secrecy or to draw attention away from the truth. When the complications involve many circular strokes, it suggests a trap that the writer uses to lure and ensnare the unwary—a graphological "roach motel," with the roach on the outside.

Exaggerations. Exaggerations of any sort draw the eye and obstruct the simple truth. You can expect self-aggrandizement, trickery, and bluffing from this writer. His need to push himself forward through these outlandish forms is a sign of insincerity and misrepresentation.

Def·i·ni·tion

> **Covering strokes:** made by laying one stroke over the other. The difference between soldering and retracing or covering is that cover strokes are made in one movement, while soldered strokes are made separately.

Double-looped ovals. When made inside the communication letters (a, o), double loops slow things down and render clear communication difficult. The extra loops are, in effect, like trying to hear someone over the phone when his hand is covering the mouthpiece. The message comes through muffled at best. We covered these in the previous chapter.

Embezzler's oval: bottoms of the letter a in the handwriting of former Enron CEO Kenneth Lay.

Kenneth Lay, Embezzler's oval

"Embezzler's ovals" are rare but a major red flag. Many whose handwriting contains them have committed heinous crimes far worse than embezzling, such as rape and murder.

Omitted letters. In a slow handwriting where some letters are omitted, the writer deliberately leaves out important information. Certain facts that might be detrimental to him if known are conveniently eliminated or swept under the rug. The same is true when ending strokes are suspended in midair, rather than returning to the baseline (in French graphology, "*trait suspendu*"). Information is dropped; the writer is not telling the whole truth.

Letters made to look like other letters. Similar to omitted letters, these represent a deliberate attempt to distort a situation and make it appear other than it is. A test of legibility is to take the word out of context and see whether you can still read it.

Felon's Claw or Cat's Paw

The so-called "felon's claw" (also known as "cat's paw") is included here because of its name. It actually has little to do with felons, and nothing at all to do with cats. A counterstroke made claw-shaped by its cramped arcade form, it is located in the middle and lower zones.

Some graphologists have reported that felon's claws appearing in the middle zone, combined with contaminated oval letters (ovals with double loops or hooks inside them), is a sure sign of the thief.

The person who chooses the claw shape has been made to feel guilty all his life. As an adult she repeatedly sets himself up for punishment by creating situations that result in the familiar feelings of shame. Deep down, the felon's-claw writer believes she is worthless and proceeds to engage in behavior that validates that belief.

Felon's Claw: Dr. Harold Shipman, convicted of killing 15 of his elderly patients, and a suspect in hundreds of other deaths

Tales from the Script

Joanna, whose handwriting contained many felon's claws, often gossiped about her friend Sandy in a way that ensured the talk would get back to Sandy. Naturally, Sandy would feel hurt and angrily confront Joanna. By putting herself in a negative light through her bad behavior, Joanna gets to feel guilty, which is what she unconsciously needs. Psychologists call this kind of behavior a "secondary gain."

In the lower zone, the claw form is associated with guilt of a sexual nature. The writer is apt to have experienced sexual abuse in childhood and feels guilty about it, blaming herself, rather than the perpetrator.

The following sample contains several red flags in a short space:

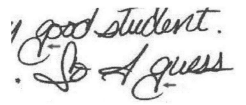

(1) Coiled form, (2) counterstroke/shark's tooth,
(3) letter a that looks like something else

No Evil d Goes Unpunished: "maniac d"

The "maniac d": In a handwriting that is moving along normally, the small letter d (or any upper-zone letter) suddenly flops over to the far right. It signifies sudden uncontrolled explosion of emotion in someone who

"maniac d" in the Zodiac Killer's writing

otherwise may appear as mild-mannered as a mouse. After he has acted out his rage, the writer returns to his normal behavior.

Mack the Knife: "shark's tooth"

The "shark's tooth," so-named for its resemblance to the eating apparatus of the Great White, is a particularly unpleasant handwriting feature. It combines a counterstroke with an inappropriately curved form and is easiest to see in the small letters r, s, w, m, and n. The final stroke of these letters bows opposite the direction it was intended to go and looks like a shark's tooth. This letter form exposes the cunning person who appears loyal and pats you on the back with one hand, while holding a knife he'll stab you with in the other. The writer tells you what he thinks you want to hear as he secretly furthers his own interests.

Shark's tooth

Unlovin' Spoonful: "spoon e"

Graphologists like giving silly names to oddly shaped strokes. The next one is called the "spoon-e." This fairly uncommon structure is a combination curve/angle where an angle doesn't belong, and is another example of a counterstroke.

The standard lowercase letter e begins at the center and makes a smooth outward motion that ends to the right. A spoon-e, on the other hand, starts with a straight stroke that is hidden by the curve. The movement requires a stop-and-turn motion, which puts a brake on the forward motion and results in the counterstroke.

The spoon-e writer' premeditated behavior is calculating and cautious under the guise of correctness. The writer doesn't show how he really feels, but acts in a way that he believes will produce the desired results. Evasive, cagey, and shrewd, his true motives are hidden behind a pleasant face. The victim never sees it coming.

The Awful Oval: "elliptical g"

As we run the gamut of unpleasant behavior, the **elliptical g** deserves a mention. The middle-zone portion of the letter, rather than being a smooth, round form, is squeezed into an ovoid shape diagonal to the baseline. The downstroke, which is supposed to go straight down, below the baseline instead, moves upward before descending with a rightward curve that looks like a backward c.

Elliptical g

Tales from the Script

Paula worked as a secretary for MediMart Pharmaceuticals for 7 years, smiling on the outside, but hating every moment of her job. One day she quit without notice. Before she left, Paul secretly sabotaged the computer system, programming complicated passwords into the most important files and deleting dozens of others that were needed on a daily basis. She also left realistic-looking plastic bugs in the desk drawers of her former boss. Her otherwise copybook handwriting featured the elliptical g.

With supporting evidence, the writer can be sly and devious, hiding his true intentions, which are to deceive and mislead. Those he deals with may not be able to quite put their finger on what's wrong because "he seems so nice!" They know only that they don't quite trust him (or her). His motivations are self-centered, and he works to get what he wants, even at others' expense. Wanting to give the impression that he is far more than what he really is, he may be a braggart who boasts and puffs himself up.

As we saw earlier in the chapter stabbing strokes in the middle of oval letters (notably, o, a, d) indicate communication problems. One high-profile graphologist calls these the signs of the pathological liar.

Stabbed oval: Dr. George Hodel, believed by his son, retired LAPD detective Steve Hodel, to be the "Black Dahlia" killer. Note the stabbed oval, wide space between the message and the signature, and the strange G in his name, which obscures the message ("letters that look like other letters").

WITH LOVE!

George Hodel

Stabbed Oval - George Hodel, possible Black Dahlia killer

Signs of Violence

Although the big picture is always more important than the small details on their own, this is one area you should not ignore the fine points. If you see any of the following red flags in a handwriting (especially when there are two or more of them), pay very close attention.

Strong variability in slant, baseline, size, and other aspects of a handwriting adds to the negative interpretation of the red flags.

Extremely heavy pressure. The writer is suffering from a buildup of excess frustration. He doesn't appropriately release his strong feelings, and may resort to drugs and alcohol which, in turn, may lead to acting them out against society in violent behavior.

Variable pressure. The writer of variable pressure is unpredictable, unreliable, and inconsistent. He blows hot and cold, and you never know when he'll fly into a rage. Variable pressure is often seen in the handwritings of convicted criminals.

Muddiness. Muddy writing is a result of unrelieved pressure and exposes extreme tension in the writer. The writer lacks the intellect or the interest in trying to finesse his way through a situation. He simply blurts out whatever comes to mind, regardless of how unlikely the story. In combination with other negative traits, such as dot grinding, the writer may be sadistic.

Be careful how you interpret muddy writing; there may be a physiological cause (see chapter 10).

Extreme right slant. Combined with extremely heavy pressure, this is a dangerous combination—Molotov-cocktail dangerous. When this writer erupts, everyone in the immediate vicinity had better duck for cover, as he goes ballistic without warning.

Bizarre t-crosses. Seen perhaps most often in the handwritings of convicted murderers, these odd forms signify the writer's willingness to go to whatever ends are necessary to achieve his goals. The violent behavior is usually extreme and may include torture.

Clubbed strokes. When pressure thickens suddenly on the ends of letters or words, it signifies an outburst of emotion. If the thickened pressure looks like a club in the middle zone, you can be sure that the writer uses his words to bludgeon.

Clubbed strokes – Former Green Beret doctor Jeffrey MacDonald
convicted of killing his pregnant wife and children

Stabbing or slashing strokes. Here's the opposite of the club stroke. This stroke starts out heavy on the left side and thins to a nasty-looking point that is made in a downward, slashing motion. The writer has a bad temper and a cruel tongue that slashes his victims. Watch out for sharp knives when he's angry.

Stabbing or slashing strokes: Erik Menendez of the
Menendez brothers, who killed their parents

Dot grinding. When punctuation is extremely heavy and actually ground into the paper, it's called dot grinding. Kathy Urbiha, a registered nurse and graphologist who works with prison inmates, reports that she frequently sees dot grinding, particularly with compulsive-type sexual offenders. Inner tension and a habit of ruminating on or reliving the offending behavior is behind this characteristic.

Fine Points

When you detect what looks like a red flag in someone's handwriting, make sure it isn't the result of illness, writing conditions, or a bad pen before deciding it is a sign of pathology.

Black spots. The "black spot" is different from dot grinding, which presses heavily into the paper. The black spot is a deliberate filling in of a loop or circle with ink. Roman identified it in people who suffer from guilt and feel that they have a "black spot" in their past that they need to hide.

Carol Bundy (no relation to Ted Bundy) helped her serial killer boyfriend by putting makeup on his victims after he had killed them.

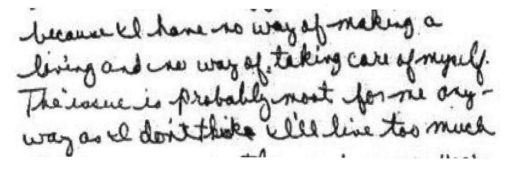

Black spots - serial killer, Carol Bundy

For contrast, here is a writing of extreme black spots but the writer is certainly not a criminal. She has taken the time to color in the letter "a."

Interestingly, this feature has been spotted in the handwritings of several attorneys. Remember our mantra: look at the whole picture.

Harpoons. These are extremely long, hooked strokes coming from below the baseline. These initial strokes, as seen in serial-killer Ted Bundy's handwriting, expose hidden aggressive behavior that is compulsively acted

Harpoons: serial killer Ted Bundy's harpoon initial strokes

out.

Extreme angularity. Handwriting in which the angle is the dominant connective form shows aggression. When combined with narrow forms and heavy pressure, the personality behind the writing is basically antisocial, having a need to dominate in relationships.

Disturbed rhythm. When rhythm is either extremely brittle or extremely slack, the inner personality lacks harmony and the behavior shows it. The writer of brittle rhythm snaps at the least provocation. The writer of slack writing gives in to every impulse. Disturbed rhythm in combination with other red flags often indicates pathology.

Jump-up letters. These are letters that pop up out of the middle zone and jump into the upper zone where they don't belong. Alone, they signify someone who is normally calm and passive, but occasionally rears up over

jump-up letters- Vandal

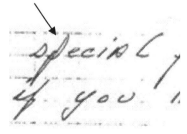

Jump-up letters - Stalker

others and asserts himself. They are a red flag when combined with other negative indicators.

Capitals mid-word. When capital letters appear mid-word in cursive writing, the writer is likely to behave inappropriately to get attention, blurting out rude remarks or generally acting like a jerk.

Changing styles. Switches from cursive to printing, or to some other style in a relatively short amount of writing (from one paragraph to the next, for example) is an indication of unpredictable behavior. You never know how the writer is going to act.

Don't Drink and Write: Drugs and Alcohol

Substance abuse involves physiological as well as psychological changes. The handwriting indicators in the early stages of drug or alcohol abuse may be somewhat different from those found later. Research shows that a low level of alcohol in the blood has relatively little effect on handwriting, which tends to become slightly more irregular and may increase in size.

Fine Points

The addictive personality encompasses far more than just problem drinking and drug addiction. For a discussion of this personality type, see my book, *Advanced Studies in Handwriting Psychology*.

When the writer is inebriated and coordination is affected, motor disturbances appear in the handwriting. The size continues to grow, breaks between letters increase, legibility is reduced. With blood alcohol around .3, the person is incapable of writing at all, and probably will lose consciousness.

Even with short-term alcohol use, motor activities can become impaired. If you've ever been with someone who had "one too many," you couldn't help but notice his slurred speech, unsteady walk, and clumsy movements. The effects of the alcohol on the motor system shows up in handwriting.

Hallucinogens, such as marijuana and LSD, affect the liver, spleen, gall bladder, lungs, and nerve centers of the brain. Used over a period of time, some types of recreational-drug use can result in tremor that carries over to handwriting. Tremor is seen in a shaky-looking writing line (ductus). LSD use is characterized by bizarre forms of letters. Overwriting is sometimes seen in the handwriting of heroin users. Overwriting is a matter of the writer literally tracing the letters over and over again.

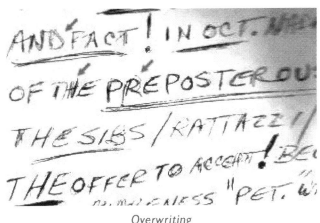

Overwriting

Believe it or not, the following two samples are from the same person, first when sober and then when using cocaine. It's not too hard to figure out which is which. This is an excellent illustration for anyone who claims that drugs do not impair their abilities.

Before and After

Last Words

Honesty is largely subjective, which makes it hard to determine for certain in handwriting. There are some specific red flags that can help you determine the level of potential for bad behavior. The red flags signify potential only. We do not know whether the writer will act on that potential. Drugs and alcohol impair handwriting.

Chapter **20**

Putting It All Together

So, you've soaked in all this wonderful knowledge about handwriting, what do you do with it? Hopefully, by now you have fully adopted the concept that no single element of the writing should be interpreted out of context.

Knowing that the writing is right-slanted might tell you that the writer is moderately emotional, but to get a good "fix" on the personality, more information is needed. Along with the slant, for example, the pressure will reveal how long the emotions stay with the writer. Add information about the margins to know whether the writer's emotions are holding him back; and all the other pieces of the puzzle that play a part in making the writer who he really is.

> Knowing that the whole is always greater than the sum of its parts is to understand the gestalt.

This chapter is intended to help you synthesize the many elements you've learned about into a coherent whole that will help your client understand themselves (or others) better.

1. The First Impression

Your first look at a handwriting sample can make it seem like a jigsaw puzzle made of a thousand pieces, all in the same color. Even though you have learned the basic principles of handwriting analysis, you may have yet to achieve the "Aha!" flash of insight that is the key to understanding the essence of the writer's personality.

Making up a "laundry list" of traits is easy. Anyone can pick out "resent-ment strokes," "yieldingness strokes," "vanity strokes," but that is simply not enough. Many students, not understanding the need to evaluate each trait against the others, never move beyond this stage. A report that speaks to the writer's heart takes more than just a superficial dusting on the sur-face of her personality. It means having a thorough understanding of the writer's motivations and needs.

The good news is, the ability to look at a handwriting and quickly grasp the core personality can be learned. There are no tricks and you don't have to be psychic to do it. Now that you understand the theories of space/form/movement, the techniques in this chapter can help you put them into a helpful report for your client. You will have mastered the art of synthesis before you can say "graphogobbledygook."

2. Finding the Guiding Image

Synthesis means making a series of deductions to arrive at the desired end, which is an accurate picture of the writer's personality. There are several methods of synthesis that apply graphological theories or principles. Trial and error will tell what works best for you.

Def·i·ni·tion

Guiding image: the writer's core personality. It's the underlying character of the writer, which you can find in the two major opposing forces in their handwriting.

One method is to *find the guiding image.* Everyone has personality conflicts or contradictions of some type, and the guiding image comprises the two major opposing forces in the personality. For example, you are examining a writing with a strong right slant, which reveals a need to move out toward others. At the same time, however, the spacing between words is very wide, which indicates a need for the writer to separate himself from others.

He needs to move toward others and also has a need for space? Sounds like a contradiction, doesn't it? I the example, these are the opposing forces or the basic conflict in the writer's personality. You will need to examine the surrounding factors in the writing to explain the apparent incon-sistency. Perhaps the writer wants to reach out to others but is afraid to (as in a tall but narrow middle zone). Once you are able to identify those opposing forces and understand the guiding image, you will have a basis for writing the analysis.

> Even if you give the analysis verbally, rather than a written re-port. It's a good idea to assemble what you are going to talk about with a written outline.

The checklist below will help to get you started by giving you some specific traits to look for in the writing. I've included some hints in parentheses so you'll know where to look in the writing. You can photocopy the list and check off each appropriate item on your copy.

3. Easy Handwriting Checklist

	Emotionally responsive (right slant)
	Emotionally reserved (upright slant)
	Retains past emotional experiences (strong pressure)
	Quickly forgets emotional experiences (light pressure)
	Detail-oriented (careful i-dots and t-crosses)
	Prefers the big picture more than small details (i-dots and t-crosses high and to the right)
	Sensitive to criticism (big loops)
	Criticism has little effect (no loops)
	Enjoys verbal communication (large middle zone)
	Tends to be secretive (small middle zone)
	Relies on intuition to make decisions (smooth breaks)
	Logical thinker (strong connectedness)
	Enjoys physical activity (large lower zone)
	Sedentary type (small lower zone)
	Well organized (balanced overall arrangement)
	Needs help getting organized (messy overall arrangement)

Once you have put a checkmark next to the items that apply, you can use statements from the checklist to get the analysis started. Write out a couple of sentences describing the writer's personality. For instance, take "logical thinker." You could say something like this: "John is a logical thinker. That means he is more comfortable having all the facts and figures before reaching a decision, and is less likely to listen to his intuition."

See how easy that is? Use the same process for each item and you will soon have a one-page analysis. Once you are comfortable doing these quickie profiles, you will be ready to go on to a more detailed analysis.

Tales from the Script

You may wish to copy the handwriting checklist and make it into a trait chart to give friends and practice your skills, or make your own. Just leave out the notes in parentheses and check off the items that apply to their handwriting. With almost no effort at all, you will have given a mini-analysis. Your friends will be impressed!

4. How Do You Do? Ask the Writing Questions

Asking the writing questions will help you get deeper into the writer's personality. Just be ready to listen to the answers, rather than trying to impose your own answers onto the writing.

How can you ask a writing question? Will it answer you? Following are some examples and clues on how to find the answers in the writing:

I.   **Is the writer reactive or proactive?**

Reactive: The writer is affected by his environment and feels good about himself only when others are treating him well.

Variable slant, baseline, middle zone height;
small or poorly formed capital letters.

Proactive: The writer responds to the environment, but makes his own choices based on an internal set of values.

Good rhythm, direction, speed; zonal balance.

2.   **Is the writer resilient?**

Resilient: He bounces back when obstacles arise to block his progress or keep him from achieving his goals.

Strong left to right movement, fluidity, rhythm.

Not Resilient: The writer is easily distracted or frustrated.

Variable baseline, dished t-bars, slack ductus.

3.   **Does the writer have initiative?**

Has initiative: The writer acts on his own without being prompted.

Simplification, lack of beginning strokes, speed, stick PPI.

Lacks initiative: waits to be told what to do.

Long beginning strokes, slowness, school type, elaboration.

4.   **Does the writer acknowledge mistakes and learn from them?**

Learns from mistakes:

Zonal balance, upper zone not too tall, lower zone returns to baseline.

Justifies and rationalizes mistakes: Blame others, make excuses?

Upper zone too tall and narrow, copybook style, complicated ovals.

5.   **Does the writer keep his feelings to himself or act them out?**

Inhibits feelings:

poorly formed lower zone, narrowness, wide right margin, narrow left margin, sharp ductus.

Acts out feelings:

right slant, elaborate capitals, moderate to large size, heavy pressure, pastosity.

6.   **Reliability: Does the writer keep commitments?**

Good rhythm, left to right movement, balance, harmony, clear middle zone, clear line spacing, no zonal interference.

Impulsive: Is he propelled by the impulse of the moment?

Wavy baseline, variable pressure, slackness, muddiness.

7. **Goal-setting: Does the writer use his imagination and will power for goal setting?**

Well-formed upper zone, strong horizontal movement, good pressure.

8. **Sense of security: Does the writer feel secure within himself?**

Good rhythm, well-formed capitals (especially the PPI), good pressure.

9. **Perspective: Does the writer have a clear perspective on life?**

Good zonal balance, overall clear spacing, good margins.

Lack of perspective:

Overall crowded spatial arrangement, especially tight word spacing.

10. **Integrity: Does the writer make and keep commitments to himself and others?**

Good rhythm, simplification of form, fluidity, moderate pressure, clear ovals, balance.

11. **Goal-directed: Does the writer have goals, a mission in life?**

Strong left to right movement, pressure, balanced margins, moderately straight baseline.

12. **What motivates the writer?**

Approval: The writer's need for approval leads to emotional dependence and vulnerability to the moods and behaviors of others. It results in a lack of power.

Rounded writing, strong garlands, long lead-in strokes, bowed t-bars, variable baseline.

Money and material possessions: If the writer is driven by a need for material things, anything that threatens his economic security leaves him vulnerable. He is restricted to what he accomplishes through his financial worth.

> Heavy pressure, overblown lower zone, pastosity.

Pleasure and comfort: The writer bases decisions on the pleasure they bring. Decisions are based on how the outcome will affect him; he wants only what feels good at the moment. He sees the world in terms of what's in it for him.

> Large middle and lower zones, pastosity, loose rhythm; ending strokes return to the left, extra-large capitals, narrow right margin, narrow line spacing.

Recognition: The writer's self-image is identified with his work and his accomplishments that bring personal acclaim.

> Moderately strong pressure, large capitals, good rhythm.

Other Kinds of Questions You Could Ask

You might not want to use these in the analysis, but it helps to picture the writer in different life situations. Ask yourself how the writer might...

- ✓ React in a traffic jam?
- ✓ Handle an irate customer?
- ✓ Deal with a child having a tantrum in public?
- ✓ Act at a party?
- ✓ Perform in bed?
- ✓ Ask the boss for a raise?
- ✓ Break off a bad relationship?

Using the Gestalt Method to Analyze a Handwriting

Let's analyze a handwriting for practice. The writer is Hillary Rodham Clinton. Whether you like her or not, you must force yourself to be objective. Put politics aside and just look at the spatial arrangement, the writing form (letter designs), and the writing movement.

How Does It Look? Using the gestalt method, we start with how the writing looks overall.

General impression: The handwriting is lively and active, with an emphasis on movement. The organization is pretty good, although it could be improved by a little more space between the lines (the paper size may have affected the spatial arrangement, if he wanted to fit his message onto one page).

Signature: The signature is congruent with the text of the sample.

Space/form/movement: In the overall picture of space, form, and movement, there is good balance.

Picture of space: Moderately good distribution of space between words, lines, letters, and well-balanced margins. The left margin is a little narrow, but again, that may be a factor of paper size.

Picture of form: Simplified, original forms with some irregularity.

Picture of movement: Rapid progression from left to right with moderate rhythmical pressure. Some of the return strokes in lower zone letters are stunted by hooks.

What is the **conclusion?** Right now, we are simply describing the handwriting, not deciding how these factors affect personality.

This is an original writing with a medium-size middle zone, largely connected, with interesting letter combinations. Garlands and arcades predominate with a mixture of curved and linear forms that are disproportionately short in the lower zone.

Dear Mr. Klein,

I did a double take when I looked at the photo you made of Eleanor Roosevelt and me, wondering what I was wearing at the time it was taken because my clothes were not immediately recognizable to me. Then it dawned on me I was looking at another miracle of modern times! What a high compliment the article and photo are — even to be compared with Mrs. Roosevelt. I will try to be worthy of that.

With best wishes,

Hillary Rodham Clinton

The Synthesis

Now we can figure out what all the pieces mean. Let's break them into four areas of personality: intellect, social skills, drives, and controls. This gives you a place to start and will provide a good overview of the personality.

Intellect: (Original, rhythmic, quick, simplified, connected) Hillary is a quick thinker who doesn't suffer fools gladly. She has the ability to come up with her own unique ways of doing things, rather than relying on the old tried and true methods that worked in the past.

Social skills: (Strong movement, right slant, good pressure pattern, stunted lower zone, some irregularity). She is sensitive and understands complex people-problems. Her strong intuition and flexibility allows her to deal with many personality types on their own level.

Drives: (Good pressure, somewhat stunted lower zone, irregularity). She's an intellectually lively, active individual whose enthusiasm is quickly aroused and discharged. Good stamina and vitality help her get through a long day.

> Always take care in the way you word negative information. Put yourself in the reader's place. Would you appreciate reading, "Joe, your handwriting shows you are suicidal and were sexually abused as a child"? It would probably be more useful to say, "I can see that you've endured some very painful and difficult life experiences."

Controls: (Tension, irregularity, connectedness, good organization). Hillary is spontaneous and may be impulsive at times, but with generally good self-discipline. She adapts well on a surface level, but is unlikely to change her value system, even under pressure.

Self-image: (Modest PPI and other capitals, medium-size middle zone, strong left-to-right, good upper zone movement). The writer is independent, with the ability to project her needs onto the world. Not afraid to reach out for what she wants on the surface, she may neglect some of her deeper needs.

Typecasting: Using Typologies

Once you understand the principles of gestalt graphology, typologies can help speed up the process of analysis by as much as 75 percent.

Typologies categorize personality types into various groups and are used by many psychologists. The Myers-Briggs Temperament Indicator, based on Jung's two attitudes and four functions, is widely used.

Fine Points

Numerous typology books such as *Please Understand Me,* by Keirsey & Bates (www.keirsey.com), *Type Talk,* by Kroeger & Thuesen (www.typetalk.com), and *The Enneagram Made Easy* by Baron & Wagele are a good place to start.

Jung described two attitudes—extrovert and introvert—and four ways of functioning—thinking, feeling, sensing, and intuiting. Although one function is used primarily, everyone uses all the functions to some degree or another.

Think of how much information you would already have if you could look at a handwriting sample and immediately decide whether the writer was an introvert or an extrovert. That's pretty easy, isn't it? Identifying thinking or feeling, sensing or intuiting, is nearly as easy and supplies a tremendous amount of information about the person. You can apply what you know about the general type, and personalize it to fit the writing you are analyzing.

Some analysts complain that typing people is like putting them into boxes. I find that people who make this claim are those who have never tried using a typology. Knowing the various types, you will be able to identify the primary type from handwriting and then pick out the aspects of their secondary and tertiary types that apply.

My favorite typology is the Enneagram, which has nine types. But each of those types has "wings" and "arrows," which show you how the person behaves under stress and their path to growth. There are many wonderful books that explain the types. After you familiarize yourself with them, you will be able to see where the personality traits are found in handwriting.

For example, the One Enneatype is the Perfectionist. The handwriting of the perfectionist is likely to include a high degree of angle, good organization, and clear spatial arrangement. That's just for starters.

Some of the other typologies include Freud's neurotic types: Depressive, Schizoid, Obsessional, and Histrionic; Fromm's Receptive, Exploitive, Hoarding, Marketing types; Adler's Comfort, Pleasing, Superiority, and Control types; Maslow's hierarchy of needs; and the Enneagram with its nine types.

One of my favorite books outlining Freud's developmental types is *The Art of Psychotherapy* (Methuen, 1979, 1980) by Anthony Storr. If you are interested in learning about the Enneagram, one of the many excellent works to get started with is *The Enneagram Made Easy* (HarperCollins, 1994) by Elizabeth Wagele and Renee Baron. Felix Klein wrote monographs describing Fromm's, Maslow's, and Adler's types and their handwriting equivalents. His late wife, Janice Bottenus Klein, published them in *Gestalt Graphology: Exploring the Mystery and Complexity of Human Nature Through Handwriting Analysis* (iUniverse, 2007).

Professional Is as Professional Does

Reports may be verbal or written, depending on your preference. One advantage to a verbal report is being able to explain what you mean on the spot (sometimes a reader misunderstands what the writer meant). On the other hand, when the client has the report in hand, he can reread and review the material easily. If writing isn't your forte, consider taking a creative or business

Fine Points

Strunk & White's *The Elements of Style* and *The Elements of Grammar* (Allyn & Bacon, 1995) and *Woe is I* (G.P. Putnam's Sons, 1996), Patricia T. O'Connor will keep you on the straight and narrow.

writing course. If verbalizing your opinions makes you nervous, try joining a local Toastmasters group.

Make sure you know what question is to be answered by the analysis. Is it a profile that needs only to cover the high points of the personality? Or a comprehensive analysis that will discuss the more in-depth issues, such as vocational guidance? Or, is the report meant to determine whether the writer's personality is suitable for a job?

> Verbal or written, the report you provide speaks for you. You
> must be able to coherently report your findings or you will have
> wasted your time and your client's.

Saying What You See—Writing the Report

Depending on the application, the written personality profile is usually between 350 and 1000 words long. That's one to three typed pages. It should consist of an overview of the writer's strengths and weaknesses, and it should answer the question for which the analysis was ordered. A comprehensive report is longer and may include charts and/or graphs, where you discuss the many aspects of the writer's background and how it helped to mold his temperament.

If you do your part to present a professional image, we all benefit. Always edit your work carefully before emailing it to the client. A poorly prepared report full of grammatical and typographical errors detracts from the message and reflects poorly on you and on graphology as a profession. Some sentences should be short and to the point, connected by slightly longer, explanatory ones. Rewrite or cut out any words or full sentences that don't read well.

Long, run-on sentences tend to be confusing and obfuscate the meaning. Try to figure out what this analyst is trying to say:

> *The writer has a desire to distinguish himself from others,*
> *at the same time enjoying the approval of others, although*
> *he is self-reliant and at ease with people, evaluating and*
> *appraising others in a critical, fault-finding way.*

Huh? This sentence was taken from an actual analysis that someone paid good money for. Let's try rearranging and rewording it:

> *While the writer enjoys the approval of other people, he*
> *wants to distinguish himself from the crowd. Once he be-*
> *comes comfortable in a group, however, he tends to be crit-*
> *ical and fault-finding.*

Read the analysis aloud. If anything sounds blurred or confusing to you, it certainly won't be clear to the client. Use easily understood language, not graphological or psychological jargon. And *never* make psychological or medical diagnoses unless you are qualified to do so. Your job is to describe behavior. If you stick to that, leaving out value judgments, you will be on the right track.

1-2-3

There are three parts common to all analyses—a beginning, a middle, and an end. Most important is to make sure that everything in each part accurate and beneficial to the client.

1. You may want to include an introductory paragraph outlining what handwriting analysis is and what the client can expect. Next, you might state the purpose of the analysis.

> Put yourself in your listener's place. Always begin and end a report on a positive note.

2. Dealing with someone else's psyche is a tremendous responsibility, and you have the power to wound with your words. If you do your job correctly, however, a well-presented analysis can have a highly favorable effect.

Even when faced with the ugliest handwriting in the world, you can find something kind to say. For example, instead of saying, "Wow, your handwriting shows you had a terrible relationship with your parents. They seriously abused you," you might say, with empathy, "I can see that you've had to deal with some very painful issues to deal with throughout your life." You want to provide self-knowledge, not a reason for self-immolation. Any negative information should be somewhere in the middle and discussed diplomatically, sandwiched between something positive.

3. End on an encouraging note that will leave the client feeling hopeful and eager to improve his life with the information you have provided. A call to some type of action leaves the client feeling that he has benefited. If appropriate (and you are qualified in that branch of graphology), you might offer some suggestions for graphotherapy, or, if called for, psychotherapy.

The handwriting will let you know how to approach the client. If the style is highly simplified, you can be more direct and candid and tell it like it is. At the other end of the spectrum is the overly-sensitive client whose handwriting has many loops and garlands. He needs kid-glove treatment.

Some Analysis Do's and Don'ts

Do:

- ✓ Answer questions directly and accurately.
- ✓ Be able to back up every statement in your report.
- ✓ Couch negative comments in diplomatic language.
- ✓ Make suggestions for developing weak areas.
- ✓ Allow the client room to disagree. You may be wrong. Or you may be right and he just isn't ready to accept it right now.

Don't:

- ✓ Diagnose physical or mental illness without a license.
- ✓ Forget how vulnerable you felt when *your* writing was under the magnifying glass.
- ✓ Be dogmatic.
- ✓ Be too hard on yourself if you miss something important or are just plain wrong. Every graphologist has a humiliating story to share.

The End of the Beginning

Here we are at the end of the book, but it truly is only the beginning of your new hobby or career as a handwriting analyst. I'd like to share some final words of advice given to me by my first teacher, Charlie Cole:

> *"If you want to learn to analyze handwriting,*
> *you have to analyze a lot of handwriting."*

In other words, don't expect to instantly know what you're doing, any more than a first-year medical student can expect to walk into the operating room and perform surgery. If you are serious about this field, be prepared to practice, practice, practice. As I've said elsewhere in these pages, after more than 50 years of my own practice, I continue to come across samples that stump me. And when that happens, I call on a trusted colleague who might just see something that I've missed. That's why it's called a practice.

Last Words

The analysis should be a synthesis of all the writing elements, not just a list of traits. A checklist will help you get started writing the analysis. Ask the writing questions about specific situations to help you get deeper into the personality. Choosing a typology will help you get lots of extra information about the writer.

I love hearing from readers and invite you to visit my website: www.sheilalowe.com

Appendix A

Glossary

Airstroke The movement of the pen as it is raised from the paper and continues in the same direction in the air.

angular forms Sharp, straight strokes that are made by stopping the pen and changing direction before continuing.

arcade forms Forms that look like arches, rounded on the top and open at the bottom. Fast arcades have a more positive connotation than slow arcades.

baseline The invisible line upon which writing "rests."

connectedness The degree to which one letter attaches to another.

connective forms The shape of the connections between letters. The primary connective forms are garland, arcade, angular, and thread.

copybook The standard of handwriting instruction taught in a particular school. The most common copybook standards in the United States are D'Nealian and Palmer.

covering stroke A stroke that unnecessarily covers over another stroke in a concealing action.

cursive writing Writing in which one letter is joined to the next.

double curve An indefinite connective form that combines the arcade and the garland. Also called a "double s link," due to its resemblance to the letter *s*.

downstroke The movement of the pen toward the writer. The backbone of handwriting, without which the writing becomes completely illegible.

figure and ground The dark space (ink) and white space (paper). In the handwriting gestalt, it refers to the balance between the ink and the paper.

final The ending stroke on a letter when it is at the end of a word.

form   The writer's chosen writing style. The way the writing looks, whether it is copybook, elaborated, simplified, or printed.

fullness   The width of letters compared to their height. The ratio of height to width in the copybook model is 1:1 in the middle zone and 1:.5 in the upper and lower zones. Full writing is wider than copybook.

garland forms   A cuplike connective form that is open at the top and rounded on the bottom.

gestalt   The German word that means "complete" or "whole." A good gestalt needs nothing added or taken away to make it "look right." Also, a school of handwriting analysis that looks at handwriting as a whole picture.

initial   An added stroke at the beginning of a letter as it moves into the word.

knots   Extra loops that appear as if tied in a knot.

letter space   The amount of space left between letters.

ligature   The connections that tie one letter to another.

line direction   Movement of the baseline. May slant up, down, or straight across the page.

line space   The amount of space left between lines.

margins   The amount of space left around the writing on all four sides.

movement   Writing in four dimensions: across the page, up and down as it goes from left to right, into the paper, and above the paper (airstroke).

narrowness   The width of upper and lower zone letters, which is less than half the middle zone height in the copybook model (see, also, **fullness**).

natural handwriting   The writing of someone who has reached graphic maturity and no longer needs to stop and consciously think about what he is writing.

pen hold   The place where the writer grasps the barrel of the pen and the angle at which he holds it.

personal pronoun I   The capital letter *I*, the one single letter in the English language that represents the writer.

pressure   There are several types of pressure: Grip pressure refers to how tightly the writer holds the pen; primary pressure is the degree to which the pen digs into the paper; secondary pressure is the rhythm of light/dark strokes produced by movement on the paper.

printed writing   Disconnected writing.

printscript   A creative combination of printing and cursive writing.

Psychogram   A circular graph devised by Dr. Klara Roman in the 1930s to provide a visual measurement of personality.

rhythm   Periodicity, alternation of movement.

school model   Same as copybook[md]the style of writing taught in school.

simplification   Eliminating extra or superfluous strokes from the copybook model.

size   May refer to the overall size of the writing or the proportions between zones.

slant   The angle between the up and downstrokes in relation to the baseline.

space   The overall pattern of spatial arrangement on the paper. Includes the width of margins, and letter, word, and line spacing.

speed   The personal pace at which the writer's pen moves across the paper.

supported strokes   Upstrokes partially covering the previous downstrokes. Originally taught in European schools.

tension   The degree of force exerted on the pen compared to the degree of relaxation.

thready forms   An indefinite connective form that looks flat and wavy.

trait stroke   A school of handwriting analysis that assigns personality trait names to individual writing strokes.

tremor   Shakiness along the writing stroke produced by poor physical health, anxiety, or external causes.

upstroke   Movement of the pen away from the writer.

variability   The degree to which the writing varies from the copybook model.

word space   The amount of space left between words.

writing impulse   The result of the pen touching down on the paper and moving across the page, until it is raised from the paper.

writing zones   The three distinct areas of writing: upper, middle, and lower zones. Each represents a specific area of personality functioning, but all work together to produce the whole person.

Resources

Sheila Lowe's Self-Study Course in Gestalt Graphology

A series of four complex lessons builds on and amplifies topics introduced in this book. While designed as a self-study program, Sheila makes herself available to answer questions and offer feedback, even after the student graduates. For students who purchase the four lessons all at once, a series of one-hour webinars is added as a bonus (no additional cost). A certificate of achievement is awarded at the satisfactory completion of the course. For information: http://www.sheilalowe.com - email: sheila@sheilalowe.com

Academy of Handwriting Sciences (Heidi Harralson)

The training includes step-by-step lessons, handwriting illustrations, flash cards, review questions, examinations, complex charts, extensive report writing, recommended reading, and more. Students can expect a personalized and thorough review of lessons and questions. A certificate of achievement is awarded at the satisfactory completion of each course. Contact: Spectrum008@aol.com

The Vanguard2 Forum Online listserv

A network for handwriting professionals and serious students, the Vanguard2 is one of the oldest private listservs in the field of handwriting analysis. Members on all levels of interest and expertise, and from both schools of thought, participate from all around the world. Membership is by invitation, recommendation, or request. To request membership contact Sheila@sheilalowe.com

The American Handwriting Analysis Foundation (AHAF)

AHAF is a non-profit educational organization that has been active in the field for more than fifty years. The go-to organization for information about handwriting and handwriting analysis, there are members in more than fifteen countries. For nominal dues, members receive access to an astounding array of resources: hundreds of newsletters, monographs, videos; a free weekly online study group, an Internet chapter that meets monthly via Zoom, online conferences, certification testing. Links to handwriting analysis organizations around the world can be found on the AHAF website: www.ahafhandwriting.org

Recommended Reading

Graphology Books

Amend, Karen & Mary Ruiz - *Handwriting Analysis, the Complete Basic Book;* Newcastle Publishing, N. Hollywood, CA; 1980

Bernard, Marie - *The Art of Graphology;* Whitston Publishing Co., New York, NY; 1985

Farmer, Jeanette - *The Theory of Contraction and Release in Handwriting;* self-published, Denver, CO; 1990

Farmer, Jeanette - *Ductus Evaluation and Stroke Quality Classification;* self-published, Denver, CO; 1990

Hartford, Huntington - *You Are What You Write*; Macmillan Publishing Co., New York, NY; 1973

Karohs, Erika - *Inner Circle Papers*: (#33) Enrichment, simplification, elaboration, neglect. (#43) Letter height. (#44) Letter width; (translation/interpretation of Pophal) self-published; Pebble Beach, CA

Klein, Felix - Collected papers, self-published; New York, NY

Lazewnik, Baruch - *Handwriting Analysis, a Guide to Understanding Personalities;* Whitford Press, W. Chester, PA; 1990

Lowe, Sheila R. – *Advanced Studies in Handwriting Psychology;* KDP, 2018

Lowe, Sheila R. – *Personality & Anxiety Disorders, How they may be seen in handwriting*; KDP, 2018

Lowe, Sheila R. - *Handwriting of the Famous & Infamous*; Metro Books, New York, NY; 2000

Mendel, Alfred O. - *Personality in Handwriting*; Newcastle Books, Van Nuys, CA; reprinted 1990

Nezos, Renna - *Graphology, the Interpretation of Handwriting*; Trafalgar Square/David & Charles, N. Pomfret, VT; 1986

Olyanova, Nadya - *Handwriting Tells*; Borden Publishing Company, New York, NY; 1969

Pulver, Max - *Symbolism of Handwriting*; Scriptor Books, London, England; 1994

Roman, Klara - *Handwriting, a Key to Personality*; Pantheon Books; New York, NY; 1975

Rubin, Roger – various self-published monographs

Teillard, Ana - *The Soul in Handwriting*; Scriptor Books; London, England, 1995

Victor, Frank - *Handwriting, a Personality Projection*; Fern Ridge Press, Eugene, OR; 1989

Sonnemann, Ulrich - *Handwriting Analysis*; Grune & Stratton, New York, NY; 1950

Psychology Books

American Psychiatric Association: *Diagnostic & Statistical Manual of Mental Disorders*, Fourth Edition; Washington, D.C.

Ewen, Robert B.; *Introduction to Theories of Personality* Fourth Edition, Lawrence Erlbaum, Associates, Publishers, 1993

A current text dealing with Introductory Psychology, Abnormal Psychology

A current text dealing with Developmental Psychology

Coleman, James; *Abnormal Psychology, & Modern Life,* Pearson Scott Foresman; 7th edition, 1984

Arnheim, Rudolf; *Art and Visual Perception, a Psychology of the Creative Eye, The New Version,* University of California Press, Berkeley and Los Angeles, CA 1974

INDEX

abbreviations, 109

Airstrokes, 7, 211

analyses, 318

   checklist, 318

angles, 97, 104, 142, 166, 204, 209, 281, 292

angular, 142, 170, 194, 195, 197, 203, 204, 239, 268, 321

angularity, 301

Balanced Word Spacing, 3, 45

baseline, 12, 72, 73, 74, 75, 76, 77, 78, 79, 80, 81, 82, 83, 84, 85, 86, 87, 88, 89, 90, 91, 93, 100, 101, 104, 110, 114, 118, 127, 137, 159, 172, 180, 197, 198, 200, 216, 225, 228, 229, 230, 231, 240, 253, 255, 256, 259, 264, 272, 276, 291, 294, 297, 298, 301, 308, 309, 310, 321, 322, 323

beginning strokes, 183, 309

Black spots, 300

Blocked pressure, 165

brainwriting, 2, 131

Capitals, 242, 251, 252, 301

Checklist, 9, 307

Clubbed strokes, 299

Communication Letters, 8, 284

connected, 172, 214, 215, 216, 218, 220, 222, 225, 226, 275, 282, 312, 314, 317

copybook, 20, 21, 101, 108, 109, 141, 180, 181, 182, 183, 184, 188, 193, 205, 217, 251, 253, 257, 266, 273, 280, 282, 297, 309, 321, 322, 323, 324

Counterstrokes, 138, 291

Cover stroke, 290

covering strokes, 172

D'Nealian, 20, 21, 108

Directional Pressure, 5, 161

Disconnected writing, 226, 323

dishonesty, 179, 200, 221, 288, 289, 291

Dot grinding, 265, 300

Double Bow, 7, 208

Double-looped ovals, 293

downstroke, 90, 100, 104, 118, 121, 122, 123, 125, 149, 183, 200, 228, 230, 253, 254, 264, 297, 321

elaboration, 109, 187, 188, 292, 309, 326

elliptical g, 9, 297

Embezzler's oval, 293

Exaggerations, 29, 142, 170, 293

Extra loops, 285, 287, 322

extremes, 44, 78, 129, 136, 144, 149, 251

fast writing, 176, 177, 200

Felon's Claw, 9, 294

figure, 0, 12, 26, 27, 29, 30, 31, 120, 167, 195, 233, 254, 255, 272, 275, 283, 303, 314, 317, 321

figure-eight g, 283

Final Strokes, 8, 262

flat-top r, 282

form, 5, 7, 25, 34, 37, 49, 55, 73, 86, 92, 103, 104, 130, 138, 139, 140, 141, 142, 144, 145, 146, 168, 170, 180, 182, 186, 187, 188, 189, 195, 197, 198, 199, 200, 201, 202, 203, 204, 205, 206, 207, 214, 221, 222, 237, 242, 248, 257, 258, 266, 267, 268, 269, 274, 278, 279, 281, 282, 284, 285, 289, 291, 292, 294, 295, 296, 297, 301, 306, 310, 311, 312, 321, 322, 323

forms, 8, 9, 10, 11, 15, 23, 54, 90, 102, 103, 104, 105, 133, 142, 145, 172, 174, 180, 184, 189, 192, 194, 195, 196, 197, 200, 205, 206, 208, 209, 224, 232, 239, 260, 266, 269, 271, 272, 275, 276, 279, 284, 287, 292, 293, 299, 301, 302, 312, 321, 322, 323

Freud, Sigmund, 1, 69

fullness, 155, 187, 189, 322

garland, 194, 195, 196, 197, 198, 199, 200, 201, 202, 203, 205, 208, 262, 267, 268, 321, 322

garland, clothesline, 198

gestalt, 5, 7, 8, 26, 27, 41, 81, 222, 253, 271, 277, 289, 305, 312, 315, 321, 322

Gestalt Method, 9, 311

graphic maturity, 167, 169, 175, 179, 180, 226, 258, 322

graphology, 3, 4, 5, 6, 7, 8, 12, 17, 19, 26, 33, 84, 101, 205, 213, 222, 278, 289, 294, 315, 317, 318

Greek E, 283, 284

Grip, 152, 323

ground, 26, 27, 29, 30, 31, 72, 74, 76, 101, 216, 300, 321

Guiding Image, 9, 306

Harpoons, 301

Honesty, 9, 289, 303

Hooks, 8, 267, 268, 269, 286

i dots, 277

Initial Strokes, 8, 258

Intrusions, 8, 285

Jump-up letters, 301

knots, 269, 322

left trend, 138

Letter Spacing, 3, 50, 51, 52

ligature, 214, 322

light pressure, 155, 166, 170, 307

line spacing, 37, 38, 39, 40, 41, 42, 43, 44, 46, 48, 53, 70, 232, 309, 311, 323

lower zone, 5, 75, 90, 93, 95, 100, 101, 103, 104, 105, 108, 110, 118, 125, 126, 127, 129, 158, 159, 160, 200, 201, 215, 225, 239, 240, 257, 264, 268, 279, 291, 295, 307, 309, 310, 312, 314

lyrical d, 283

margins, 18, 29, 30, 36, 54, 55, 56, 57, 58, 59, 61, 70, 71, 75, 77, 85, 86, 138, 142, 172, 182, 305, 310, 312, 322, 323

medium pressure, 153, 172

middle zone, 4, 75, 89, 90, 94, 95, 96, 98, 101, 104, 105, 107, 108, 109, 110, 111, 113, 114, 115, 116, 123, 125, 160, 198, 215, 223, 230, 231, 234, 237, 240, 251, 253, 257, 259, 260, 264, 268, 269, 272, 280, 284, 291, 294, 299, 301, 306, 307, 308, 309, 312, 314, 322

movement, 4, 7, 11, 25, 36, 37, 63, 74, 80, 90, 104, 108, 120, 130, 131, 132, 134, 135, 136, 138, 139, 140, 141, 142, 145, 147, 149, 150, 151, 153, 158, 162, 167, 169, 170, 175, 179, 195, 196, 198, 200, 202, 203, 205, 208, 211, 212, 219, 222, 237, 248, 250, 257, 276, 278, 280, 293, 296, 306, 308, 309, 310, 311, 312, 314, 321, 322, 323

Muddy, 163, 298

narrowness, 69, 113, 115, 127, 309, 322

needle point r, 282

Palmer, 20, 21, 108, 253, 321

pastosity, 162, 163, 164, 165, 309, 310, 311

persona, 0, 191, 192, 193

personal pronoun I, 242, 252, 256, 322

PPI, 8, 242, 252, 253, 254, 255, 256, 309, 310, 314

pressure, 0, 5, 51, 80, 112, 125, 143, 148, 150, 151, 152, 153, 154, 155, 156, 157, 158, 159, 160, 161, 162, 163, 164, 165, 166, 170, 172, 174, 178, 179, 195, 197, 200, 206, 207, 228, 237, 253, 254, 264, 274, 279, 287, 290, 298, 299, 305, 307, 309, 310, 311, 312, 314, 323

pressure, heavy, 103, 156, 157, 162, 166, 203, 274, 276, 292, 298, 299, 301, 309

Primary Thread, 7

printed r, 283

printed writing, 219, 222, 323

printing, 180, 222, 223, 237, 302, 323, 332

printscript, 222, 323

Psychogram, 18, 323

Punctuation, 8, 265, 270

red flags, 9, 65, 288, 289, 290, 295, 298, 301, 303

retracing, 122, 293

Rhythm, disturbed, 301

Right Trend, 5, 137

samples, 1, 15, 30, 31, 32, 33, 35, 55, 60, 80, 83, 85, 150, 200, 223, 263, 265, 303, 319

sexual abuse, 101, 284, 295

Sham Garlands, 6, 198

shark's tooth, 9, 205, 296

signature, 12, 13, 197, 212, 242, 243, 244, 245, 246, 248, 249, 250, 252, 256, 277, 298, 312

simplification, 42, 142, 182, 186, 187, 193, 310, 323, 326

size, 7, 12, 25, 36, 37, 56, 58, 93, 96, 107, 129, 137, 142, 146, 172, 179, 180, 182, 249, 256, 268, 276, 298, 302, 309, 312, 314, 323

skeletal writing, 187

slant, 14, 18, 42, 73, 84, 93, 137, 172, 180, 182, 192, 227, 228, 230, 231, 232, 233, 234, 235, 236, 237, 238, 239, 240, 241, 247, 276, 298, 299, 305, 306, 307, 308, 309, 314, 322, 323

Slow arcade, 172, 291

slow writing, 9, 61, 75, 86, 148, 170, 171, 173, 174, 175, 179, 198, 200, 202, 268, 291, 293, 321

slowness, 167, 173, 174, 175, 309

soldering, 172, 221, 293

space, 7, 26, 29, 30, 31, 32, 36, 37, 38, 39, 43, 45, 46, 47, 49, 50, 53, 54, 55, 56, 58, 59, 63, 70, 71, 75, 113, 114, 129, 130, 138, 140, 141, 142, 145, 146, 190, 217, 220, 222, 255, 256, 257, 263, 266, 295, 298, 306, 312, 321, 322, 323, 324

speed, 0, 125, 167, 168, 169, 170, 171, 173, 175, 176, 178, 205, 268, 290, 308, 309, 315, 323

spoon e, 9, 296

Stabbed oval, 298

Substance abuse, 302

t bars, 172

tension, 73, 74, 80, 92, 143, 149, 150, 152, 157, 158, 198, 260, 298, 300, 323

thread, 172, 195, 205, 206, 207, 208, 209, 232, 291, 321

Thread, 7, 195, 205, 206, 207

thready, 194, 195, 205, 206, 281, 323

ties, 8, 101, 214, 268, 269

tools, 18, 282

trait stroke, 277, 323

tremor, 170, 302, 323

upper zone, 4, 90, 95, 98, 99, 101, 105, 108, 117, 118, 120, 121, 122, 123, 124, 126, 160, 192, 200, 217, 229, 231, 234, 240, 250, 257, 261, 264, 268, 274, 282, 301, 309, 310, 314

upstroke, 90, 100, 104, 118, 121, 122, 149, 156, 183, 200, 229, 253, 323

variability, 69, 93, 96, 117, 124, 298, 324

Violence, Signs of, 9, 298

word spacing, 38, 45, 47, 48, 49, 50, 142, 237, 310

writing impulse, 210, 211, 212, 217, 220, 253, 324

About the Author

Sheila Lowe began her study of handwriting in 1967 as a senior in high school. After ten years of reading as many books as she could find, she discovered the Handwriting Analysis Workshop Unlimited courses offered by internationally recognized handwriting expert, Charlie Cole.

Sheila joined the American Handwriting Analysis Foundation, a nonprofit educational organization, and passed their certification examination in 1981. She served on the board of directors as newsletter editor for eight years, and as a chapter president. In 2012, she was elected president of the organization and as of this printing continues in that position, as well as editor of *The Vanguard*.

Sheila is also a Certified Forensic Document Examiner who has been court-qualified since 1985. She currently serves as Ethics Chair for the Scientific Association of Forensic Examiners. Having been appointed to the Judge's Panel of Experts for Los Angeles County, she is retained by various offices of the Public Defender and District Attorneys, and continues to work with private clients and attorneys.

As a frequent speaker for professional and civic groups in the US, Canada and her home country, Great Britain, Sheila teaches on many handwriting topics. She has appeared many times in the media when there are questions about handwriting.

Sheila has authored several books and monographs about handwriting analysis. Her Handwriting Analyzer software has been in use worldwide since 1997. She offers a self-paced online study program in Gestalt Graphology. Her award-winning Forensic Handwriting Mystery series featuring fictional handwriting expert Claudia Rose and her partner, LAPD Detective Joel Jovanic.

Sheila lives in Ventura, California with Lexie the Very Bad Cat. She welcomes your emails: sheila@sheilalowe.com

Made in the USA
Middletown, DE
26 February 2021